THE GIFT OF LIFE

Female

Spirituality

and Healing in

Northern Peru

The Gift of *Life*

Bonnie Glass-Coffin

University of New Mexico Press
Albuquerque

Library of Congress
Cataloging-in-Publication Data

Glass-Coffin, Bonnie, 1957–
The gift of life : female spirituality and healing in northern
Peru / Bonnie Glass-Coffin. — 1st ed.
p. cm.
Includes bibliographical references and index.
ISBN 0–8263–1892–4 (cloth). — ISBN 0–8263–1893–2 (paper)
1. Shamanism—Peru—Chiclayo (Province)
2. Women shamans—Peru— Chiclayo (Province)
3. Women healers—Peru—Chiclayo (Province)
4. Rites and ceremonies—Peru—Chiclayo (Province)
5. Chiclayo (Peru : Province)—Social life and customs.
I. Title.
GN564.P4G53   1998
291.1′44′098514—dc21   98–49887
CIP

Designed by Sue Niewiarowski

Contents

Acknowledgments

The list of those whom I must thank for making this research possible is long—my gratitude extends back more than twenty years and spans three continents! My first trip to Peru—where my love affair with this enchanted country began—was only possible because my parents were willing to "let go" of their teen-aged daughter. Without their support and encouragement, none of what follows would have happened. My interest in Peruvian shamanism began when Sonia Pajares and María Pérez opened their lives to me. My Peruvian "family" gave me much as they struggled to socialize me into a completely new life, and I shall never forget their patience or endurance. From the very beginning of my graduate career, my dissertation advisor at UCLA, Dr. Johannes Wilbert, gave me encouragement and direction. His Thursday night seminars provided a forum in which to explore new ideas and built a sense of community among graduate students that is rare, indeed. During those seminars, Johannes instilled his sense of dedication to students to those he mentored as well. It was two of his former students—Donald Joralemon and Douglas Sharon who took me under their wings when the time came for my dissertation research. Without their invitation to work with them on their NIMH-funded grant, my field research would not have been possible. In addition, I want to thank Carole Browner, who insisted that I listen to my own voice at a time when I felt most frustrated and who has encouraged me continually in the time since. The dissertation-writing stage of this project was supported by monies from the Upaya Fund, for which I am also grateful. For permission to study documents on file at the Bishopric Archives in Trujillo, I am grateful to Monseñor Manuel Prado Pérez-Rosas, but it is also thanks to the kind assistance of Imelda Solano, Bishopric Archivist, and to Rafael Vásquez Guerrero, that I was able to collect this material at all. The ideas expressed in chapter 2 have been presented in several conference papers and have benefited from my discussions with Iris Gareis, Norman Jones, and Nicholas Griffiths, among others. Conference travel was made possible by the Department of Sociology, Social Work, and Anthropology, as well as the College of Humanities, Arts, and Social Sciences and the Office of the Vice President for Research at Utah State University. A trip to the Archivo Histórico Nacional in Madrid and the Archivo General de Indias in Seville, Spain, to study related documents, was made possible by generous support from a Utah State University New Faculty Research Grant. Additionally, a trip to Lima, Peru, to present information from chapter 2 and to conduct archival research at the Bishopric Archives in Lima was facilitated by travel monies from the Women and Gender Research Institute at Utah State University.

Likewise, chapters 5 and 6 are the products of much rethinking and rehashing of the data. Earlier incarnations were presented in several conference papers, and one of these was recently published in the *Journal of Ritual Studies*. These incarnations benefited from the comments of Diane Bell, Laurel Kendall, Anne Butler, and the anonymous reviewers at the *Journal*.

The personal sections of this manuscript have also undergone much revision. How much or how little to share were issues that I did not have to grapple with alone, thanks to friends and colleagues like Stacy Schaefer, Peter Furst, Johannes Wilbert, Barbara Walker, Randy Williams, Steve and Ona Siporin, Bob Desjarlais, Lydia Degarrod, Fran Morgan, and Ken Stahl. For their help and encouragement in pushing and prodding me onward when I lost heart, I would also like to thank Eddy Berry, Susan Dawson, Art Rubel, Audrey Shillington, Douglas Sharon, and most especially the late Carol Loveland. I also owe much to my undergraduate and graduate students at Washington State University and at Utah State University, especially those in my "Shamanism and Traditional Medicine" class. In addition, I have had excellent editorial assistance from my husband Dan Coffin, whose competence as a published author and professional editor I abused on more than one occasion, from Larry Durwood Ball of the University of New Mexico Press, and especially from Ruth Steinberg, also of UNM Press.

To Rafael Vásquez, my erstwhile *compañero* in both field and archival research, as well as a colleague, friend, and confidant, I owe a special debt. To the *curanderos* Eduardo Calderón, Nilo Plascencia, and Victor Flores, to the women of Fanny Abanto Calle who shared their lives with me, and especially to my friend through it all, Nora Rivas Vásquez, I am grateful. To Clorinda, Vicky, Yolanda, Flor, and most especially to Isabel and Olinda, I owe the largest debt of gratitude, and these pages are a testament to their faith and confidence in me. But it is to my husband Dan—whose love, patience, and belief in me have never wavered—and to our son Ian—the product of my healing experience in Peru and the greatest gift of my life—that I dedicate these pages.

Prologue

"I want you to learn something very well," Isabel told me. It was the first night that I had participated in the all-night healing ritual that she and other *curanderos* in northern Peru refer to as a *mesa*. "Whenever you help another person here [at] my *mesa,* whenever you contribute, you are living. You are experiencing, and *that* is the way you enter into the movie [of life]. . . . To live is to experience. . . . You should save your tapes. They are expensive and you will learn very little from them. What you write won't come from what you record but from what you live—from what you *experience*. Reality isn't observed or recorded, it is lived!"

Experience. This became the metaphor by which my understanding of female healing in Peru was organized. But because experience is one of the most problematic concepts in contemporary anthropology, writing about the healing philosophies and therapeutic strategies of these women has been most difficult. In part, the problem emerges because experience is a way of knowing that is grounded in reflexive engagement with the world. The origin of the term itself suggests that experience requires interaction of the experiencing subject with the object-world in a way that is processual and emergent.[1] Experience eludes abstraction and analysis because these distance the experiencing subject from the context and process through which experience occurs.

Another part of the experience problem is that the link between experience and its perception never reflects a one-to-one correspondence. Rather, one's perception of the world "out there" changes according to the way the senses encode received data. Emotional and interpretive landscapes also influence how reality is perceived. For example, one's experience of a room with an ambient temperature of seventy degrees will depend upon—among other things—the season, the time of day, and the

amount of conscious attention given at that moment to external surround-
ings. Experience shapes perception, but perception also shapes experience.

Furthermore, experience is personal and, to a large degree, unshare-
able. If the numinous could be adequately expressed to others, there
would be no need for faith. As Geertz recently summarized it, "Whatever
sense we have of how things stand with someone else's inner life, we gain
it through their expressions, not through some magical intrusion into their
consciousness. It's all a matter of scratching surfaces" (1986, 373). In
other words, the articulation of experience—however well crafted that
may be—is not the same as the experience itself. Rather, experience lies
somewhere *between* the encoding of sensation and its expression (Bruner
1986, 6; Jackson 1989, 1).

Additionally, while an accepted definition of experience, although inef-
fable, is one in which we all participate equally as we pass through life
(Ayto 1990), the healers in my research emphasized that experience is
something else altogether: it cannot be passively received but must be
actively engaged. It is through this engagement that we both transform
and are transformed by life. It is through experience that both agency and
subjectivity are defined.[2] As Isabel notes, not all who pass through life
"experience." Instead, one may eat, drink, and die without ever engaging
life—without ever experiencing it. And, according to Isabel, I was one
who suffered from this malaise. As she told me that first night,

> You are a good woman. I have looked within you and have seen the
> beating of your heart. But—there is a "but" here—so many years
> studying for your degree, just a piece of paper! And yet, you take nothing
> with you. You have studied a lifetime and yet you have nothing, you are
> worth nothing. All of us want to own our own lives . . . to create something
> that we can call our own. . . . That is why you have been studying. . . .
> But you walk around empty. . . . For all you have studied and all that you
> have seen, you have actually experienced very little (Glass-Coffin 1992a,
> 309–10).

Finally, the dilemma of how best to portray my work weighed heavily for
personal reasons. Trained as an anthropologist at the same institution and

in the same program as Carlos Castañeda, I feared the consequences of writing a first-person experiential account because of the dubious legacy left by that master of ambiguity. While his books revitalized interest in both shamanism and cultural anthropology among the general public, questions of authenticity, of validity, and of comparable worth still swirl in academic circles whenever his name is mentioned.[3] I did not want to be painted with the same dismissive brush—especially since I was headed for a career in academe. So I clung to the mantle of "objectivity" that is the problematic legacy of the social-scientist. As an anthropologist interested in understanding the impact of gender on healing philosophies and therapeutic strategies, I found myself seeking out parallels and contrasts that could be objectified, analyzed, and ultimately compared to answer the research questions I had posed. Yet, Isabel kept insisting that objective reporting would only distance me from this goal. Indeed, while the emphasis given to experience did emerge as a key to understanding gender differences in healing, by its very nature this phenomenon defied the generalization and comparison that objectification demands.

Thus, when it came time to write up my results, I was faced with a dilemma. First, how might I write about "experience," if, as discussed above, experience is always emergent and therefore defies representation. And second, how might I write about my own role in events, since not only was I a social-scientist trying to live the paradox of participant/observer, but I was also the one who had been transformed by this awakening to experience! Could any portrayal of my research possibly be faithful to Isabel's exhortations to be actively engaged with my own experience? Further, would anyone be interested in the things I had to say, or would my portrayal suffer the inconsequential fate of so many other so-called confessional accounts.[4] Finally, how best could I satisfy the requirements of academic discourse without essentializing these transformational processes. Certainly, what Van Maanem (1988) refers to as a "realist" portrayal, where the transition from lived experience to written account is uncontested and transparent would be inappropriate. In these accounts, the author invokes the "evidence" of experience to claim a position of privilege and distance from the context in which the tale unfolds. Through this process, cultural descriptions are reified or, in ethnographic terms, salvaged. Similarly, cultural processes are essentialized, so that these appear more patterned, homogenous, coherent, and static than they actually are (Abu-Lughod 1991). Also, separations rather than affinities between subject and object (between producer and produced) predominate. The distance which separates writer, reader, and written-about masks the fact that the observer never "simply stands outside" (Abu-Lughod 1991:141) that which s/he describes.

So, in the pages that follow, I've chosen to present an ethnographic account of female healing practices on the north coast of Peru through two separate lenses. The first lens is the comfortable lens of traditional ethnographic description and analysis. Although the reader can see the author at work occasionally within the scenes being described, this first lens shows its subjects after they've been organized, edited, pondered, and otherwise crafted and shaped into an academic "representation." The second lens is the uncomfortable lens of first-person experience, as it has been reconstructed or as it was originally captured in my field notes and letters home to friends. This lens focuses on my own lived experience with my principal informants, Isabel and Olinda, as they worked to heal me of a spiritual illness. Even this lens fails to adequately present direct experience; it is, of necessity, only another kind of representation of my experience—in the form of words that can only partially convey my observations, thoughts, terrors, and dreams. Like all real spiritual journeys, my own does not reveal itself in a tidy, straight-line movement from abject illness to rosy health, but rather, moves fluidly between insight, confessional despair, catharsis, and analysis. Nevertheless, it represents the only case study of a patient's healing experience to which I have legitimate access.

These two lenses yield a bifocal view of contemporary female healing practices: one focus is that of the anthropologist outside looking in and the other focus is that of a patient inside looking out. This approach manifests itself in the book as two separate threads, interwoven as alternating chapters. The analytical chapters, with their bias toward observation, are designated by Arabic numerals (1–6). The experiential chapters, with their bias toward participation, are designated by Roman numerals (i–vi) and the Epilogue.

In the analytical thread, chapter 1, "Sorcery and Dependence," presents the northern coast of Peru in its modern social, economic, and environmental contexts and introduces the concepts of both sorcery and shamanic healing. Chapter 2, *"Madre, Mujer, Bruja,"* reviews the dynamics of history that have contributed to perceptions of contemporary *curanderas* as "witches" instead of healers. Chapter 3, "A Call to Healing," introduces five female ritual healers (*curanderas*) and tells their tales of how they chose their vocation. Chapter 4, "Healers at Work," presents a case study for each of the healers, as they cure a patient using ritual techniques. Chapter 5, "Spiritual Tools," is a detailed examination of the religious and symbolic space in which the healers perform, including the specific epistemologies they use to manipulate spiritual energy. Chapter 6, "Gender, Healing, and Experience," returns to the question of what is specifically female in the healing practices of the women studied and attempts to distinguish between male and female healing tropes.

In the experiential thread, chapter i describes my introduction to Peru and my initial dependence upon the well-defined, traditional Peruvian roles of "daughter" and "sister" to provide a touchstone for my own identity and sense of self. Chapter ii describes a moment of experiential crisis which led me to question that identity and also sets the stage for the reader's understanding of why Isabel thought of me as a patient in need of a cure. Chapter iii describes my first ritual contact with Isabel, her assessment of my illness, and the steps she outlined for my cure. Chapter iv illustrates how illness and healing are not linear, goal-oriented behaviors when subjected to the idiosyncrasies of human experience, but are instead personalized, cumulative, and sometimes irrational processes which are profoundly affected by perception, attitude, and affect. Chapters v and vi apply the conceptualizations of illness and therapeutic strategies for healing (including acceptance, purification, penance, awakening, and empowerment, which are described and discussed in the analytical chapters of the book) to the context of my own experience. The Epilogue brings the reader from the "ethnographic present" of 1988–89 to 1996 and presents a final statement about the ongoing relationship between experience and analysis in ethnography.

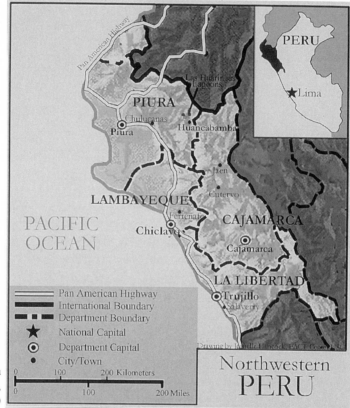

Map of Peru
(FACT Center,
Utah State University.)

1 Sorcery and Dependence

No matter how many times I ride along the Pan American Highway from Lima to Chiclayo, I am stunned by the aridity of this coastal ribbon of land which snakes northward, wedged between the Pacific Ocean to the west and the towering Andes to the east. The mean temperature of 20–25°C is milder than would be expected of a region only a few degrees south of the equator. The tropical heat is tempered by the cold Humboldt current just offshore, which flows northward from Antarctica. The Andes, rising abruptly from 50 to 200 kilometers inland from the beach, prevent the moisture-bearing winds, which blow westward across the continent, from reaching the sea. Only the rivers, born high above the desert floor in the highest peaks of these rugged mountains, feed the parched soil of the lands to the west. Where they touch the desert, grays and browns turn to green, and the landscape becomes lush and full, sustaining life for those who live within the reach of the rivers' life-giving flow.

Between these oases of green, the bus lumbers past adobe shrines and temple mounds that rise above the desert floor. Furrowed and weathered like the faces of the very old, many of these *huacas* are at least 1,500 years old. The remnants of ancient civilizations, some contain opulent burials, painted and sculpted pottery, and woven tapestries that suggest legacies of homage and conquest (Donnan 1976). Here on this arid plain, city-states, regional cultures, and, finally, panregional empires gained power and wealth as they learned to channel the water from these life-giving rivers. Evidence suggests that by 1,000 years ago, this complex system of canals was controlled by an authoritarian politico-religious elite. Large-scale agricultural projects sustained large numbers of people, and control of water resources influenced the development of social, political, and economic relations among inhabitants of this desert region.[1] After the region's most recent conquest in 1532, the Spanish fetish for planting water-intensive monocrops like rice and sugar cane, crops destined for export rather than consumption, only exacerbated these relations. Today, 70 percent of the arable land is still planted in rice and cane sugar (Montoya Peralta 1988, 48). Although the single-owner *haciendas* were broken up into cooperatives in the 1960s and subsequently privatized, water scarcity continues to create an atmosphere of dependence, economic insecurity, competition, and conflict among agricultural producers throughout this desert landscape. These relations are only intensified by the mercantilist focus of economic activity in the region.

Until 1988 my trips from Lima had ended in the colonial capital of Trujillo—four hundred kilometers to the north. In that year, however, and largely because my attempts at locating female healers in Trujillo had been unsuccessful, I headed to Chiclayo. This city of 250,000 people, three-and-a-half hours north of Trujillo on the Pan American Highway, had been described to me by a friend who knew of my interests as the "sorcery capital" of northern Peru. As soon as I stepped from the bus, it was not hard to see why. In Chiclayo, even more than in Trujillo, it is commerce and not industry which sustains the local economy. Because the Andes rise more gently here than farther to the south, export-destined goods from the mountains and the tropical forest beyond find their way to the coast over roads which have their outlets in Chiclayo. Early in the morning on any given day, trucks filled with coffee and bananas, tropical woods, cacao, and other tropical forest products jockey for space to unload their goods on the narrow and dusty streets surrounding the immense warehouse and wholesale district known as Mercado Moshoqueque. Locally produced goods like rice and sugar from nearby cooperatives, dried and salted fish from nearby ports, and goats and pigs and fruits and vegetables from nearby family farms are also brought here for resale and shipment, either to faraway markets or to retail markets only a few blocks away. By mid-morning the streets of the market district are choked with *carretillas*, loaded up with goods that will be resold to smaller markets around the city.

Along the wide arterial which connects the main square to these central markets, traffic flows more easily, but here the sidewalks are impassable. Street-hawkers, who prefer to sell their goods "informally" rather than pay the taxes which would give them official status and protection, sit in the shadow of doorways. Strings connect them to their portable display cases so that these can be pulled from the regulated public space of the sidewalk to the unregulated privacy of the stairwells and doorways should a policeman attempt to confiscate their goods. Organized by product type, the six-block length of sidewalk yields everything from toilet paper and shampoo to ratchets and hammers to high-fashion jeans. Imported radios blare and watches gleam—contraband from Ecuador smuggled over the border to avoid the 100–200 percent import tariff. Beyond the doorways, formal retail businesses have the feel of warehouses or large distribution centers rather than retail outlets. Across from one corner of the central market, several stores compete to sell bolts of cloth. Farther up the block, half a dozen furniture stores attempt to draw passers-by from the street, hardware stores sell lengths of rope and wire by the reel, and a huge showroom stocks every conceivable size of plastic tub. Everywhere there is a feeling of commerce and an emphasis on attaining profit through redistributive rather than productive activities.

Traveling from the city center to any of its three open markets gives the feeling that this "Heroic City"—as its motto and shield proclaim—is now in decline. Over half of the city's population lives in marginal neighborhoods which are inadequately supplied with water, electricity, sewers, and other public services (Forsberg and Francke 1987, 230). Still, the population continues to balloon, as more and more people move to Chiclayo from rural areas in search of a better life.

While I was in Chiclayo, from September 1988 to September 1989, electrical outages—the product of outmoded circuitry as well as terrorist bombings—occurred at least once a week. Holes for sewer lines, dug in dusty streets, gaped like toothless grins. The once-paved streets, now little more than dusty paths, appeared to be playing connect-the-dots between innumerable, impassable pot-holes. Parks that once sported a covering of grass appeared to have been reclaimed by the desert, and garbage was heaped on corner lots, waiting for pickup by broken-down trucks that often didn't arrive. In the newer districts of the city, like La Victoria just south of the city center, the garbage mounds were often shoulder-high and dozens of yards long. In the older districts, they might be twenty or more feet high. As the putrid mounds decomposed and were reclaimed by the desert, they came to look more like ancient adobe-temple *huacas* than heaps of garbage. No wonder they were often referred to by this term.

In this environment the emphasis is on redistribution rather than on production (De Soto 1987, Montoya Peralta 1988). Capital amassed from commercial ventures is reinvested in other mercantile activities rather than on development of a productive infrastructure that would support a more diversified domestic economy. The result is unequal development and a dependent economy, wherein an entrepreneurial and bureaucratic "elite" becomes wealthy at the expense of the rest of the population. It is also an environment in which thrive the frustration, suspicion, envy, and projected hostilities that are the hallmarks of sorcery.

Daño

Throughout northern Peru, extraordinary shamanic healers called *curanderos* (curers) or *maestros* (teachers/masters) conduct all-night curing rituals in order to heal their patients of the sorcery-related illnesses from which they are believed to suffer.[2] Although its roots are ancient, this tradition continues to thrive today throughout the region, especially in or near coastal cities like Chiclayo.[3] In spite of the myriad doctors, clinics, hospitals, and other healthcare facilities available here, shamanic healers are rarely without clients. As one healer told me, this is because "sorcery is more prevalent, now that the economic situation is so bad. There is more envy now than ever before and more sorcerers who are ready to kill for a price." Unlike "natural" illness, sorcery intentionally harms and is directed toward specific victims. It evens the score, removes competitors from the marketplace, or avenges perceived inequities in resource distribution. It may be carried out by a *brujo* (sorcerer), but s/he is just an agent, contracted to do the "job" by an enemy of the victim. Most often, this enemy is not a stranger but rather a close family member or friend— a business partner, mother-in-law, sister, or even a son. All those upon whom one depends for economic, social, and emotional survival may be aggressors because mistrust and suspicion underlie the most intimate social relationships. This is especially true in the urban and peri-urban centers, where accusations of sorcery are most prevalent. Here, wage laborers and merchants compete fiercely in a market where both jobs and buyers are limited. Moreover, wage work has changed the individual/ household dialectic, so that individual success at accumulating wealth directly clashes with social obligations to family and community. Thus, those upon whom one most closely depends for economic support cannot always be trusted to "do the right thing."[4] Accusations of sorcery are a culturally meaningful expression of this ambivalence.

Women and Dependence

Women are especially at risk in this environment of dependence and insecurity. In Peru, where unemployment rates were above 20 percent in 1988, only one in four "economically active" Peruvians were women (Forsberg and Francke 1987, 228). In other words, three out of every four Peruvian women depended on husbands, fathers, or other male relatives to support them.

One reason for this disparity is that men and women are both raised to frown on independent, strong-willed women and to believe that a woman's place is "in the home" rather than "on the street" (Grandón 1987, 18). This is due, in part, to cultural models that emphasize separation of gender roles into domestic and public spheres of influence. Traditionally, throughout the Andes, women have been charged with organizing and administering domestic affairs. In the agrarian, subsistence-oriented setting of the rural highlands, women's gardens, flocks of chickens, ducks, guinea pigs, rabbits, and other food animals provide the food, and their weaving provides the clothing which helps sustain their families. They attend to their children's health (see Finerman 1985) and are responsible for all aspects of childcare. Men believe that "the children are their mother's . . . they are her obligation"[5] (Pimentel Sevilla 1988, 175). At the same time, women have traditionally been expected to defer to male authority in the public sphere. They have been excluded from the political and economic workings of the broader community.[6]

While this emphasis on separate and complementary gender roles may

5

function well in the subsistence-oriented, agrarian economies of the high-lands, where the household is the basic unit of production, it is less adapted to the increased dependence on wages that is typical of the coastal areas. House plots here are too small to sustain much of a garden or the sheep or llamas that have been the traditional source of wool for clothing. So women in coastal cities who do not work outside the home are forced to depend upon the daily allowance that they receive from their husbands in order to feed their families. And because feeding and clothing the family has been traditionally understood to be part of the woman's responsibility, it is typical for men here to give their wives only a portion of their wages.

As buying power has shrunk—it decreased by nearly 60 percent between 1979 and 1988—many women have thus been driven from their homes and into the public sphere in order to fulfill their domestic obligations. Some have begun to organize with other mothers in grassroots organizations that have sprung up to address the problems that they all face. In the last ten years, using funds obtained from international development agencies, the Catholic Church, and service organizations like Rotary International, these women's groups have organized efforts as varied as communal soup-kitchens, infant feeding programs, family-planning and low-cost health clinics, dispensaries, informal credit organizations, cooperatives that produce and sell handcrafts, and community gardens (Grandón 1987; Alcalde Lucero 1988; Barrig 1988).

El Bosque

One such community organization is *El Grupo de Mujeres, Fanny Abanto Calle,* created in 1983 to address the problems that women face in a poor neighborhood called El Bosque on the southernmost edge of Chiclayo. Over the years, this women's group has worked with Rotary International, CARE, Caritas, Perú Mujer, and a German-sponsored development group on various projects for the benefit of all women in the community. As international donations of food and money have swelled and then dried up, membership in the group has also fluctuated. At the height of participation in 1984–85, the group had a membership of 62 women who cooperatively prepared three meals a day for 224 children using the food rations donated by international development agencies. In 1989, when I was invited to interview 15 of the group's members about their concerns as women, the group was preparing breakfasts only for about 60 children.

The women I interviewed were quite a diverse group. They ranged in age from twenty-four to fifty-nine years and were mothers (in one case, a grandmother) of from one to seven children. Two of the women had completed the equivalent of a high school education and one had studied beyond high school. Many of the women had not completed grade school. Some lived with their husbands, some were separated or had been abandoned, and one was widowed. Their homes ranged from very humble adobe structures, which the women themselves had struggled to build, to two-story homes constructed of brick and cement. Some of the residences had water service and most had electricity. These women spoke with me about their life-histories, their relationships with husbands and children, and the economic problems they faced, as well as their thoughts about what they most valued in their friends and about the characteristics that define "good" and "bad" women. In spite of the differences in their personal stories, many shared the same concerns.

Roberta,[7] a thirty-eight-year-old woman with six children, like many of the women I interviewed, had joined the *Grupo de Mujeres, Fanny Abanto Calle*, in spite of her husband's objections. She described him as *machista*:

> *Just because he is a man, he says that he is the one who commands and orders and that [the children and I] are under his rule. Sometimes when I go to the group meetings . . . he says no, that woman was made to be in her house and shouldn't be going out into the street. . . . Sometimes, he doesn't tell me this when he is sober, but when he is drunk. He comes and causes problems . . . insulting and yelling. . . . Well, sometimes, in spite of the fact that he has hit me, and he has told me not to go, I don't give in. I can see that the things I do are for my children and for my home. . . . I know it is a good thing.*

Machismo—the typically Latin American expression of male dominance, authority, and superiority over women—limits women's abilities to look beyond the home for supplemental sources of income. In the poorer neighborhoods, where "women's husbands cannot afford to prohibit their wives from working" (Figueroa and Anderson 1981, 15), men often resist rather than support them. And this resistance causes increased economic, social, and emotional conflicts within the household (Pimentel Sevilla 1988).

Daniela's story about the conflicts between her husband's lack of economic support and his insistence that she not work is particularly poignant. At the age of twenty-two she had fallen in love with a well-known local poet whom she described as, "educated, quiet, and reserved." Like many poor couples, they had set up housekeeping together as common-law partners. Their first two children were born while the couple was living in Daniela's mother's home. Although Daniela's partner had some training as a radio repairman and owned his own tools, he didn't have a steady job. When he did work, he gave her money, but seldom enough to cover the cost of daily meals. Even on a good day, Daniela told me, he would leave her only enough to buy a half-kilo of rice, an egg, and a handful of noodles. As she recalled, "I cried, I suffered. When he would arrive I pleaded, 'Don't be so mean . . . look for steady work, if not for me, then for your two daughters.' " He got steady work for awhile but was fired by the company because he was "lazy." When she cried her frustration, he snapped at her, "I am nobody's slave. . . . Not for you—you're not even pretty—nor for your children will I work."

Eventually, he told her he had decided to go to Lima to look for work. She thought it was a good idea and that her luck might change, so she lent him some money. He left and didn't send her any money for months, so she borrowed some money from a cousin and began to make food to sell, which she would put on a table in her doorway for sale to passersby. As she looked after the children and the housework, her mother helped her with the sales. With this money, she was able to buy the food she needed to feed her mother, her children, and her two nephews. She was happy working and says things were much better than when her husband was around.

When he came back to Chiclayo, Daniela's husband insisted she quit working. "What will people say?" he told her. "I have come back home and you have become a *zamba causera*."[8] Daniela argued, saying that if he didn't give her money, she had no choice but to make it on her own. Because he insisted things would change, she agreed to shut her business. After only a week, she told me, he quit providing for her yet again and everything returned to the way it had been.

Later, when he began having an affair with another woman who was living in the household, he exchanged his quiet, if lazy, demeanor for insults and swearing, which Daniela attributed to the affair. His character changed, she told me, and he verbally abused her. When he hit her one day, she left. "I will put up with poverty, but I will not put up with this," she told him. Her children were school-aged by then and her mother was at home, so she was able to find a more stable job working in a photography studio retouching photographs. Once she had a steady income, her husband came to try and get her back but she refused, convinced that he must be thinking, "I'll conquer her and take her to live in a room that she pays for. She will keep feeding me and I'll live like a king." She told him she would prefer to marry another man a thousand times over rather than return to the suffering that she had with him. He kept after her, but she refused, until she finally met her current husband and they were married.

I heard similar stories from the other women that I talked with. Although they expressed different strategies for dealing with these inequities. Even though Alexandra complained that her husband spent all his money on drink and that he beat the children, she preferred to stay with him and endure rather than risk the social and economic stigma of being a woman alone. As she put it, "So many times I thought of separating from him, but I put up with everything. . . . I raised my children. . . . I have had to be husband and wife. . . . [Even so] I, like my children, have to ask permission from him. . . . He is the boss." Lorena also endured her husband's beatings rather than leave him when he took a mistress so that she would not lose her house. She found consolation in the fact that, now that her children were older, they were taking care of her. "Thank God," she told me, "I had boys. This way, I have the security that they will someday repay me." When their husbands took other women, Reina and Delia both left them. At the time of our interview, Reina's husband was contributing 30,000 intis (about $10) monthly to family expenses, but she was afraid to ask for more, fearing that he might cut her off entirely. Even though she sells *Yambal* (similar to Avon in the United States) and makes frequent trips to Ecuador to bring back contraband items for sale around the neighborhood, she says she can't afford to feed her five children without her husband's help.

Even when there is no resistance from their husbands, poor mothers often find it difficult to earn enough to break their dependency on husbands, neighbors, or family for survival. When Rigoberta's husband left to find work in Lima, they had two small children and she was pregnant with their third. The responsibilities of caring for young children while pregnant, as well as marketing, cooking, washing, and cleaning, would put serious constraints on any mother's time, but attempting to keep up with domestic responsibilities where there is inadequate electricity and no running water adds additional strain. Thus, when her husband sent no money and she was evicted from their rented home, Rigoberta had to depend on the economic and emotional support of her parents to cope. She cried as she recounted how her mother and brothers had treated her when she was forced to move back into the family home with her children. She had no money for food, but instead of welcoming her to share their rations, her brothers accused her of depriving them of their share and treated her children like dogs. Although she was angry and ashamed, Rigoberta felt she had little recourse, dependent as she was on her family for lodging.

When there are older children in the household—and when there is no resistance from the husband—a mother has more flexibility in the type of job she can take. No longer restricted to the home, she may find work for a specific employer as either a domestic servant, a washer-woman, a cook, or a nanny, or she may become a street-seller.[9] If she has no one to help with childcare at home, she may decide to take her children with her to her work. Opportunities for even more lucrative or more stable employment are often denied poor women because they do not have the necessary education. As Roberta and others who had grown up in the countryside before moving to the city told me, "Our parents kept us out of school because they believed that if we [women] learned how to write we would just be more able to write to our boyfriends."

Celina, a thirty-eight-year-old woman with three children who worked at the Mercado Moshoqueque, told me that she was kept out of school to help look after her younger siblings for the thirty days of her mother's confinement after delivery. Then, because her father wouldn't go to the school to officially explain her absence, the teacher wouldn't take her back. The next year she was unable to go back to school because they had "thrown her out." Now, she was working in the market from 7:00 a.m. to 6:00 p.m., selling bananas, plastic bags, cleansers, and a variety of other goods. On good days, she might make enough to buy food for herself and her children, but some days, like the day I interviewed her, she didn't even make enough to cover her bus fare to and from work. Similar to Rigoberta's experience, Celina told me that even though her parents lived nearby, they didn't give her much support. As she put it, "Sometimes, when my father sees that I haven't worked for three or four days, he loans me a bunch of bananas, which he can buy wholesale because of his job counting fruit trucks, . . . but none of my brothers or sisters help me at all."

Unlike Daniela's husband, Rigoberta's husband had supported her efforts to work outside the house after the children were older. Although he refused to give her any money for household expenses or to help out at her fish-selling stall, he did get up early every day to make the trip to a nearby port where he could buy fish wholesale and then bring them to her stall at the local market. Still, he apparently felt that it was his prerogative to spend her income as he wished. After four years working in the market, Rigoberta had managed to save enough money to buy a lot and to begin buying building materials for a house for her family. One day, however, she discovered that while she had been working at the market, her husband had been stealing from the growing pile of supplies and selling them behind her back. When she confronted him, he at first denied that he had sold anything, but then he snapped that the money was also his. Since she didn't give him money from her market sales, he had gotten it from selling the building supplies. In this way, he had reasserted his authority in the household and had shown her "who was boss." When I interviewed Rigoberta, she reported that she no longer felt any love for her husband but that she continued living with him because she needed him to buy the fish every morning at the port. Her children were still young, she explained, and if she had to leave them alone while she went out to the coast, someone might sneak into the house and hurt them. Besides, she was afraid of traveling in the early morning hours by herself, since she could easily be attacked and the money for the fish stolen.

Rigoberta might have been better off economically had she been able to leave her husband, but the social constraints on a woman living alone were—for her, and for many of the women I spoke with—a deterrent. When I asked Celina what she felt was most important in a woman's life she responded, "A husband's support. If one has no husband, there is no respect. People will try to abuse you, even in your home." Outside the home, where public opinion is an important sanction for social behavior, what people will say—*que dirán*—is also of vital concern. Roberta explained to me that, even though her husband's beatings were somewhat legendary in the neighborhood, she sometimes felt little support—even from other women. She told me that other people said it was good that her husband took charge and beat her. They felt his wrath was legitimate because she works outside the home instead of keeping to her house like a "good woman" is expected to do.

According to Peruvian scholars, the physical, psychological, and even moral abuse that Peruvian women endure when their behavior does not conform with expected norms debilitates their sense of self-worth (Pimentel Sevilla 1988, 43) and encourages the formation of a "dependent personality" (Pimentel Sevilla 1988, 117). Decisions, opinions, attitudes, and ways of perceiving reality depend on external mechanisms; subordinance is imposed, and women come to accept their domination by others as a natural and legitimate state of affairs (Pimentel Sevilla 1988, 47). In Peru, women's social roles, their economic dependence, and even their very identity are "other-directed" and "overdetermined."[10] Emotionally, the fear of "what others will say" is especially great because women are subjected to extraordinary external pressures that condition the way they feel about themselves should they not be able to live up to social norms.

Not surprisingly, almost all of the women I interviewed described a "good friend" as one who knows how to keep a confidence, is not a gossip, and is not a hypocrite or two-faced. These women preferred to keep to themselves rather than share their troubles with other women for fear of exposing the gap between the society's ideals and their own behavior to outsiders. As Mirta explained it,

> *I'm not very open. I don't get involved with anybody. . . . But I prefer*
> *people who are frank and who tell it like it is. If I have to find out third- or fourth-hand [what somebody is saying about me], I don't like that. That's why I don't do much visiting. It's difficult [if one goes from house to house, talking with the neighbors], not to be gossiped about.*

Also, the women expressed a real fear of being "shamed" in public. As Mirta added: "It makes me ashamed to yell or fight with another person. When that happens, I would rather die. I might yell at my son here in my house, but not with outsiders."

Almost all of the women shared examples of how they had been shamed by someone they had confided in. Marta, age twenty-four, told me a story about a friend whom she had helped through difficult times, often giving her plates of food. Later, when her friend's situation improved, not only did she not return the favor when Marta needed money to buy medicine for her sick baby, she "went around saying that we eat pig-slop."

Roberta, like Marta, had learned through painful experience that other women in the neighborhood can be egotistical and *interesada* (interested in friendship only when it benefits them economically). Once, a friend whom she had often helped in the past demanded that Roberta pay her back immediately some money that she owed. It wasn't that her friend needed the money, Roberta explained. Her friend's husband had been passing her everything she needed since he had quit drinking and become a member of a Protestant evangelical sect. Still, her friend insisted so firmly that she had to have the money back that Roberta gave it to her, thereby causing her own children to go hungry that day. Marta and Roberta both felt abandoned and rejected by these women whom they had helped in times of need, and both said that they no longer mixed with their neighbors, preferring instead to keep to themselves and suffer their pains in silence.

When I asked why they felt most people were so *interesada*, I was told that this sense of competition, instead of cooperation, had intensified as the economic crisis had deepened during the previous year. Neighbors, friends, and family barely had enough money to care for those who legitimately depended on them, and were certainly unwilling to share with women less fortunate than themselves. On the other hand, economic stresses had intensified the relations of dependence for many of the women, and the possibilities for releasing frustration through overt means had been thwarted. Instead of frustrations being expressed openly, they were often projected onto others as accusations of *daño*.

Daño *in El Bosque*

Many of the women interviewed in El Bosque invoke *daño* as a way to explain the misfortune in their lives. Roberta's story is particularly telling. In a previous marriage, her husband had treated her well, always giving her enough money with which to run her household. Then her husband had fallen in love with another woman, and this woman, out of envy, had effected a *daño* against Roberta, so that her husband would leave her. As she described it,

> [From one day to the next], I got sick. When I went to the doctor, he gave me medicines but it only got worse. I was filled with a tremendous desire to leave the house, and I began drinking. I wasn't interested in taking care of my children, I wasn't interested in anything . . . I just wanted to go out. I had never in my life drunk more than a glass of alcohol at a time, never had I gotten drunk before then. . . . It all started when I found a bottle sitting on the window ledge and I smelled it. . . . After awhile, anytime I smelled that smell I just wanted to drink. . . . I more or less knew that it was my husband's girlfriend [who was behind the problems] . . . because one day he told me, "Roberta, I don't know what it is with that woman. One day she gave me some liquor to drink, and now I can't get her off my mind. Why don't you go and tell her to leave me alone, that you're my wife." . . . I went and told her and she denied it. . . . Then, my six-month-old daughter got sick. I had gone one day to visit some relatives of my husband with the baby, and I had put her in a crib. He came in with the woman while I was in the other room . . . and she took the baby's

diaper. Right away, the baby got sick, from one moment to the next [she became paralyzed]. . . . She died when she was six years old; she couldn't move at all. She was just like a newborn.

After exhausting all other health resources, Roberta's godmother took her to see a *curandero.* Since she didn't believe in sorcery, and would not have consented had she known, the godmother lied and said that she was taking her to a birthday party. When Roberta discovered the ruse, she felt very angry. But when the *curandero,* who had been singing and walking among those present, stood in front of her and spoke, she had been amazed at the precision with which he had described her situation. He told her she had a great desire to drink. Then he described her daughter and her husband, saying:

He has another woman . . . and he will stay with her his whole life. She has harmed you with the intent of killing you, so that you will become an alcoholic, so that you will take up with other men just like a street-woman. . . . You shouldn't spend any more money paying doctors, but rather spend money to buy your daughter good food because . . . you lost a diaper and this diaper has been trabajado *[magically "worked" by a* brujo *to effect the* daño*] and* enterrado *[buried or thrown into the sea]. . . . Your daughter won't recover. Right now, we must concentrate on your recovery so you [can] have another child and another husband to take care of. . . . Your life from here on out will be a trial. You will become involved with a man who . . . will make you suffer greatly.*

According to Roberta, everything that the *curandero* predicted that night came to pass. That's why she believes in *daño:* "When bad people want something, they get it, one way or another—even if they have to resort to *daño.*" Because of her newfound conviction, she now tells her children not to be confrontational and not to fight with others. She has often heard her neighbors openly threaten one another with *daño,* as they shout, "You'll soon see who you're dealing with because my uncle is a *brujo,* and a really good one from Ferreñafe! Just you wait and see."

Both Lorena and Rigoberta also believe that the problems with their husbands have been caused by *daño*. Lorena believes that her husband's new wife was able to steal him away from her through *daño,* and that perhaps one of the reasons he has been treating her better in the last year or so is that the *daño* is wearing off. Rigoberta believes that a photograph she once gave her husband was used to do *daño* to her, and that this explains why she has suffered so much torment with him.

While interviewing the women of El Bosque, I heard many such stories of intended harm. Still, since I had not yet witnessed a sorcerer at work, it was easier to assume the threats were more figurative than real, and that accusations of intended harm provided the "escape valve" for social pressures that could not be expressed more directly.[11] This assumption changed on the day I accompanied two of the healers with whom I worked on what, for them, was a weekly journey. Every Monday the two women would visit the grave of a relative at Chiclayo's main cemetery. Afterward, they would walk among the dead, looking for "packages" among the freshly buried corpses or among the bleached bones of *ánimas* whose bodies had long since rotted away.

On the Monday I accompanied these two healers, we walked into the main cemetery gate and past the posh miniature houses, complete with picture windows and recessed lighting, that are the tombs of the wealthy families of Chiclayo. We passed the main cross and turned left into the rows of more utilitarian crypts—long, double-sided, cement vaults that stood open, ready to receive the dead, their empty niches gaping like ulcers in a pock-marked face. We had no trouble locating the tomb of my friends' dead relative, and after they had replaced its flowers and prayed for his soul before the cement and plaster marker which sealed the sepulcher, we walked along the length of the vault searching for other familiar names in the long rows of the seven-level structure.

Satisfied that we had properly paid our respects, my friends led me away from the honeycomblike tombs and we struck out across the open ground. Here lay those souls whose families could not afford the modest sums required to buy a niche in the above-ground vaults, their graves marked only by weathered, wooden crosses and rusted tin cans or plastic jugs that had once held flowers. Maintenance of these irregularly shaped plots was nonexistent; any grass that may have once covered the mounds of earth had long since turned to dust. Dogs and other creatures of the night had obviously been busy digging at the shallow graves. In some places, body parts were strewn above the ground, tattered rags that had once resembled clothes now clinging to them by threads.

We picked our way among the debris, in search of the grave of a man called Pedro Palomino—a healer whose spirit had once presented itself to my friends during a healing ceremony. He had told them that he had been killed by a sorcerer and that his body was now lying on top of the ground. Because it was unburied, another sorcerer had found it convenient to conceal within the rib cage of Palomino's cadaver a "package," in the shape of a doll made from the unwashed clothes of a man that this second sorcerer had been hired to magically harm. Since this package lay within his cadaver, Palomino had explained, he, as well as the intended victim, was suffering. The next day, my friends had gone to the cemetery and found Palomino's body, with the doll just as he had described it. They followed Palomino's instructions to undo the *daño* and then paid for a Mass in his name. From that time on, Pedro Palomino's spirit has regularly come to them during their rituals, to help them locate the "packages" of persons suffering from this type of *daño*.

As they led me to Palomino's final resting place, we stepped around the remains of a body: the skin was dried and clinging to the broken ribs of the exposed torso—the sun-bleached limbs lay several feet away. From the underside of what was left of the ribcage, one of my friends freed a clothing bundle with a long, pointed stick. It was completely stuck-through with sewing needles—twenty or more pins sticking arms to torso and chest to stomach on the soiled shirt. A few paces away, another package was found. This time, a newspaper parcel wrapped in plastic concealed a woman's blouse. Within the folds of the blouse lay a picture, dried, crushed herbs, and what appeared to be slivers of human bones. A tiny, fractured, human-looking skull lay nestled in the fragments. "My God," exclaimed the healer, "how can people be so evil." She sprinkled the Holy Water that she carried for such purposes over these packages while praying to God that both victims might be delivered from the evil intended by the sorcerer.

The Healing Tradition

Sorcery and healing are two sides of a single coin. The sorcerers who effect the harm, and the *curanderos* who heal it, both utilize the forces of an unseen world beyond the realm of normal sensory perception. Both make ritual use of a ritual altar called a *mesa* (often translated as table [Giese 1989, 61]) and ingest an infusion of the mescaline-bearing San Pedro cactus (*Trichocereus pachanoi*) so they can psychically see or "travel" into this world. Over the last fifty years or so, social scientists have studied the healing traditions of northern Peru, which have been developed to counteract this antisocial magic.

The San Pedro cactus—also called *huachuma* or *achuma,* and *gigantón,* is a "smooth relatively thin, night-blooming columnar cactus of the genus *Cereus*" (Sharon 1978, 39) which grows to a height of 4 meters. It can be found at sea level and at altitudes of up to 3,000 meters from Ecuador to Bolivia. In this region of the world, as suggested by the pictorial representation of this cactus on pre-Columbian pottery, San Pedro has probably been used by shamans for at least 1,000 years, and possibly as long as 3,000 years.[12]

Written evidence associating the use of San Pedro with shamanic practice appears shortly after the arrival of the Spaniards. Sharon quotes from colonial sources written by seventeenth-century priests who were associated with the Church-sponsored campaigns to "extirpate idolatries." In 1631, one Father Oliva wrote:

> *The principal* Caciques *and* Curacas *[leaders] of this nation . . . in order to know the good or bad will of some to others drink a beverage they call Achuma which is a water they make from the sap of some thick and smooth cacti that they raise in the hot valleys. They drink it with great ceremonies and songs, and as it is very strong, after they drink it they remain without judgment and deprived of their senses, and they see visions that the Devil represents to them and consistent with them they judge their suspicions and the intentions of others. (In Sharon 1978, 43)*

In northern Peru, this practice continued throughout the eighteenth century, despite Church efforts to exterminate pagan, idolatrous ways, and it continues still. In 1768, for example, one Marcos Marcelo, an Indian born in Ferreñafe near Chiclayo, was accused of cooking and imbibing the hallucinogenic brew by an ecclesiastic court. The detailed account of his actions so closely matches the way in which San Pedro is used today that there can be no doubt that Peruvian shamanism both accommodated and resisted the Church's attempts to eradicate such pagan practices. When asked the nature and process of the cures that he conducted, Marcelo's testimony was recorded by the notary as follows:

19

> He said that when a sick person who believed he was bewitched solicited
> the Declarant in order to cure him, he first cooked an herb that he
> always has; which is called Gigantes; which usually is found on
> mountain slopes, and that he drank the juice of this herb, well cooked,
> with which he came into full awareness and patently saw with his eyes
> the sick person's maleficio and if he had a frog, a snake or another
> animal in the gut, and that with this certain knowledge he gave the sick
> person the news about his condition and also whether his illness was
> sorcery; and he also recognized the sorcerer who had done the daño,
> and that being thus assured the sick one of the state of his illness he
> begged the Declarant to cure him; and then, to proceed with the cure,
> what he did was to give the sick person of the same herb to drink; after
> drinking it the sick person became drunk, and fell exhausted and that
> if the sick person could be cured he got well and if not he died. (AAT
> 1768)

The "drunkenness" associated with ingestion of San Pedro infusions, often referred to by modern healers as *remolino* (whirlpool), may be explained scientifically as one of the plant's psychotropic effects. Mescaline (trimethoxy-phenilethilamine) is contained in the skin and rind of the plant in a concentration of 0.12 percent (Polía 1988b, 221). However, modern-day healers, who use the plant to see the causes of a person's affliction, describe the plant's powers in quite different terms: "It is the [plant's] power or *virtud* (virtue) that permits one to see. The power is a spirit that is in the plant, if it weren't there it would not be possible to see" (Polía 1988a, 54).

20   What does one "see" upon ingesting San Pedro? Some *curanderos* describe seeing events occurring at a great distance (these may belong to the past or the future) and passing before their eyes, as in a movie. Sometimes, this look into supernatural realms is described in terms of spiritual flight, in which the *curandero's* shadow, or spirit, is unbound from his body and projected in time and space to the places that are home to the spirit forces responsible for the affliction. As one of Polía's informants told him:

> The spirit of San Pedro takes one wherever it wants. If you have had a
> susto [spiritual shock], the San Pedro takes one to the place where
> the susto happened. It's not the person who travels, certainly, but the
> spirit. . . . One can see many things according to the illness, or when a
> person has been magically harmed one sees who it was that did the
> job. One sees what type of daño one has and where it was made.
> (1988a, 56)

The altar around which the ritual ceremony revolves—both the altar and the ceremony are referred to as *mesa*—consists of power-objects called *artes,* which are also perceived as containing a spirit-essence or power. These include staffs of various kinds of wood, including palmwood, quince, and bamboo. These staffs are used to defend against attacks from sorcerers and spirit forces as well as to launch counterattacks against these. Swords and knives of steel and bronze serve a similar function, attacking and defending as the healer commands. The staffs and swords are also used to cleanse the patient of evil and illness, absorbing the *daño* from the patient's body and trapping it until it is dispatched into the air by the *curandero* or his assistant.

The staffs and swords, when not carried by the *curandero,* his assistants, or by the patient for personal defense, are to be found standing on their points in a row along the length of the cloth on which the other *artes* are placed. Although this cloth may be laid out on a table that is permanently set up against a wall inside the *curandero's* house or office, it is more frequently taken out after sundown on the night when the ritual will be held and set upon the ground—in a corral, patio, or pasture where the *maestro* will perform the ritual. Most of the rest of the *artes* are arranged on top of the cloth. These may include framed pictures of religious images or sculpted statues of these images, rocks, crystals, seashells, rattles, animal hoofs, pre-Columbian ceramic pots, skulls, crucifixes, and *seguros*—the herb-filled bottles that are said to contain the *curandero's* shadow-spirit. In addition, the other indispensable tools for conducting the ritual are set around the groundcloth: containers of sugar, white corn meal, cane alcohol, champagne or other sweet wines, perfumes and colognes (especially floral fragrances like *agua florida* and *agua de kananga*), macerated leaves of white or black tobacco, bitter herbs which cause vomiting, and, of course, the pot containing the boiled mixture of San Pedro—.

Preparations for the ritual generally begin in the afternoon on the day of the ceremony. A length of the San Pedro, which has either been purchased, gathered from a hillside where it grows wild, or cut from a garden, is sliced into cross-sections like a loaf of bread or a cucumber. After it has been placed in water, perhaps with other psychoactive plants like *misha* and with purgatives, the cactus is prayed over and put on the stove to boil for anywhere from two to seven hours.

The ceremony itself begins sometime between sundown and midnight with the *curandero* setting up the *mesa,* saying or singing the opening invocations, and serving the San Pedro to all present. The *mesa* ritual is usually divided into ceremonial activities and curing activities, which end before the sun's rays strike the curing altar the following the morning. Ceremonial acts include invocations to God, the Virgin, other Catholic saints (especially Saint Ciprian), and to the spirit of San Pedro to give the healer the ability to see into the spirit world. In addition, offerings of sweet perfumes, aromatic seeds, and floral-scented waters are made to the spirit-essences of the lagoons, mountains, and the four cardinal points, to the spirits of the dead, and to the spirit-essences of all the power-objects on the *mesa.* These are also "raised," by nasally imbibing *tabaco*—a mixture of tobacco leaves, cane alcohol, and perfumes in order to activate their power and to call their spirits to the *mesa.* Any negative influences that may affect the *mesa* are dispatched or "thrown away." Perhaps the most important ceremonial act is the serving of the San Pedro to all present after blessing it and invoking its spirit to attend to the special needs of each of the patients. The *curandero* may speak, chant, sing, whistle, shake a rattle, strum a guitar, sound a bell, play a harmonica, or remain silent during the ceremonial parts of the ritual. The sound of the rattle is especially good for "calling" the *curandero's* tutelary spirits to the *mesa.*

The curing acts of the ritual include the *rastreo* (divination/diagnosis) of the *daño,* as well as several therapeutic acts, including the *limpia* (cleansing), the *chupa* (sucking), and the *levantada* (raising), all of which help destroy the *daño. Limpias* involve the vigorous rubbing of the victim's body in an up-to-down motion with various *artes,* especially staffs and swords. After each *limpia,* the patient is instructed to shake him- or herself vigorously by jumping and fully extending the arms and legs so that elbow and knee joints "pop." This action helps to disengage the evil from the patient's body. Meanwhile, the healer and/or assistant, using their mouths, spray the patient and/or the *arte* with cane alcohol, rubbing alcohol, or another liquid appropriate to the particular healer's ritual, so as to send the evil from the patient's body. *Levantadas* require nasal-ingestion of the *tabaco* by patient and/or healer or assistants so as to pull out the evil from deep within the patient's body. Generally, the *tabaco* is nasally imbibed through first the left and then the right nostril. If healer and/or assistants are "raising" the patient, they do so from his feet to his head. As with the *limpia,* the patient is instructed to shake out the evil after the raising. Sometimes, the healer employs strong language or instructs the patient to shout profanities during the *levantada* or while shaking-out so as to counterattack the influence of the evil in his life. *Chupas* act to suck the *daño* from specific parts of the victim's body. The healer places his mouth—or the end of a staff—against the body part to be sucked. The person performing this act holds in his mouth an infusion of water, either a special mixture of Holy Water that combines herbs, tobacco, perfumes, lime, honey, flowers, and other ingredients, and/or water from one of the sacred lagoons of Las Huaringas. The water acts as a kind of barrier that captures the *daño* so that it does not pass into the healer's body. He sucks the *daño* out of the victim's body and then vomits or spits, being careful not to swallow any of the liquid. The healing activities also may include calling or pulling one's shadow from the place where it has been captured to the *mesa* so that it can be reintegrated with the body.

Toward dawn, after the patient has been diagnosed and cleansed of the *daño* from which he suffers, the healer turns his attention from curing to *floreciendo* (flowering), or raising the patient's luck. This often involves another nasal ingestion of *tabaco* on behalf of the patient, as well as orally spraying perfumes, sweet lime, flowers (or flowered waters), white sugars, and other substances over the patient.

If the patient is to receive a *seguro,* which the *maestro* has previously prepared, he will receive it now. The *seguro* is a jar of ritually prepared herbs that protects against *daños* and pulls luck and good fortune to its owner. It consists of a clear glass bottle (often a discarded rum or perfume bottle) which has not been in contact with garlic, onion, or other strong seasonings. This bottle is filled with magical herbs that have been collected from enchanted locations, especially the sacred lagoons of Las Huaringas. The bottle is also filled with water from one or more of the sacred lagoons, perfumes and flowered waters, honey, sugar, fragrant seeds, and it may contain liquid mercury, small figurines, crystals, and other miniature *mesa* objects. The spirit-powers of all the objects that it contains are called upon by the *maestro* as dawn approaches. The patient—whether or not his own hair, nails, and/or photograph have been placed within the *seguro*—is instructed to breathe into the bottle three times so that his shadow is symbolically entrusted to the spirit-powers of the herbs, water of the lagoons, and other ingredients bottled up in the *seguro.*

The remaining moments of the *mesa* ritual are usually devoted to blessing the *mesa artes* and the personal possessions (keys, money, photographs, clothing, hair, fingernails, jewelry) which the patient has placed on the *mesa* during the night and which serve as talismans once they are blessed. All present are also blessed, usually receiving a good drenching of perfumes, flowered waters, petals of white roses or carnations, sugar, white corn meal, sweet lime, and other substances that refresh and sweeten. This final oral spraying (often followed by a symbolic "meal," where small amounts of these refreshments are consumed by all present) serves a double function. Not only does it refresh and sweeten to bring good-fortune to all present, it also cuts the effect of the San Pedro because it counteracts the "hot" nature of the hallucinogen with its cool or "fresh" properties.[13] After a final benediction thanking God, the Virgin, the spirit of San Pedro, and that of the highland lakes and mountains who have helped the *curandero* throughout the night, the *curandero* closes the ceremony, often asking the patients to greet the morning and each other with applause, hugs, or handshakes. If the *mesa* has been set up in the open air, it is gathered up and stored in a dark room before the sun rises. If payment for the evening has not already been received, the *curandero* may now retire to a room where the patients will approach him privately to receive any last-minute instructions about the status of their condition, and to pay for services received.

In order to understand the power of the *mesa*—and of the San Pedro also—it is necessary to understand the perceived relationship between body and spirit articulated by those who heal.[14] The *curanderos* believe that each individual has a spiritual essence (also known as one's vitality, volition, or will), without which life would not be possible. This spirit-essence is separable from the body. As one of my informants added, this vital essence leaves the body during sleep and travels in what we know as "dreams." When it is time to awaken, the spirit returns. Were it not for this temporary separation, the body could not rest, but were it not for the reintegration of body and spirit at the beginning of the new day, the body would die.

This duality—and separability—of spirit-essence and physical manifestation permeates the natural world as well. The spiritual essence of caves, springs, mountains, and highland lagoons is understood in two ways. First, it may be an inherent feature of the particular place. Second, it may be the accumulated spiritual essence of humans who lived and died at that place—on the mountain, in the cave, or at the lakeshore—in previous eras. Both definitions of this spiritual essence are referred to generically as the "charm," or the *encanto,* of the place.[15]

The *encanto* and the physical appearance of an object or place are different. In the highlands of Piura, for example, there is a "charmed" lagoon called Chicuate. According to legend, this lagoon was once an Incan city whose streets were paved of gold. But, when the Christians missionized the area, their God became angry at the libertine ways of the inhabitants and caused the city to sink into the ground and become covered with water. Today, the physical manifestation of Chicuate is the highland lagoon that remains, but to those who see the *encanto*, this charmed city, with all of its inhabitants, is apparent below the surface of the lake.

These *encantos* have a kind of power that exists in symbiotic relationship with humans. Mountains, waterfalls, lagoons, and other expressions of nature provide humans with food, water, and shelter in exchange for periodic offerings.[16] But, when not propitiated, their *encantos* may attack humans, capturing the life-essence from unwary passersby by "opening" to reveal treasures of gold and silver, or even whole cities like the city of Chicuate described above.[17] The *encanto* thus lures the passerby into approaching. Then, and especially if the victim becomes frightened when s/he realizes that the "treasure" is not real, the victim's spirit may be jarred loose from the body. The *encanto* captures and imprisons the loosened spirit, which in turn adds to the aggregate power of the place.

The power of *encantos* to capture and possess human spirits makes possible the practice of sorcery. The person desiring to effect the harm provides a sorcerer with something that contains an image of, or something that belongs to, the victim. What constitutes the victim's "image" is loosely interpreted and may include the imprint left when walking across a dusty road, the victim's signature on a letter or other document, or even a photograph. Similarly, the thing that "belongs" to the victim might be a lock of hair, a bit of fingernail, or even a piece of the victim's unwashed clothing. These appurtenances facilitate the sorcerer's ability to call the victim's spirit from the body and to commend it to the spirit of the *encanto*, with whom the sorcerer has a special relationship or "pact."[18] Sometimes, this pact is not with a "charmed" place but with an *ánima*, or tortured soul, of a human who has died but who still wanders the earth.

In either case, to complete the process and "bind" the victim's spirit to the *encanto* or the *ánima*, the sorcerer prepares a potion or powder containing an appurtenance of the *encanto* or *ánima* to which the victim's spirit has been commended. For a pact with the *encanto* of a particular mountain, a bit of dirt from that place will suffice. Similarly, for a pact with an *ánima*, a bit of ground-up bone from a human burial will be included in the potion. This potion or powder should somehow come in contact with the victim, so that s/he might absorb the magical effects of the sorcerer's work through contagion. It might be slipped into the victim's food or drink. In this case, it is called *daño por boca* (harm that is ingested) and is usually fatal. If placed in the victim's path so that s/he unwittingly steps upon it, flung into the air so that s/he unwittingly breathes it, or placed on the victim's clothes so that s/he comes in contact with the magic when next wearing the garment, it is called *daño por aire* (harm that is carried through the air and comes into contact with the victim in this way).[19] Similarly, a "package" containing the victim's clothing, hair, photograph, and so on, might be prepared and buried at the place where the *encanto* resides. This binds the victim's spirit and causes the body to suffer the effects through sympathetic action. *Daño* is thus a kind of "soul loss." But, unlike *susto,* it requires the intervention of sentient beings who orchestrate soul capture. For this reason, *mal daño,* literally, "evil-harm," falls under the heading of sorcery.

To cure the sorcery, a healer must be able to ascertain which shaman and which *encanto* or *anima* is responsible for the harm, as well as the techniques by which the victim's spirit was commended and bound. Similarly, the healer must somehow locate the victim's spirit, persuade or force the *encanto* or the *anima* who holds it to release it, assist in its reintegration with the victim's body, neutralize the harm, alleviate the symptoms, and provide some kind of defense against future *daño.*

It is to this end that the healer ingests an infusion of the mescaline-rich San Pedro cactus and calls upon the spirit-power of the *mesa* objects for help. Since the *mesa* objects come from "charmed" places, they embody the spirit-essence of these *encantos.*

The above generalizations are based on studies of the lives and ritual practices of male *curanderos* in northern Peru. However, the picture is still far from complete because women's contemporary participation in this tradition is completely missing in the analysis. This omission is puzzling for several reasons. First, the archaeological record suggests that women utilized the psychoactive cactus, as well as objects such as those found on contemporary *mesas,* long before the arrival of the Spaniards brought the written word to Peru. Second, as will be discussed at length in chapter 2, early written records suggest that women made offerings to Andean deities and ministered to the sick both before and during the colonial period. Yet, with but one exception, little has been published about the role of contemporary women in this ancient tradition of sorcery and healing.

Do female healers perceive human affliction similarly to their male counterparts? Do their therapeutic strategies differ from those of the men? In the social and economic setting of present-day northern Peru, does becoming a healer empower women in significant ways? Further, how (if at all) does growing up female in a patriarchal society reflect, shape, or constrain the emergence of an explicitly feminine model of healing in this region? Finally, does a "gendered" model of shamanism offer any redress for the dependence and suffering of women living under patriarchy? In an effort to unravel the dynamics of gender and healing in northern Peru the following chapters address these questions.

i *Families and Emotional Dependence*

I kept a journal as a youth, trying my hand at poetry and other romantically tragic essays that reflected the self-indulgent melancholy typical of early adolescence. Looking through those poems, letters, and essays as an adult is painful and embarrassing, but it also reveals much about why I became so enamored with Peru, about the origins of the emotional dependence which still plagued me as an adult and which served as the catalyst for my own experience with sorcery and healing. In that journal, when I was thirteen, I wrote my first poem.

If I could sing a song to you
I'd sing of love and of hope anew,
Of peace and joy and of brotherhood
But I have no words to sing with.

I've found the truth and I've seen the light
I know the answer to mankind's plight,
The world must know, oh they've got to be told
But I have no words to sing with.

This feeling inside, I'm yearning to tell
My silent world, it's like living in hell
But I have no words to sing with . . .

Today, I understand the reasons for my frustration and my silence, but at the time, I was confused about the melancholy and frequent lack of energy which so worried my mother. Although I have two older brothers, from the time I was nine or ten, when they left home for college, I had grown up like an "only child," surrounded by my parents' affection but without the company of siblings. In many ways, I was a lonely, introspective child, spending much time alone with my essays and poetry, as I tried to sort out who I was and what I might become. I often felt isolated and alone, as though no one understood me. I remember sitting in my room one day, feeling like a sprig of wheat, blowing in the wind, changing and reacting according to the whims of the gusts. I felt empty, and I felt somehow at the mercy of the world around me.

In high school, I compensated for the emptiness which was growing within me by becoming involved in every club and every school activity that I could handle. Externally, I was exuberant, but as a perfectionist, I didn't like myself very much. I heaped criticism upon myself every time I didn't live up to my own, often unrealistic expectations. Additionally, I was eager to please, changing and reacting according to the whims of others, all the while feeling empty and somewhat at the mercy of the world around me.

The moral lessons I learned from my parents expressed that legacy of hard work, self-abnegation, and sacrifice so typical of western farm-families: "Don't be selfish." "Your commitment to others is more important than your own needs." "Do your best." "Be good." "It's important to be appreciated." They were lessons that gave little room for enjoyment, while speaking volumes about the importance of what others think. Whether because of constitution, upbringing, or simply because of having too much time to think, these were years in which I felt confused and angry, guilty and responsible, self-righteous and unlovable, all at the same time. I deeply envied my friends' families, where I saw laughter and play, communication and forgiveness. I longed to repeat my childhood as part of a large and boisterous family, where there was room for laughter and growth, imperfection and change.

So, I was more excited than nervous when I was selected to participate in the American Field Service high school exchange program. Soon I was told that a family had been found to host me in Peru, and that the family had eleven children, ranging in age from eight to twenty-eight years of age! The youngest seven children lived at home. I was ecstatic. I memorized the family picture that had been sent to me and counted the days until I would be among them. During the orientation in Lima, we were told that Peruvian families were not as liberal as U.S. families with regard to dating and other issues, and that there were more-narrowly-defined roles for both men and women than in the States. Girls were expected to be virgins when they married, we were told, and we should expect to be more sheltered and protected than the boys. While some of my AFS friends balked at these new rules, I felt strangely safe and comfortable with them. I looked forward to the security of having the roles well pre-scribed, and I looked forward to living up to these well-defined expecta-tions. I also looked forward to having eleven new "brothers" and "sisters" to share in my adventures.

In Trujillo, I met my new family and began the process of adjustment. In spite of my eagerness, the first few months of my new life were hard. I knew no Spanish and although three of my new siblings had taken exten-sive English courses at a private institute, they had agreed not to use their English with me until I had a firm grasp of the language. I again felt frustrated at my inability to communicate. But this time, the silence was an obstacle that could be overcome and I was determined to be victorious. My little dictionary and my vocabulary notebook for writing down the new words that I discovered were with me always. When one sibling would walk away, his or her patience worn from my constant pointing at objects and asking "What is that?" I would seek out someone else to be my temporary tutor. I was lucky to have so many people close at hand to help me! At the dinner table, I was merciless, so anxious was I to partici-pate in the rollicking and boisterous conversation. During my first two months in the Catholic girls' high school in which I had been enrolled, I understood little, since the classes were in Spanish. But I was determined to finish my homework in spite of the language barrier. I would often spend ten or more hours struggling at the upstairs table with my note-books and my dictionary. It wasn't until much later that I realized the ire and the envy that I aroused in my new siblings. I was being held up as the example against which their father compared their lax attitudes toward their schoolwork.

That year, there were only three exchange students in the entire city (of 250,000 people) so I was the focus of attention in almost every social encounter. My arrival had inspired a new commitment to family outings, holiday dinners, and social gatherings among the large extended family of cousins and uncles, aunts and nieces who lived both in and beyond Trujillo. Before the novelty wore off, I was invited on every trip to the store, every drive around town in the new family minivan, and every Sunday-night walk around the town square.

During those first months, I was so thrilled with the attention and approval that at some point I thought my dream of being part of a loving, exuberant family had been realized. Although I knew that my adoptive kinship status was fictitious, I wanted to believe that it was real at some level. As I slowly mastered the language, I experienced problems that should have tempered my identification with the family. After the novelty of my presence wore off, for instance, I began to realize that jealousies and envy were brewing which I had not recognized at first. My apparent preference for one sister caused another to stop speaking to me for several weeks. A trust that I had given yet another sister was betrayed, and I was publicly humiliated. Inexorably, I became part of the complex machinery of trust, betrayal, and calculated appeals for attention which probably afflicts many large families, where emotional resources—as well as material resources—are often limited.

Despite the battles for attention and affection, the children were taught obedience and respect to elders, loyalty to family, and duty to society. Most of all, they were taught to bring honor on the family by protecting the family's image. When ideals could not, for whatever reason, be upheld, they were taught to project the appearance that all was well and to keep knowledge of the gaps between ideal behavior and actual occurrences within the household.

I recognized that once I learned the codes and as long as I conformed to expected behavior, I could be confident of winning the approval which I needed to feel good about myself. Over the next months, I watched and learned and became proficient at the behaviors expected of me. My confusion abated and I began to feel reintegrated—but my allegiance passed from my home culture to that of my new home. In anthropological terms, I "went native."

After my year in Peru, I returned to the States, but I found it difficult to readjust. I longed to return to Trujillo—to a world which didn't confuse me and in which I knew who I was. There was a more personal reason to return as well. In Trujillo, I had fallen head-over-heels in love with one of my Peruvian brothers. His name was Carlos and he was only seventeen, but I was absolutely smitten. It was a bittersweet romance, bolstered by an idealism which did not withstand even the first obstacles of separation. At one point, soon after my departure, I wrote him suggesting that because of the time and distance which we would need to endure before seeing one another again, we should consider breaking up. What I secretly wanted was to know that he still loved me, that he would fight to continue our relationship. He didn't. I felt hurt, guilty for trying to manipulate him, abandoned, angry, and confused. There was something about the feeling of belonging that I had felt with this young man that I wanted back. I sensed that the old frustrations at not being able to honestly communicate my feelings had tragically betrayed me. He haunted my thoughts, and I was unable to move on. Even when I married my college sweetheart, I couldn't get him out of my mind. I think I began to study anthropology so that I could find a way to fill the void left by our breakup.

I returned to Trujillo in 1982 (on vacation with my new husband), in 1984 (to conduct research for my Master's degree in Anthropology), and in 1987 (to begin dissertation research while working as a Research Associate for a study designed by Joralemon and Sharon to document the efficacy of *curandero* ritual therapy). In all these visits, I lived with the same family I had stayed with in 1975. I suffered silently as I watched Carlos fall in and out of love with other women.

In the intervening years, the children had grown, but five of the original seven, including Carlos, still lived in the family home. They still lived under the same house rules, deferring to parental authority in ways which seemed similar to those I had witnessed twelve years earlier. The girls still sometimes hid their romantic relationships from their brothers and their parents. Even those who had finished college and embarked on their careers still answered to their father when work responsibilities or a date kept them out too late. The boys had much more flexibility. They had keys to the house, which the girls did not, and came and went with impunity. But they, too, were careful to maintain decorous relations with their parents and to carefully disguise their adventures.

I found it difficult to adapt to these controls, especially since I was married and had managed my own household affairs for several years. When my husband Dan came to visit, my Peruvian "mother" would chide me if he decided to iron a shirt or make himself a sandwich in the kitchen. When he showed no anger at my sleeping until noon on the mornings after I had attended an all-night *mesa*, she would chide me for my laziness and warn him that he was being too soft.

Although certainly the most vocal, she was not alone in her criticisms of both my marriage and my behavior as a married woman. The brothers often counseled Dan about proper male and female roles, expressing both disgust and pity that he was henpecked by his wife. I earned a new nickname—*la loca,* the unbridled "crazy" one—because of my nocturnal comings-and-goings. After Dan returned to California, suspicions about behavior mounted. Irritated at the innuendoes and lack of confidence, I flaunted my independence like a rebellious adolescent. I spent less and less time at home. When I did arrive for meals or in the evening, a growing gulf prevented all but the most polite conversation. Mostly, I ate in silence, then slipped unnoticed to my room. I felt more and more like a boarder, and less a part of the family. I pretended not to care, but inside I mourned.

Then, in September of 1987, I learned I was pregnant with Dan's child. I embraced my new, culturally appropriate, role of expectant mother. This Peruvian household—with its eleven children, numerous grandchildren, and great Peruvian/Catholic family ethic—had, after all, helped shape my understanding of social and gender roles. I felt glorious at being able to finally fulfill such a basic expectation of the married woman and I basked in their approval and concern. Once again, I felt comfortable with my identity as a member of the family. Once again, I was at ease with the rules and codes of behavior the family imposed upon my Peruvian persona and felt more allegiance to these than to those of my home culture. The tensions that had darkened the previous months melted away for a time. I was treated to sweets and affectionately teased about my bull of a man. I quickly forgot the shadow of rejection that had threatened my status just weeks before. When a friend asked me what I planned to do after finishing my degree, I quickly responded that I would find work in Peru. "This is where I belong," I told him. "Others may come here in passing, but I intend to stay."

2 ❖ Madre, Mujer, Bruja

Introduction

In May of 1785, in the Doctrine of Trujillo, Peru, a twenty-year-old woman named Manuela de la Resurección de la Cruz accused her biological mother as well as her adoptive mother—María de la O—of having a pact with the Devil. According to the story Manuela told her parish priest,

> [She said] that she often saw some married women with their husbands and other women who were not married gather at midnight in María de la O's house. When they were all there, they would strip and all go naked to a big abandoned field full of water. . . . They would bathe and anoint their underarms with white powders and turn into ducks. And all did the same thing. . . . And [then] they would fly to where there was a large lake tucked in among some hills and when they got there they got in the lake to swim. Afterwards a huge red goat would come down, shooting flames from his anus. Then all would get out of the lake and would form a circle and one by one they would go to kiss the goat's ass. When all had finished . . . they would dance. [They would fly] back to town and then enter [the house]. . . . To turn back into people they would cross themselves and say a "Hail Mary." And each would take their clothes and go home. . . . [signed] Fray Agustín Delgado.[1]

As a result of Manuela's accusations, the two women were imprisoned. When questioned by the Ecclesiastic Judges, they denied the charges, but the interrogations persisted. Neighbors were interrogated and were asked to affirm gossip and hearsay that proclaimed María de la O to be a witch. Still the accused denied the charges. Finally, María de la O convinced the

Judges to allow her to face Manuela and to contest the charges. At this, Manuela recanted, claiming that she had been persuaded by her husband's aunt (a long-time enemy of the two) to approach the priest with this fabricated tale. Finally, after nearly three years, María de la O's transfer from the Royal Jail was approved, and she was apparently released.

This account—one of twenty-nine proceedings brought against parishioners in the Doctrine of Trujillo by Ecclesiastic Judges between 1752 and 1924—is remarkable for several reasons. First, it illustrates the social dialectics of history. In these cases, the power of the Church to influence the way these women were perceived and to remake them into witches is evident. Second, it shows how European ideologies of witchcraft—which portrayed women as Devil-worshipping and evildoers—had passed from the realm of Church dogma to that of Peruvian popular belief by the late eighteenth century. María de la O was accused of these acts, *not* by the church fathers, but by her own adoptive daughter. Finally, this case is remarkable because, together with the other folios on record in the bishopric, it opens a new chapter in the analysis of the impact of the Church on the construction and manipulation of gender identities in northern Peru.

In contemporary northern Peru, participation in the *mesa* tradition of sorcery and healing is perceived as a primarily male occupation. In part, this view may stem from the fact that researchers into this tradition have been primarily male.[2] Inaccessibility to female practitioners, who tend to emphasize the private nature of their healing practices, by male researchers may partially explain the lack of women documented. But this perception also stems from popular beliefs. Indeed, when I began my search for female *curanderas,* months passed before I found anyone who would admit to participating in this profession. When I asked friends, colleagues, and even the male *curanderos* I had met over the years for their help in locating female *curanderas,* I was told that most women who *do* work with the supernatural world practice negative magic. In fact, as I was told by one of the male healers of Joralemon and Sharon's study, the most powerful sorceresses are female *brujas,* who transform themselves into black cats, ducks, pigs, and goats as they cast their spells and who might take to the air on brooms to attend their secret reunions with the Devil. Time and again, when I asked the question, "Do you know any *women* who are *curanderas?*" the reply was emphatic: "No, all the women who work with magic are *brujas!*"

I will show that, contrary to these views, women do work as *curanderas* in contemporary northern Peru. They participate now—and have participated historically—in the same traditions as male *curanderos,* utilizing both the curing *mesa* and the ingestion of the San Pedro cactus, just as their ancestors did fifteen hundred years ago. So, the question becomes "Why?" Why did this transformation in the perception of women *curanderas* occur? What were the social dialectics of history that typed women not as healers but as witches? And why did this ideology pass from official Church dogma to popular lore?

Women and Shamanism before the Conquest

We know from the archaeological record that prehistoric women utilized both the psychoactive San Pedro cactus and some ritual paraphernalia which bear a resemblance to the contemporary *mesa* to cure the sick. In the portrait-style pottery of the ancient inhabitants of this region, women are depicted, with San Pedro in their hands, in an attitude of ecstatic trance, for example. They are also depicted healing the sick, who lie prostrate before them. And they are depicted performing the *mocha*— the sacred "kiss," a ceremony that was later recorded and described by Spanish priests during the early 1600s.

Today, the earliest chronicles for northern Peru provide the only written insight we have into the content of pre-Columbian ritual there. For a variety of reasons, however, they must be viewed with caution—especially as a means of reconstructing women's precontact roles as healers, diviners, priestesses, or even sorceresses. First, it should be remembered that by the time of the Spanish conquest, the peoples of northern coastal Peru had already been conquered and reconquered many times. Between the time these pots had been created and the first appearance of written descriptions of coastal religious and healing traditions, these traditions had been co-opted, repressed, or transformed many times. Moreover, during the first fifty years after the Spanish conquest, coastal populations had been drastically reduced by both disease and military action, and the chronicles of northern Peruvian lifeways were mainly written after this decimation had taken its toll.[3] Finally, the only written record of indigenous life prior to the Spanish conquest is told by chroniclers whose perceptions of the pre-Columbian past were colored by their experiences of the colonial world. Those who tell us about Andean women's lives before, during, and even after the Spanish conquest are not other women but men, men whose superior position vis-à-vis women in Spanish society certainly affected their views. As Irene Silverblatt reminds us, "History making (which includes history denying) is a cultural invention. . . . History tends to be 'made' by those who dominate—by chiefs, noblemen and kings" and then universalized to celebrate their heroes and to silence dissent (Silverblatt 1987, xxi–xxii). The result has been to either factor women out of the picture altogether or to present them in a context that justifies and confirms views which are politically and socially congruent with the needs of the dominant class.

Considering the problems, it is no surprise that few attempts have been made to compile information about either the historical or pre-Columbian roles of women as magical religious specialists, especially in northern Peru.[4] Nor is it surprising that scholarship that attempts to fill these spatial, temporal, and translational gaps is only partially complete. Nevertheless, a partial (and critical) reconstruction of female healing in pre-Colombian Peru is certainly more valuable than no picture at all. It is to this end—and with these caveats—that the following summary of recent scholarly contributions on female healing in pre-Colombian Peru is presented.

According to colonial reports, before the arrival of the Spaniards, Andean social, economic, and political organization emphasized the complementary and parallel roles of men and women (Silverblatt 1978; 1987, 3–39). Even the cosmological organization of the universe reflected these parallel and complementary roles.

Inca cosmology basically divided the world into two equal halves, separating the masculine concepts of virile strength, force, conquest, and power from the feminine concepts of fecundity, reproduction, and sustenance.[5] Representations of these ideas were deified: the sea, lagoons, rivers, and aspects of the womblike earth were associated with the sustaining qualities of woman, while lightning, thunder, hail, and other "penetrating" manifestations of virile power were associated with man. The Sun and the Moon comprised the top of the hierarchy of the Inca pantheon of gods,[6] each presiding over a gender-specific half-world. The Sun, creator of men, presided over the conquering empire, while the Moon, creator of women, presided over the earth and the sea, the mother of all waters (Rostworowski de Diez Canseco 1983, 79–80). Proper functioning of the Empire needed both halves, as is evidenced by the numerous manifestations of the sacred that were paired, or even married (Arriaga 1968, 25, 79, 89; Huertas Vallejos 1981, 83–85; Rostworowski de Diez Canseco 1983, 88–96; Valcarcel n.d., 116, 164). Even in the Incan origin myths, the progenitors of the world were husband/wife pairs who emerged from Paucaritambo, "the house of origin," to rule the earth (Cieza de León 1959, 30–33).[7]

Similarly, in the Central Andes, the *ayllu* (the territory-based, extended family that forms the basis of productive relations even today) was conceived in terms of common descent from oppositional but complementary mythological ancestors. The legendary founder of the *llacuaz ayllu* was said to have come from far away and to have conquered the original inhabitants of the region, who claimed descendence from the god *Huari,* a cave dweller who was part of a race of giants. While the former *ayllu* was symbolically associated with maleness, fertility, and conquest, the latter was symbolically associated with the wet darkness of the underworld and of the fecund earth (Duviols 1986, lvi–lxvi; Silverblatt 1987, 67–72).

According to colonial accounts, indigenous peoples worshipped an entire pantheon of deities including the sun, moon, stars, wind, sea, mountains, caves, springs, rivers, lagoons, and oddly shaped rocks and plants, as well as the mummified remains of their ancestors. Outstanding individuals were consecrated to the care and worship of these deities, whose divine power—called *huaca*—was harnessed on behalf of the human community by means of frequent offerings of blood, fat, fragrant seeds, bird plumes, ground corn meal, seashells, guinea pigs, llama fat, coca, silver, and corn beer. The human guardians of these *huaca* had multiple tasks. They "fed" the gods in expectation of reciprocal acts of protection and nurturance. They divined the future and interpreted the acceptability of sacrifice. They also healed the sick—cleansing, purifying, and confessing those who were afflicted with disease because of their transgressions against the gods or against their human peers.

Women as well as men served as priestesses and *huaca* guardians. They were priests and healers, diviners, and, especially, confessors. As such, they led the purification rituals. As *huaca* guardians, women were consecrated to the care and worship of the *huacas*. They cared for the *mallqui,* the mummy-bundles of the ancestors, who were venerated by descendent lineages. They cared for the *conopa,* the household gods. They made offerings to all of these.

Women also made offerings to the gods when illness struck. Andean Indians believed that illness was a sign of punishment from the gods caused by sins committed against one another, against the land, and against their deities. To effect cures, the *huaca* guardians would invoke the gods with a kissing noise and sacrifices would be poured, aspirated, or burned at the site of the *huaca.* The Indians would confess their sins saying "Hear me, ye hills . . . and ye plains and flying condors, and the eagle owl and the barn owl, for I wish to confess my sins" (Arriaga 1968, 48), and the confessors would rub their heads with a small rock called the "pardon" stone (Arriaga 1968, 48) or with a rope twisted of black and white threads, both to purify the patient and to "capture" the illness in this object. Powders would be put on top of the stone and "blown into the air as a signal that sins had flown away" (Valcarcel n.d., 33). Then supplicants would be washed with corn meal at the confluence of two rivers so that their sins would be carried by the river's current to the sea (Valcarcel n.d., 268).

In addition, therapy included "sucking" to extract foreign substances (including blood, worms, rocks, toads, snakes, and other animals) from the victim's body (Valcarcel n.d., 62). After this, "The Indians (would) stay awake all night, singing, dancing, or telling stories. Even the children (were) punished if they fell asleep" (Valcarcel n.d., 33). Then began a fast in which the men would eat neither salt nor pepper, nor sleep with their wives (Arriaga 1968, 46–49; Duviols 1986, 64–65, 91–92, 280–81; Valcarcel n.d., 33–44, 88–89). All of these elements of therapy—the pursing of lips and "blowing" of alcohol, the use of corn-based products and water, the sacrifice of guinea pigs, the "rubbing" of patients with stones, ropes, and other objects to both purify and absorb illness, the association of illness with sins committed against community and against earth and sky deities—can be seen in the contemporary healer's *mesa* (see chapters 5–6, this volume).

While sorcery may have its origins in the pre-Colombian era, by the mid 17th century there is already much similarity between sorcery beliefs and behavior of today. Then as now, it seems that the origins of *daño* are attributable to a kind of intentional "soul-capture" facilitated by obtaining some object from the victim or constructing an image in his likeness.[8] In one 1656 account, for example, upon making a doll in the victim's likeness,

> . . . [the sorcerers] call the one they want to kill. They say that his [shadow or] soul . . . appears before them and they speak with [it . . . then] stick the shadow [who has taken residence in the doll] with some spines . . . and then they wrap it in every color of wool and they put it in a jar and . . . they bury it in a big hole and the person who they have wanted to kill begins to sicken . . . and seeing this [the victim calls on] others to undo the harm which they do with other sacrifices . . . they make another doll . . . and do another magic spell to the sick-person's soul saying, "come, we are here to help you." (Duviols 1986, 67–68)

Duviols's detailed transcriptions of cases such as this one—cases in which ecclesiastic judges interrogated Indians during their repeated seventeenth-century "visits" to local hamlets in order to "root-out" pagan practices—provide much information about the roles that women played as priestesses, *huaca* guardians, confessors and healers, diviners and interpreters of oracles, and midwives.

The cases of Catalina Guacayllano and Francisca Poma Carhua are instructive. The former, called "doctor and teacher of sorcery, rites and ancient ceremonies" (Duviols 1986, 18), was guardian of a community *huaca* called *pucara,* but she also worshipped the god *Huari* and carried out sacrifices to other idols as well. She carried out these sacrifices and interpreted as its oracle. When she cured the sick, she would offer a guinea pig to the idols, called *Choqueruntu* and *Raupoma,* slitting the pig's throat with her fingernails and saying, "Eat this so that my patient will get better" (Duviols 1986, 8). She taught others—men as well as women, and including her daughter Catalina—how to cure and how to propitiate the gods, and when the "visitors" came and destroyed the idols, she put others in their place. When she died, her followers dressed her body in finery and she was buried in the *ayllu's* traditional burial cave. She was worshipped as a *mallqui.* She was venerated with sacrifices of llama and guinea pigs, coca, and balls of llama fat and ground corn (Duviols 1986, 5–39).

Francisca Poma Carhua was a *curandera* who specialized in curing her patients by taking from their bodies rocks, toads, snakes, and spiders. She was known as the "great sorceress" and was accused of receiving her powers from a pact with the Devil (Duviols 1986, 25–26). Like Catalina Guacayllano, she also divined the cause of illness by examining the entrails of guinea pigs and cured with the help of guinea pigs, colored corn, and hot peppers (Duviols 1986, 13–39). She would rub the bodies of the sick with guinea pigs, fat, and coca to heal them, and she would tell them that their illness had come to them because they had neglected their adoration and worship of the gods of the upper world and the underworld (Duviols 1986, 58–59).

These women, and others, were commonly categorized as "sorceresses" and "witches," since the Catholic priests who evaluated them equated idolatry with witchcraft. For reasons discussed below, these Church fathers *expected* women who worshipped traditional gods and divined their discontent, who healed the sick, or who had "secret" knowledge about human reproduction to be "witches."

Colonial Transformations and the Persistence of Female Healers

Diverse interests and mandates characterized the colonial domination of Peru. The Crown sought to expand its wealth and to strengthen its economy by adding new markets and new products from its colonies across the ocean. The Church sought to expand God's kingdom on earth by Christianizing the "pagan" peoples of the New World. The roguish adventurers who set sail for lands beyond the horizon hoped to line their pockets with the gold and silver which they had heard paved the streets of native kingdoms in the "Indies." For the indigenous peoples inhabiting the region, these divergent interests resulted in attempts to expropriate their lands, to extirpate their religions, and to exchange the logic of their world for new ideologies and meanings.

One of the results of conquest was the literal and symbolic conquest of women. Stripped of liberty and dignity, women became creatures to be possessed, often sexually. Rape became a very real fear for indigenous women, since it was one way of cementing "alliances" in which the wealth and property of the victims could be transferred into their "husband's" names. Another way of neutralizing any social, political, or economic power that women might have enjoyed was to accuse them of witchcraft.[9]

According to the *Witches' Hammer,* a fifteenth-century official guide to the conduct of witch trials, women were by their very nature given to witchcraft. Because of their insatiable carnal desires, they embraced the demonic alliances through which God's kingdom on earth would be destroyed. This misogynist dogma, increasingly codified during the sixteenth and seventeenth centuries, was particularly perilous for women.[10]

In the idolatry cases that I examined in the Archives of the Archdiocese of Trujillo, most of the confessions involving women were molded, through beatings and unrelenting interrogation lasting as long as two years, to fit the picture that the interrogators expected to find. With this type of interrogation, the Ecclesiastic Judges imposed their own ideologies on the material presented to them, insisting on diabolic pacts and alliances and interpreting traditional rituals in the context of devil worship.

Women, much more frequently than men, were made to confess to standard European-style "witchcraft"—that is, that they had participated in midnight covens; had transformed themselves into demonic animals; had had relations with the Devil, who appeared as a man dressed in white, as a monkey, or as a goat; and that they had intentionally tried to kill their victims through enacting a *daño* against them, often employing excrement or other filth.

In fact, in the Ecclesiastic records of idolatry on file in Trujillo, only one of the ten male idolaters processed by the Ecclesiastic court is accused of having a pact with the Devil. By contrast, six of the ten women against whom cases are brought are accused of such a pact, or of transforming themselves into animals, or of night flights and attendance at witch's Sabbaths, or of conjuring the appearance of the Devil in animal or human guise. Furthermore, all ten of the women are accused of having committed some kind of intended harm, whereas the men are more often accused of acts of "healing" or of divining the source of buried treasures for their clients. Finally, four of the ten men are said to have utilized *mesas* and San Pedro to heal their clients, whereas none of the ten women is said to have done so.

44

If one is to believe the documents, one must believe that women did not often participate in the healing tradition described in chapter 1. But the apparent lack of *mesas* or of the ingestion of San Pedro by the women can be deceiving. In one case (AAT 1771a), Juan Catacaos, who is mentioned as a very powerful *curandero* in conjunction with several other cases on file both in Trujillo and in Cajamarca, claims to have inherited both his *mesa* and his knowledge of how to cure from a woman named María Angulo of Guadalupe. His *mesa* included a rattle to call the winds and hills, a gourd in which to put the San Pedro potion, a small, heart-shaped rock to cleanse bellies and ease pain, three pointed rocks the color of crystal which represented the power of the hills from which they had been taken, and two seashells in which to serve chewed tobacco. Similarly, Juan Pablo Arispa's wife (AAT 1804) apparently worked as an assistant at his *mesa*. Furthermore, a Huanchaco woman called María Antonia seems to have used a *mesa* to cure her patients. Finally, in a case brought before the Holy Office of the Inquisition in Lima in the 1730s, the accused—a *mestizo* by the name of Juan Santos Reyes—claimed to have learned his craft and to have inherited his *mesa* from a woman (AHN 1738).

Still, the apparent belief in gender differentiation—that men use San Pedro and the *mesa* but that women don't; that men may cause harm or heal but that women only do evil magic—is itself an important clue concerning the dynamics of history. For "to grasp history as part of societal process and not outside of it requires a conceptualization of social dialectics: of the human construction of society shaping, in turn, society's construction of human possibilities" (Silverblatt 1991, 154).

Certainly, the written (and spoken) word has often been used as a powerful tool to manipulate assumptions, perceptions, and perspectives, which create as well as reflect "historical fact." In colonial America (both North and South), social and political biases as well as fears about women's latent power led to women being accused of "witchcraft" much more frequently than men (Ehrenreich and English 1973; Klaits 1985; Karlsen 1987). According to this view, the women most likely to be accused of witchcraft were (1) independent rather than "protected" by men; (2) competing with men in the marketplace or for political power; (3) challenging the "inherent right" of men to rule; and (4) asserting power over men via their knowledge of regeneration and their unique ability to bear children (Karlsen 1987, 157–59). Those most in danger were those who asserted themselves by voicing their discontent with a system of structural inequality which presumed their inherent inferiority and prevented them from achieving equality with men. This is certainly true in many of the Trujillo cases.

On the northern coast of Peru, for example, it has been suggested, women had enjoyed substantial political power at the time of the Spanish conquest. Called *capullanas* because of the hooded dresses they wore, the *capullanas* had remained as local heads of power when first Chimu, and then Inca, overlords had called their husbands, brothers, and sons into military and imperial service (Fernández Villegas 1989, 45). The custom of female rule was still felt in this region two hundred years after the Spanish conquest, now paired with the colonial propensity to cry "witchcraft." In 1778, for example, a widowed woman named Antonia Azabache (she was also known as the *India principal* and the *cacica mayor,* or overlord, of Huanchaco) tried to take control of some land owned by another neighbor. She was accused of being a witch by the neighbor's sister-in-law, as a means of disputing the land claim (AAT 1778). In two other cases, women accused of doing *daño* claimed that they had merely provided refuge and charms so as to keep their husbands from beating them. Finally, a close reading of the case brought against María de la O also suggests that she, too, had angered and frightened her neighbors because she owned land and was a powerful member of the community. After her husband's death, the enemies that she had made—and one woman in particular—sought revenge by accusing her of witchcraft.

Thus, by the mid-eighteenth century when these cases were presented in Trujillo, the imposed ideologies that defined women as witches no longer reflected the mindset of clerics alone. Rather, as had happened in previous centuries in the witch trials of both the Old and the New World, these ideologies were now being used as a political tool by the populace as well. As long as economic, political, and social institutions limit women's ability to exert autonomy over their lives, it should not surprise us that independent women—and especially independent women who have "supernatural" powers and who cure sorcery—are perceived in nefarious or ambivalent terms. Given their understandable consternation about the accusations that can be leveled against them—accusations driven by hidden agendas of fear and anxiety—I now understand why I had such a difficult time locating women who would agree to work with me during those first months.

In pondering how (and why) contemporary perceptions of women's roles continue to be formed, we need to understand the limitations that still affect women's ability to exert autonomy over their lives. We need to understand how contemporary perceptions have been shaped by those with the power of record. We must also remember that, for the most part, this record has been devoid of the female healer's voice. In the chapters that follow, I address these issues, locating my perceptions and experiences as an investigator while giving the five women who shared their lives with me the opportunity to add their own perceptions to the record.

*O*ctober 24, 1987, Trujillo

Dear Liz,

I've been thinking about you a lot lately, though, as usual, I've been slow to put thoughts to paper. Much has happened in the last four months of my life, so much, perhaps, that I'm not exactly sure how to begin a chronicle. I always envied your disciplined daily entries in those steno notebooks that became such a record of your life when we were in college. There is so much identity locked in one's daily record. As usual, my writing has been erratic and less than documentary. Pretty intense confessions for a budding anthropologist. Actually, I'm not at all sure I wear the hat willingly.

Forgive the maudlin quality of this treatise. Both lack of practice and skeptical respect for the power of words to recreate emotion that is voiceless and fleeting invade the current attempt at bracketing time on paper. (The semi-drugged state of my current existence may also influence the prose.) I'm writing this from my single bed, in the upstairs back room of the home in Trujillo which has been both victor and villain in the shaping of a personality which is finally going out of season, after having fully bloomed and almost died on the vine. In another week I shall be gone from this house, moving on to another phase of my "life and times." I am in this bed recovering from an inflamed ovary and fallopian tube—complications of a spontaneous abortion on October 8–9. I was just a few days over two months pregnant in the mountain town of Cajamarca. Dan had already left for the States, so the miscarriage happened without his support or love. I had gone there with friends for a brief holiday from interviews and all-night curing sessions, quarrels with coworkers, friends, and "family."

The bleeding started soon after my arrival in Cajamarca on Wednesday. I didn't try to stop the miscarriage—part of me even felt relieved when it began because it was such an inopportune time to have gotten pregnant. By Friday it was mostly over, except that, when least expected, I dropped the fetus and stared into its eyes. When I saw that perfectly formed face I felt the guilt of complicity and then the confusion of duplicity. Instead of relief, I just felt alone.

Saturday, I flew back to Trujillo. When I walked in the front door of the house, I was a physical and emotional wreck. My Peruvian mother and the oldest sister were in the kitchen, preparing for a family gathering. They were completely stunned when I told them. I guess they implicitly blame me for the baby's death—Mamá warned me against traveling to the mountains so early in the pregnancy. While I understand that the burden was on me to make them understand, I neither wanted nor was able to put out the effort so I limped alone to the clinic on Saturday afternoon for the D&C that my doctor insisted upon.

After returning from the clinic, I limped upstairs to my room and waited—in pain, half-drugged, postoperatively depressed—for someone to come and check on me. No one came that day or the next except María. I felt like a banished child, so I reached out beyond the perimeter of the household for help, deciding to recuperate in the company of some friends living in Huanchaco.

Returning home three days later, I caught the wrath and guilt which had been fermenting since my departure. Civil war had broken out between parents and children. The excuses were contrived. I imagined the real reason was my untimely departure and their self-indignant conclusion of rejection. I felt weaker and more needy than ever but summoned the strength to apologize and try to put it right. Afterwards, I could not eat and cried at my total lack of control over my life. Mamá and Papá both chided me, counseling me on the obligations of Christian forbearance and the need to overcome. Then the conversation turned to another indiscretion: in my absence one of the daughters had entered her boyfriend's boarding house alone, exposing the family to accusations that she could have slept with him. One of her brothers was so incensed that he struck her—no questions asked—when she returned. The others quickly chose sides, defending and admonishing: "What will people say?" the accusers demanded. "I believe my sister's innocence," the defenders countered. In the ensuing din, I realized my error. This unrest had nothing at all to do with me. I had assumed their wrath because I had internalized the idea that I truly was a daughter whose indiscretions could threaten their honor. I excused myself and limped back up the stairs to my room. The arguing continued uninterrupted, my absence barely noticed.

I buried myself in work, half-crazy with loneliness and pain. . . . I left again, this time to deliver a paper at a professional conference in Huaraz. By the time I returned, I was in such pain that I finally went to the doctor. I had developed a postoperative infection, he told me, and he sent me straight to bed.

Because of the infection—or maybe it's just an excuse—I've decided to leave Trujillo and return to California. I don't know if I'll come back or not, but if I do, I know my relationship with this family will be forever changed. I can no longer elude myself. I have given up the illusion of being a daughter, and a sister, as well as that of being a mother, in Peru. Emptiness has now mingled and become one with the pain and the loss of my child. I don't know what is next. I just hope I recover soon, so I can continue the process, which has become my number one priority, of "finding Glass-Coffin." In the meantime, whoever I am, I know that I need to write it out; perhaps in the written word I'll capture an identity. Take care and drop me a line. I would treasure hearing from you.

Much love,
Bonnie

3 ❋ A Call to Healing

From early June to October of 1987 I searched without success for women whose use of San Pedro and the *mesa* paralleled that of male *curanderos*. Time and again the "leads" which had been given me by colleagues, friends, and patients of the male *curanderos* I had been interviewing resulted in interviews with women who denied such knowledge—although they did admit to being *curanderas*. But their use of the term translated as participation in roles socially appropriate for women, something other than what I sought. Two women I interviewed specialized in guinea pig cleansings. Others specialized in the treatment of soul-loss and evil-eye in children, for which they did "cleansings" with saltpeter, raw eggs, or newspapers and charcoal. I met midwives who massaged and "fixed" the position of the fetus within a woman's womb to assure an easy birth. One old woman, known simply as grandmother, specialized in cures for infertility and vaginal infections. In addition, almost every woman with whom I talked had a repertoire of home remedies and traditional cures which she used to attend to the aches and ills of her family. Finally, I talked with four women who specialized in the diagnosis of sorcery through tarot card readings but who claimed not to heal such ailments. I began to fear that what I sought was borne more of imposed expectations than a reflection of any reality. In a manner akin to that of the ecclesiastic judges described in chapter 2, I kept believing that I was not getting the entire picture because the women didn't trust me with their secrets.

Then, in April of 1988, my luck began to change when my good friend Rolando Vargas[1] asked me to go to Cajamarca to help him. He had become quite ill and had been told by a female healer named Yolanda that sorcery was to blame. Further inquiry revealed that Yolanda did use a kind of *mesa* as well as San Pedro as part of her ritual cure. I traveled to Cajamarca and during the next two months became deeply involved in his cure. Shortly after, a colleague apparently decided he trusted me enough to introduce me to Isabel. Not only did she use a *mesa* and San Pedro in her ritual cures, she had been his family's preferred *curandera* for years. A few months later, I was told of a third woman, Flormira, and then my contacts began to snowball. In all, I met and studied with eight *curanderas* between April 1988 and September 1989.

My relationship with each of these women—and the amount of time I spent studying their healing techniques—varied considerably. At one extreme, there was a single two-hour visit with a woman who demonstrated a ritual performance (orchestrated entirely for my benefit). At the other extreme, there were daily conversations, participation in more than twenty ritual *mesas,* and hundreds of hours of taped conversations collected over eleven months with Isabel and her assistant Olinda. Of the eight women I met, five are presented here. Each of these women shared their life stories with me. Each allowed me to participate in at least one ritual. Each of the women included here also impressed me with her sincerity and honesty. In the following pages, I introduce these five women in the order in which we met and briefly discuss how they became *curanderas.*

Yolanda

My trip to Cajamarca that Sunday was filled with excitement mixed with trepidation. Rolando and his wife Laura were family members of my closest Peruvian friend, so we had often socialized. They were also close to my Peruvian host family: Rolando's parents were originally from the same highland town as my host family, and the children of the two families treated each other almost like brothers and sisters. I had been named "godmother" to Rolando's and Laura's youngest child shortly before I left Peru in 1975. My return trips to Peru in 1982, 1984, and 1987 gave us several "touchstones" from which to build and renew our friendship. Although they had lived in Lima as long as I had known them, I eventually came to think of Laura as one of my closest friends in Peru. I often stayed with them when in Lima. When I arrived at their home on my way to

Trujillo in 1987, Laura surprised me with the news that their fifteen-year-old marriage was in jeopardy. She was afraid that Rolando's loyalties to her and to their children had been compromised by what she feared was a long-term affair with his secretary. She sought my advice—because of my familiarity with sorcery and healing—about whether or not her husband might be a victim of love-magic by "the other woman." Female members of her husband's family and I counseled her about actions she should and should not take to regain his affections. We even went to visit a diviner in Lima to see what he might say about Rolando's condition. The rumors continued, but nothing about the situation had been resolved by the time I returned to the United States in November.

Now, Rolando had summoned me to Cajamarca because of a diagnosis by a woman who asserted that his political enemies were trying to "make him disappear from the face of the planet." I was determined to help if I could, but now mine was the disapproving eye. After traveling all night on the bus, I arrived in Cajamarca at 6:30 a.m. Rolando was to arrive from a business trip later that morning, but a last-minute change in plans forced the timeline back. The cure would have to wait a few extra days. In the afternoon, Laura called. She recounted her version of the events leading up to Rolando's initial interview with Yolanda and told me she had decided to leave him if he didn't fire his secretary. I listened sympathetically, but begged her to wait until after his cure. I only felt competent to deal with one crisis at a time, I told her. Over the next month, I became deeply involved in Rolando's cure, trading my role as ethnographer for that of advocate, intermediary, and friend to help him recover. In retrospect, since participation is one of the cornerstones of Yolanda's healing philosophies, this decision was probably a good one. But the complicating nature of my relationship with Laura, with Rolando's family, and my role in his cure also highlight the difficulties that can develop when the anthropological researcher intentionally mixes these two approaches to knowledge.

Rolando knew of my study, but like many well-educated, middle-class Peruvians that I have talked with over the years, he considered sorcery to be part of the type of ignorant and backward thinking that had prevented his country from entering the age of science and reason. A recent series of events in his life had caused his attitude about the subject to change, however. He had become ill, and medical treatment had not relieved his suffering. He had finally decided to submit to Yolanda's therapy because he was at a loss to explain the illness in any other terms.

Upon arriving in Cajamarca, I went to visit Yolanda and her common-law husband José, who accompanies her in her ritual cures, to describe my project and request their help. Their two-story house stands at the end of a dirt road on the edge of Cajamarca. On the first level, a small dry goods store supplements the family income—well appreciated since their family includes the four children from Yolanda's previous marriage as well as their own six-year-old son. During my first visit, I spoke with José as he leaned upon the counter and waited on the occasional customer. José agreed that I might interview his wife, but he cautioned me. Theirs was not folkloric medicine: that kind of healing was the Devil's work. Theirs was spiritual medicine, guided by God alone. They had turned their faces away from the Devil long ago.

Behind the store is a large room furnished only with a few chairs that stand against the walls and, at one end of the room, an elaborate altar covered with images of the saints and virgins as well as crosses. Here, they perform their weekly rituals, and it was here, as we faced each other in two straight-backed chairs placed just in front of the altar, that I asked Yolanda to tell me how she came to be a healer.

Originally from a rural district of San Miguel, in the mountainous department of Cajamarca, Yolanda was born in 1946. José had been a friend of her father's, so she had known him most of her life, though she didn't begin working with him as a healer until long after she had reached adulthood. Unlike Yolanda, José was originally from the coastal plain. He had grown up in Zaña, which is renowned for its *curanderos* and *brujos*. In addition to his occupation as a merchant and a trader, José had also been trained as a *curandero*. He decided to become a healer as a result of his own experience with *daño* as a young man. He had been the victim of love magic and, as a result, he had become a real womanizer. As part of his treatment, the *curandero* had given him a *seguro*. Later, José discovered that the "healer" was actually using his magical abilities, via the *seguro*, to keep him dependent on his ministrations. From the moment José destroyed the *seguro*, he found that he was freed of the *daño*. That experience had convinced him that *brujos* who traffic in *seguros* are deceitful and two-faced, using their diabolic magic to prey upon their own clients and to line their own pockets.

Yolanda's father had been a carpenter and her mother kept busy with the household duties required of country wives and mothers. When Yolanda was just twelve years old her mother fell ill and began to hemorrhage. The doctor couldn't help her. About that time, José came to their home to commission her father to build a chair for him. As she explained:

> He [José] came to my house every year, many times. Every year he came
> to my house and talked about his cures to my father and he realized that
> the life that we were living was Evil, that we were bewitched, but my
> father didn't realize it. So when my mother fell ill . . . my father . . .
> without knowing what to do asked [José's sister] to recommend a
> curandero from Chiclayo—since José was from the region. She answered
> him, "Why haven't you said something to my brother? Hasn't he told you
> that he cures? And you want to go see a brujo? My brother can't stand
> those brujos."

Thus, Yolanda's father took them to José's so that he could cure her mother. She and her sister watched him cure her, but they laughed at the strangeness of it:

> I was twelve years old. . . . During the time he cured my mother, we
> laughed, without knowing what things these were. Then, while we were
> laughing, he told me, "What children, laughing." He told us, "I know you
> are going to return home. Don't go, because it will go badly for you. Go to
> Chiclayo, to Trujillo, or wherever you want, but don't go back there." He
> told my mother, "Don't take the child back there, because it will go badly
> for her."

In spite of José's warning, Yolanda's parents went back to San Miguel. Four years later, when she was sixteen, her parents wanted to fix her up with the man who became "the father of my children." As she explained, "He came to my parents asking for my hand, but I knew nothing. It was the custom back then, but it was new to me, so I said no, that I didn't want anything." He left empty-handed and she learned from some cousins that his family was incensed. She heard that they had decided to take another

tactic to get Yolanda for their son. As she recounted:

> They bewitched me, and without even making plans to marry I ran off
> with him. He "robbed" me, as they said in the old days, because I was
> bewitched. . . . They bewitched me so that I would run off with him. . . .
> When he came, [even though I had rejected him before], I ran off with him
> as though that hadn't happened. Afterwards, my parents arranged the
> marriage.

This was the beginning of her problems. Soon after she ran off with him, she became ill, little by little. She became weak, got headaches, and finally began suffering "attacks." Everything went badly. When she had her first child, she almost died. Her husband told her to go to a doctor, but as she told me, "How could he say that, knowing the cause of my illness. Why didn't he take me to be cured by the same person who had done [the *daño*]?" Finally, her brother, tired of seeing her ill, took her to Zaña to be cured by José. There, she took San Pedro for the first time and saw the love magic with which her husband had captured her to his side. She remembered:

> I saw everything he had done to me. I never would have imagined that it
> was brujería. . . . I saw myself in a cemetery, I saw some open tombs. It
> seemed like one soul was pulling me, then another, then another, and in
> the play of the entire curing ceremony, I saw my ex-husband. He was
> there. He flew this way, he was flying, and I had realized. I related it all in
> my mind, how he had done it, what method he had used, everything,
> everything, everything.

During that first *mesa*, she realized that her feelings for her husband had been manipulated through the use of love magic. But, instead of turning her cure over to José, allowing him to intervene with the spirit world on her behalf and to "undo" the magic, she felt obliged to take an active role in her cure. As she put it, "I decided it wasn't right to continue with [José performing] the cure, in other words I began to defend myself alone. . . . All alone I asked God and I asked the Most Holy Virgin [for help]." Instead of blaming those who had manipulated her emotions, she felt responsible, "My life had been joined [with my husband] by the Devil." To undo the evil, she felt she also had "to move ahead, little by little, with my faith [in God.]" The cure took years. She was twenty-four when she began it, but "the sickness didn't disappear until God was sure that I would turn my face towards that living road."

As she began forging a new relationship with her God, she began to see the cause of her illness more clearly. She also began to see that she should build a life together with José and accept him as her teacher. But, even though he began to teach her, she emphasized that her power to see the afflictions of others and to cure comes directly from God. As she told me, "I have experienced God in me. I can say he has become flesh in me to do—to recognize—good and evil."

After completing her cure, she and José began to work together to cure others. They traveled extensively, and Yolanda indicated that they have helped patients from all over Peru as well as from North America and Europe. Although it is Yolanda who has the ability to see and diagnose the patient's problems, she and José work as a team, practicing their spiritual healing. They hold curing sessions in their home, once a week, on Saturday afternoons. During my stay, I attended six of their rituals. The perspective I gained about their healing practices was filtered, not only through the lens of my role as anthropologist and "researcher," but also through the lens of my role as Rolando's advocate and friend during his cure.

Isabel and Olinda

It was still quite early morning as we traveled the wide arterial which connects the main square of Chiclayo to the market district and Isabel's house, but the street was choked with traffic and the sidewalks looked im-

passable. Street-hawkers sat in the shadows of doorways, peddling everything from toilet paper to hammers to high-fashion jeans. Imported radios
blared and watches gleamed—contraband from Ecuador.

My good friend Tomás had finally agreed to introduce me to Isabel and
I was anxious as we bumped along dusty, dirt-packed streets that passed
the market. We held our noses as we passed a huge mound of burning
trash which flanked a city park. If grass had ever been planted there, it
had long ago abandoned any hope of clinging to the bone-dry dust which
covered the square.

We turned right, onto a street about twelve blocks long. Brightly colored houses of brick and cement gave way to more humble dwellings of
unpainted adobe. Stretched out before us, the deeply rutted street disappeared beneath pools of seeping mud and stagnant water, evidence of a
poorly designed sewer line which had been built to serve the residents.
The driver grumbled that he would have to charge us extra for asking him
to traverse this maze of dust and mud.

Ten blocks later, we left the sewer—and the electric poles—behind as
we neared the edge of the city. Just ahead, the dust and mud ended
abruptly and green fields spread out toward the horizon. There, one house
stood out among the drab adobe dwellings. It was painted a pleasant
peach color. Tomás told the driver to stop. This was Isabel's house.

It had taken a year of almost constant companionship to convince
Tomás to introduce me to Isabel. His mother was one of Isabel and
Olinda's *comadres,* and his brother had assisted them at their *mesas* in the
past. When Tomás had finally trusted me enough to approach Isabel about
an introduction, she had hesitated. She explained to him that she knew of
a *maestro* who had consented to let two foreigners attend his ritual. During
the night, they had stolen some of the power objects off his *mesa* to take
home as souvenirs. This had resulted in his being unable to defend himself against the attack of a rival *brujo,* and he had, according to Isabel, died
at his *mesa* that night. She told my friend that the foreigners then cut off
his head and his hands and took them to a museum in the United States
for display!

But now Isabel had agreed to meet me and we were finally here. The
dark brown wooden door bore a paper sticker with a picture of the Virgin

and a statement: "This family is Catholic, no religious soliciting here." Our knock was answered by a young woman who recognized Tomás, but who informed us that Isabel wasn't home.

The next day, I returned alone and knocked on the thick wooden door. Almost immediately, a window was opened in another door to the left of where I stood and a pert, round face with laughing eyes and a huge, warm smile looked out at me. I was surprised at this woman's youth and wondered if she could really be the *curandera*. In another moment, the same young woman I had spoken with the day before answered my knock and ushered me into the living room to wait for Isabel, who was just finishing up a consultation with a patient in the next room. While I sat on the hard-back chair that, along with the dining table and some low benches made up the room's furnishings, I contemplated the care with which this house had been finished and decorated. The clean-swept cement floor had been recently swathed with white petroleum to keep down the dust, the green-painted walls had been expertly stenciled with rows of fish, outlined in red, and the cane-and-reed ceiling had been plastered over and painted a crisp white. It was a comfortable, cheerful room and it put me at ease.

Isabel came in a few minutes later and welcomed me. She is a small, stout woman, and I was again struck by her wide smile, and particularly by her eyes. They were not large or wide or particularly round, their deep brown color was not compelling, and her full cheeks made them squinty when she smiled, but they radiated a kind of clarity and openness that I had not seen in any of the other healers I had met before. They seemed to exude goodwill and honesty, and I was drawn to look directly into them. She introduced herself and asked after my friend, who, I explained, was sorry to have missed her but had had to travel back to Trujillo that morning. After a few more pleasantries, I began explaining my study to her. She invited me to come to a *mesa* the following Saturday so that she could see, with the help of San Pedro, my intentions and determine whether or not she could help me in my study.

That *mesa* had been successful and Isabel had agreed to help me however she could with my project. As it turned out, my long wait was well worth it because Isabel and Olinda became what anthropologists have traditionally referred to as "principal informants." Our relationship grew and deepened over almost a full year as they shared their lives and taught me about their work. With them, I attended over twenty *mesas,* and additionally I was able to tape over one hundred hours of both formal interviews and informal conversations.

Isabel was born in 1948 in a small village in the province of Huancabamba in the highlands. As a young child, Isabel had spent many days pasturing the family herds with her sisters. She had had her first taste of city life when her elementary school teacher convinced her mother to let her spend summers in Huancabamba, where she provided childcare and domestic service to the teacher. During the school year, she attended school, but only through the third grade. Then, instead of allowing Isabel to continue with her education, her teacher took advantage of her by making her teach the younger children. It was during this period of her life that Isabel had met her curing assistant and her housemate, Olinda, but their paths did not cross again until much later, in Pucalá. Disillusioned with the treatment that she had received from her teacher, Isabel went back home to the farm when she was ten to keep company with her mother, who was alone with the younger children. Her father had run off with another woman, and her uncle who had helped her mother administer the farm had died.

Isabel stayed with her mother until she was thirteen and then ran away to the coast with her cousin, where they both worked as domestic servants for a family who exploited them cruelly. Finally, after escaping from that household and then working for some people on the *hacienda* of Pucalá, where members of Olinda's family also lived, she had gone to work for a Chinese family in Chiclayo who were very good to her. They sent her to night school, where she finished her elementary education, and then to trade school so that she could learn to become a seamstress. She worked for them for the next eleven years, until in 1977 she eloped with the man who would father her two children.

Isabel told me that this union must have been the result of love magic since she made the decision to run off with him almost from one day to the next, and only a week after breaking up with her boyfriend of four years, whom she loved very much. The boyfriend was a medical student

and had been sent to Bagua. While he was away, the man who would become her husband began making a nuisance of himself. As Isabel related
the story, "He followed me around for about a year, but I didn't love him.
I detested him. I said, 'Why is he following me around.' I refused him, I
scorned him, I didn't like him." One day, unaware of her boyfriend's
return, Isabel ran into him in the park, talking with another woman who
was a fellow student at the university. She told me:

> *I had never been jealous of him in my life, never . . . the whole time we*
> *went out. [That day] I don't know what got into me, it made me angry to*
> *see them talking together, so I didn't talk to him. . . . Then he [saw me*
> *and] ran after me saying, "Isabel, what's wrong, what's the matter with*
> *you?" "Nothing, man," [I told him]. "Go to hell!" And I scorned him.*
> *Never had that happened to me before. . . . Afterward, the idea came to*
> *me . . . so what, he has surely been with another woman, besides, what*
> *am I to him. He is finishing the university and I am just finishing high*
> *school, my family doesn't know him. . . . I began to think like a fool. I got*
> *up early and erased him from my mind. . . . From that moment on, I*
> *couldn't stand the sight of him. Inside myself, I thought, how strange. . . .*
> *[When he came looking for me] I told him, "I have another boyfriend. . . .*
> *I don't want to have anything to do with you. . . . I think I'll break up with*
> *you."*

Her boyfriend told her that she had better be sure of her decision
because he wouldn't come begging her later, and she insisted that that was
what she wanted. Within a few days, she had accepted the other man's
proposal that they be boyfriend and girlfriend, and a few days after that
they eloped. After she returned home with her new husband, her employ-
ers had tried to talk her out of her decision, even offering to take her to
China if she were pregnant, but, as she told me, "At that time, I loved him,
and it was something even I didn't understand. I had hated him so much
and then I loved him."

After they had been living together for a few months, Isabel told me,
she really began to suffer. She was pregnant. Her husband was extremely
jealous of her and beat her. When he took her to meet his family, they

hated her, calling her "old woman" and "hillbilly." Isabel and her husband began to fight continually, even before the baby was born. As she recounted: "I came to hate him. . . . I didn't even want to sleep with him. I don't know, but I hated him. I wanted . . . to destroy him." She concluded the story, saying, "The father of my children did a hex on me so that I would love him. What a wretch!" Finally, Isabel said, she decided to split up with him and strike out on her own. But after a time, and because of the insistence of her mother-in-law that their baby deserved to have both a mother and a father, she reunited with him and soon became pregnant again. The arguing and the problems continued and again she left. It was then that she went home to Huancabamba to have the second baby and it was then that she decided to form a household with her friend Olinda, who had recently been widowed.

It was during the time that Isabel was merging her household with Olinda's that she began to suffer from headaches that did not respond to medical treatment. Isabel recalled going to one doctor, who asked her if there were other members of her family who had occult powers and who concluded that her headaches were the result of a very well developed "sixth sense" and that she should try to develop this. Although Isabel's great-grandfather and grandfather were both *curanderos*—her great-grandfather had a solid gold *mesa* that still stands in an enchanted garden, according to her account—Isabel had known neither of them in life and had never before attended a *mesa*. So, she asked her friend Olinda how to proceed with her doctor's advice.

It was at this time that Isabel's cousin, Miguel, came to see them, believing that he was suffering from a *daño*. He had already traveled throughout the mountain region looking for a cure, and had even gone to *la jibaría*.[2] Recalling that Isabel's doctor had said she should develop her psychic potential, she and Olinda decided to cook some San Pedro to see if they could help Miguel. Their recent experience at a *mesa* in Huancabamba had confirmed that Isabel had good psychic vision. The *mesa* had taken place just prior to the birth of Isabel's second child. Because she was too pregnant to drink the San Pedro, the *maestro* there had simply dipped his fingers into the glass and spread the San Pedro on her forehead, in the shape of a cross. That night, even though she had not ingested the potion, Isabel had been able to see with astonishing clarity. She had even divined the amorous designs the *maestro* had on Olinda, and she told Olinda not to drink the potion that the *curandero* had prepared for her, supposedly to help her regain the psychic vision that she had lost the previous year, warning her that the *curandero* had really designed the potion to "charm" her into sleeping with him. Then, the spirit of San Pedro had told her to quietly take certain *artes* from the *mesa*. When she did, the *brujo* had fallen fast asleep!

If Isabel had the psychic vision, Olinda had the practical knowledge of healing because she had participated in scores of *mesas* with various *maestros* during her youth. She knew the proper procedures for preparing San Pedro, for invoking its help, and for safely disengaging oneself from its power at the completion of the ceremony. Also, Miguel was familiar with the ways of warding off the spirits or shadows that might assail them during the night—he had previously worked as a *maestro's* assistant in the mountains and in the high tropical forest to the east. For this first occasion in which they would combine psychic vision and practical knowledge in order to cure themselves, they bought a few *artes* to defend themselves from harm and to destroy the *daños* from which they were suffering. These included a steel knife, a wooden staff carved with the image of San Cipriano, a quincewood staff, and three seashells for raising the *mesa*.

That night, after taking the San Pedro, Isabel saw just how Miguel's *daño* had been effected. A woman had sprinkled some powder into his shorts before washing them and returning them to him to wear. The result was an inflammation of the testicles which caused him considerable pain and which the doctors he had consulted had confused with cancer. Isabel was directing the cleansing of her cousin with the few *artes* they had bought for the occasion. She remembered:

> *A plane flew by so low that it seemed it would land on the house. That was the illness. . . . [We] tore up the clothes [which had been hexed and which he had brought with him in a suitcase] and with scissors cut them up . . . destroying the illness. . . . Then we burned them and he was cured.*

That night, the San Pedro also told Isabel that she should continue in this work as a way of resting her head and heart, and in order to alleviate her headaches. Also that night, they learned that their *mesa* should be

called *novata* ("rookie") to reflect their inexperience.

Miguel, understanding the many problems associated with the taking of San Pedro, discouraged them from using the cactus for any but the most intimate of family members. He argued that they were too inexperienced, that they wouldn't know how to defend themselves against magical attacks. Isabel remembered Miguel saying, "You know nothing of *daño*. Any *brujo* will grab you, 'flip' you and kill you [if you take San Pedro and lay the *mesa*]."[3] But despite Miguel's objections, they decided to continue taking the San Pedro and laying their *mesa*.

The next time Isabel and Olinda cooked the San-Pedro and conducted a *mesa* was on the twenty-ninth of June—the festival day of San Pedro. Olinda had suggested this date because she knew that many *maestros* in Huancabamba took San Pedro on this day. As she told Isabel, just as the saint called San Pedro is "keeper of the keys . . . [and] guardian of the doors of Heaven," so the San Pedro plant is called "guardian of the doors of remedy." And on this day especially, the San Pedro plant was likely to help them see the appropriateness—or not—of the path they had chosen.

This time, when they took the San Pedro, Olinda recounted that it was as though San Pedro himself had actually possessed Isabel. During the *mesa* she began speaking with the voice of a very old man. As Olinda told the story, "Her entire body was like that of an old man and her voice was of an ancient one. She sat, she didn't work standing but sitting." Isabel continued the story:

I sat in the clouds, not on the earth. . . . If I reached out my hand, I felt nothing, I touched the emptiness [of the sky] in spite of the fact that I was really sitting on the ground.

Also under the influence of the San Pedro, Olinda too saw Isabel as though she were in the clouds. She told me, "Her spirit wasn't [at the *mesa* but there in the sky]. . . . It was as though from there she looked out over all the problems that the patients would have." So when Miguel came back through town the following week, the three of them laid another *mesa*, in which:

> *San Pedro appeared in the sky like a light, like an exploding star . . . and the clouds came together and formed the body of a person . . . and the clouds came down [to the mesa]. The clouds seemed to come down. We were there in the middle of it and it seemed as though they were descending. . . . And the mesa was lit up . . . everything was lit. And then, at that moment when the clouds descended . . . she [Isabel] fell unconscious . . . [and began speaking] with that old man's voice.*

In that voice, Isabel commanded them all to kneel and to take the oath, by the *mesa*, that they would commend their bodies and souls to their healing work. She told them to "promise before the *mesa* and before God to always be faithful, to do good works and to always cure; no matter how much money one might need, never to do *daño*. It is better to be in need than to sell your soul." Then they were told to raise the *mesa* in a single seashell, as they became like the Catholic Trinity—Father, Son and Holy Spirit—three persons in one. Afterward, the San Pedro indicated that they must give offerings to the *mesa* of Isabel's ancestors and travel every year to the lagoons to bathe and purify themselves and their *mesa*. The San Pedro told Isabel, Olinda and Miguel that they would receive the strength and power of that ancestral *mesa*. Then they began to cleanse themselves and to "raise" their families and the house in which they lived.

In the morning, before they finished working, San Pedro showed them the exact location of the sacred lagoons. They also saw, reflected in the sky, a path of people who would come in search of their services. San Pedro told Isabel that she would become famous and would cure many people. Isabel remembers that they asked for guidance, saying "How are we going to cure? and that San Pedro had responded:

> '*When you take your patients there [to the lagoons], you will bathe them thus.' Then the lagoons became a kind of spirit that was passed between the people. Then we saw the lagoons there, the waterfalls, we saw all as spirit.*

Isabel also explained that during the first years of her work as a healer, her cures were much different than they are now. Then, she didn't use *mesa* objects to defend herself from the attacks of other sorcerers and spirit powers, as she does now.

> *When I took the San Pedro it lasted twelve hours exactly. . . . I was unconscious . . . ; it was like something possessed me, and I saw much more than I do now. I sat [on the ground] . . . but I felt as though I were in the clouds, I wasn't here. . . . I felt myself to have the face of an old man more than two hundred years old. I touched my wrinkles, my beard and hair were white. . . . I didn't move and I didn't utilize the* mesa. *. . . I didn't use the staffs to cleanse [patients]. . . . I simply touched them and that was that [they were cured]. . . . But I was afraid, because I thought that I would not return to earth. I felt bad, I felt bad for my children, [afraid] of leaving my children. . . . I said to myself what if I don't return to this world one day and I remain like this. I remembered that in Huancabamba there was a* maestro *who is dead now. [I went there] and I told him that I had this problem and that I had to drink three glassfuls of the San Pedro, which were Father, Son, and Holy Ghost. He told me no. . . . He said you have to be conscious because if they come [and attack you in the* mesa] *to do* daño *to you you might be left dead there. . . . Then he told me, I am going to cleanse you and he "cut" the remedy. . . . Now I am conscious [when I take San Pedro], and the hours that it affects me have been shortened. . . . [He also told me] that I should use saints [and other* artes] *to protect myself against evil. . . . Evil, one has to strengthen oneself against evil. . . . When you cure strong* daños *you have to be surrounded by [the objects] of your* mesa. *. . . It is since then that I have begun adding [them].*

Flormira

In January 1989 I learned about Flormira—she refers to herself as Flor for short—from a former patient of hers. Using the directions that this patient gave me, I went to try to locate her in a poor neighborhood on the outskirts of Chiclayo. She lived in a very modest adobe structure which was the most dilapidated-looking one in the entire block. A clatter of children and dogs erupted inside as I knocked on the rough wooden door, and it was only after some explanation that I was admitted into the gloomy, windowless room beyond. There, the hard-packed dirt-floored "living room" was bare, except for a wooden bench and a *carretilla*. Flor looked much older than her years, withered by the responsibilities of raising two generations of children. With the paltry income that she made working as a washerwoman and sweeping streets for the city, she was often unable to feed them more than one meal a day. Her daily wages might buy her a quarter-kilo of rice, a little oil, a few vegetables, and nothing more. She rarely took the bus because she could not afford the fare, and she spent much of her time walking back and forth to the town center from her home. Flor was, without question, the most destitute of any of the healers that I talked with during the course of my study and the story of her life was punctuated by poverty and tragedy.

That first day, Flor listened to my nervous rendition of what I wanted and why I had come to her with what seemed a mixture of interest and caution. She agreed that I could return to talk with her again and that she would consider my request to work with her and would "put it before God," to determine whether or not it was possible. The next time we met, I was able to win her faith and trust because of a set of circumstances which still surprise me.

She was in the middle of a problem, she told me, and implored me to help if I could. Her son had apparently left for the high jungle earlier in the week, leaving her in charge of a tape recorder and a television set, both of which he had pawned from two of his friends because they desperately needed money. Apparently, the appliances had been stolen and the friends had been accused of the crime. As part of their confession, they told the police where the stolen items could be found and the police had arrived earlier in the day and raided Flor's house. They had taken the appliances—as well as another television set, an iron, a bedspread, a porcelain serving tray, some cassette tapes, and a towel, all of which Flor claimed were hers. They had also threatened to detain her as an accessory to the crime since her son was not at home, and they told her they would return in the afternoon to do so. She asked me to go to police headquarters with her, apparently hoping that my status as a *gringa* would give her the "pull" she needed to get back the goods that belonged to her and to discourage further police action. I tried to explain that I didn't think that I would be much help, but I agreed to go with her anyway.

When I arrived at police headquarters with Flor that day, it turned out that the single friend I had acquired in the department, the result of a previous police investigation of my own activities, was the very man who had been assigned to Flor's case. Within twenty-four hours of the time that Flor and I spoke with him, her television and the other goods that had been taken from her in the raid were returned and we had secured the lieutenant's word that he would be an advocate for her son in the department should he be arrested in connection with the robbery. Whether or not my acquaintance with the case officer influenced the outcome of her case, Flor was convinced that I had somehow been sent to her in this hour of need ("God is so good"). From that time on, Flor opened her arms and her heart to me and invited me to share in her life.

Originally from Cutervo (in the Department of Cajamarca), Flor was born November 3, 1944. She was orphaned by the age of ten and shuffled between relatives for the remainder of her childhood. Perhaps because of this, she never learned to read or write. When she was fourteen, she married and went to live with her husband's parents in Bagua. Her husband died after they had been married only four years, leaving her with two small children whom she had to raise however she could. He died from *daño,* Flor told me. Another woman fell in love with him and when he refused to abandon Flor and the children to go with her, the other woman told him, "If you won't be mine, you won't be anybody's." Flor said that before he died, he told her that it was this other woman who had killed him, giving him *daño por boca* by means of a poisoned piece of pork. He died in agony. As he lay dying, he hugged his wife and said, "I kept my promise, I never left you . . . until death, I never left you. Now, having kept the word I gave you, my word returns to me. Good-bye, good-bye, Flor, good-bye, forever."

After her husband's death, Flor stayed on in her in-law's house as a domestic servant, cooking, washing clothes, ironing, and picking up after them. Her mother-in-law treated her harshly, she told me, chasing her on one occasion with a knife, and on another with a whip. After some time, Flor decided to leave and took her two young children to a nearby town where she began working as a domestic servant for another woman who was very good to her. She stayed with that family for eight years. Then her mother-in-law convinced her to come back and live with them because, as Flor recounted, "I worked hard, they got used to having me around." After a time, Flor explained, her mother-in-law began "turning my daughter against me. . . . Her grandmother had told her that if I ever got hold of her [the daughter] I would throw her into the river . . . imagine such a thing, Señorita." So, Flor ran away from her mother-in-law, taking her children to another town, where she set up housekeeping and opened a restaurant to support the family.

Five years later, when her daughter was thirteen, she was "stolen" away by a boy who was in love with her. As Flor explained:

She didn't know about her period, she didn't have breasts, she didn't know about any of those things that God gives woman. That boy came from Bambamarca and he stole her, but with the help of a cousin who got some of her hair. [The cousin] took that hair and they "worked" it so that my daughter would fall in love with him.

The day of the elopement, Flor recalled that she was lured outside by the cousin and as soon as she stepped out of her house, the other boy popped out from behind the counter where he had been hiding and stole her daughter away. They went to live with his parents in Bambamarca.

Two years later, Flor told me, she had had a dream in which God told her that her daughter needed her, that she was dying, that she must rescue her. She was instructed to call out to her daughter by going to a high hill above where she lived and by waving a red rag. Flor followed the instructions and found her daughter, who told her that her in-laws had been very mean to her . . . [and that] they had often made her pasture the family's cattle all day long with only a handful of toasted corn to eat.

Flor, her daughter, and her son-in-law then all moved to Chiclayo. Then, at the age of twenty-one, her daughter was killed on the highway between Chiclayo and Ferreñafe, leaving behind four children without their mother. The son-in-law left, saying to Flor, "My children are now yours. . . . Sit down and raise them, I'll help you with what I can but you will have to raise them." He contributed money toward their care for a month but then disappeared, and Flor was faced with the responsibility of childcare and economic support for her grandchildren. Flor's son had become the main provider in the household, but he was gone during most of the time I spent with her. He had left his two young children with Flor as well.

Before her daughter died, Flor had been much more active as a healer, and she had been able to supply most of the family income from her profession while her daughter took care of the domestic responsibilities of cooking, cleaning, and childcare. "I was like an invited guest at home; I never had to do anything," Flor remembered. Now that her daughter was gone, that had all changed. At the time that I met her, she could only describe to me how things had been in the past. But, because words were her only medium for making me understand, she was especially articulate at describing her life as a healer to me. She could speak for hours at a time with little prompting. I would turn on the tape recorder and simply listen to her life unfold as she recounted her childhood, how she had learned to cure, her methods and techniques, the cases that stood out in her mind, her run-ins with the police, and her dreams—in which God indicated the course of action that she must take with patients. God, she told me, is "my only teacher," and she claimed never to have undergone an apprenticeship.

According to Flor, God's first gift was a revelation about the roots, leaves, and flowers she should use to cure those around her. As a very young child, when her mother was still living, she would often play with flowers and God had shown her how to prepare remedies for those who were ill. "I began curing, and people said, how is it that this child learned to cure? How beautiful! We must help her, and give her any little thing. . . . The Lord revealed [these things], indicated [these things] to me." Later, He gave her the gift of the *baraja,* the tarot cards, which she uses to divine her patient's illnesses:

> *I was about ten or eleven years old when He gave me the revelation. He said, you will be a good person, you will be well thought of . . . and since you are good, and [since] you have a good heart, I am going to give you a*

*present. . . . Go tomorrow at five o'clock in the afternoon to a field of
straw. From there, you will arrive at a sugarcane field. When you are by
there, you will arrive at a path that enters the cane . . . a very narrow
path . . . like a thread. Go on down this path until the canefield ends.
Don't be afraid. When the canefield ends, you will enter a corn field
where the corn is golden; go in a little way, then turn off the path into the
middle of the corn. The big corn stops and you go on into where the corn
is small. . . . Go in there, to a part where the corn has been weeded. Keep
going and you will come to the foot of a mountain, and when you get to
the foot of the mountain, look at the ground.*

Flor followed the instructions given in her dream and she found the
baraja, spread out on the ground as she had never seen before, in lines of
ten cards each. She picked up the cards and ran back home. That night,
in another dream, God reproached her for her fear, telling her that she
should have gone on up the mountain; all that she wanted, she would have
found there. The next day, she began to learn how to read the cards and
how to lay them out, again in revelations from God which came to her in
her dreams.

According to Flor, God taught her everything that she knows. He has
guided her choices and put limits on her ambitions. As she said:

*Nobody, nobody, Señorita, nobody showed me. . . . God is the one who has
given me this profession to cure; it is of God. He gave me this beginning,
the flowers to cure . . . and later he gave me the cards so that I would
[have a profession]. From there have come all the powers that God has
given me. I began to know. I began to learn, to do any little thing. . . .
Whenever I make a mistake, he says, "No, not that way; that's not how it
is; this is how it is." He guides me. . . . He always advises me. When I
have wanted to change things, he says "No, be happy with what I give
you. . . . Don't want what others have; be happy with what I give you. I
am God."*

Even though daily living is a struggle for this valiant woman, Flor
doesn't worry about things: she has confidence that God will provide. "I
ask God and He helps me. I don't have anything and I say, 'God, God,

what will I do, with what will I feed these innocent children?' And then their bread appears." She has had this faith since the time that God visited her in person.

According to Flor, God appeared to her after she had left her children at home one day and gone to visit a friend. A whirlwind had come up and she had run back home to check on the children. The tin roof had been blown off their house, but the children were fine. As Flor looked up to the sky and prayed to God, lamenting her poverty and her tragedy, she says she saw a man kneeling on her roof, replacing the tin. He was tall and white, with a thin face. At first she thought it must be the local priest come to help her, but then the man came down off the roof in a single step and walked to the end of the block with another step, then came back into her house through the front door. He wore a white habit tied up with a cord and he had a thin sickle in his hand. The man then spoke to Flor, asking her why she traveled so much, and she had replied it was because they were poor. Then he asked her if she wanted to know who he was and she said "yes," to which he responded, "I am God." Flor thanked him for answering her prayer in person and invited him to sit and rest awhile, which he did. When the man commented that she had very little food and furniture, she said that it was because they were poor. "We only have a little manioc," Flor told him, to which he replied, "But I see a lot of manioc." Then, as she looked to where the man pointed, Flor saw that it was true: there was a whole pile. The man then listed other food items that she needed and told her not to worry but to live happily, even if she was hungry, and that he would provide for her needs.

Then God asked her for water. But as she ran to get him a glass of fresh water, he proceeded to drink from a wash basin full of water that she had been using to wash hot peppers, which caused him to choke. When she ran to put the fresh water to his lips, he waved her off, saying that she couldn't touch him. He then asked her if she had given her children breakfast, and when she replied that she hadn't, he ordered her to prepare it and to feed them. Then he rose to leave, indicating that he would return. Next, she saw him enter a nearby house, from which she heard screams as the inhabitants fled. But God followed them with the sickle and cut off one of their heads. Then, she said, she was afraid, thinking to herself that he would come back and kill her also.

As she saw him cross the street, she ran back inside to finish preparing the breakfast, afraid that he would kill her too for not carrying out his orders. Although the fire was hot, the water had not yet heated. When he came back through the door and asked if she had given breakfast to the children, she said that she hadn't, lying that the water was too hot and that it had to cool off for them to be able to drink it. This satisfied him, and he took a seat to wait. Then he asked her which she preferred, a long life or a short life. She responded that she wanted a long life. He told her that her life would be long and then admonished her to finish serving the children their breakfast. He told her not to worry, even if she had no food, and he blessed her, saying, "You will have nothing, but you will eat. You will have nothing, but you will live." He told her to put a little salt in the water and that something would come to her for lunch while the water was heating. Then he left. Afterward, she said, she was sad, but just as the water got hot, a neighbor came to the door, offering her rice, fresh corn, and bananas.

Later, when Flor's daughter died, she prayed to God and he appeared again in a picture, saying, "Don't worry. I didn't know about your daughter's death. It was a surprise to me. But don't worry, I am going to help her. Raise her children, help them, and I will help you. Don't cry anymore because you need strength and courage to take care of her children." Because of these promises, Flor lives in the faith that God will provide. Whenever there is no hope in sight, she says, a patient will appear in need of her services, asking for a cure because of the power that she possesses. As she told me, "This is my happiness, in the name of God."

Vicky

In late June of 1989, Martín, a friend from Ferreñafe who knew of my study and my interest in expanding the sample of female *curanderas*, offered to introduce me to his cousin's wife Vicky. She cured with a *mesa*, he told me, and was quite famous in the area in which she lived.

About seven miles outside of Ferreñafe, we hopped out of the open-bed pickup truck we had been riding in and began the half-mile walk to Vicky's house along a road which cut through the deep gold of the rice fields that were almost ready for harvest. A little way beyond a turn in the

road, we found a green house with a broad cement patio with its doors
and windows open. Three small children were playing on the patio, and
Martín shouted out his greeting to them as he stood at the wrought-iron

gate. A young man who introduced himself as Martín's cousin Emilio
appeared at the door and invited us in, calling for his wife, Vicky. When
she appeared, I was somewhat surprised, for she was eight months pregnant with what I learned was to be their fourth child.

Martín and I were invited to sit in the comfortable living room. After
greeting Vicky, Martín began to explain my interest in talking with her at
length about her profession as a *curandera*. She responded that, as a favor
to him—since he was her husband's cousin—she would be happy to help
me. Then, she corrected him, saying that while she was, in point of fact,
a *curandera,* she worked more specifically as an *espiritista,* or one who
employs the aid of the spirits of her ancestors to help diagnose and cure
sorcery-related illness. This, she explained, was different from the work
of those *curanderos* she called *hierbateros,* who, she said, work with the
spirit power of mountains and lakes. She told me that *hierbateros* are much
more common in the highlands, whereas *espiritistas* are much more common on the coast.

Vicky told me that she knows many secrets, including how to do *randas*
(cleansings with a chicken) in order to free a victim of the evil spirits
which have possessed it. The chickens, once they are cut open and stuffed
with purple and white corn, are fed to the *huacas,* together with three
bottles of corn beer, salted fish, and hot peppers, in order to quench their
thirst and placate their hunger, thereby saving the victim's soul.[4] I was
anxious to talk with Vicki further, but she reminded us that we should be
returning to Ferrañafe. Catching a ride back to the city would be difficult
if we waited much longer.

During my next visit, Vicky told me that her father had grown up in
Ferreñafe, and her mother was from Morrope. Both are small communities
near Chiclayo, and both are reputed to have many *brujos* practicing sorcery and many *curanderos* who cure the sorcerers' victims. Vicki came
from a long line of healers. Both her maternal and paternal grandfathers
had worked as *curanderos* in their respective communities, and both her
parents had inherited the profession from their parents. They had worked

together as a team after they married, although their special talents were somewhat different. Vicki's mother had the vision, while her father "dominated the *artes* of the *mesa* [which he had inherited from his father], and he was the one who prayed to the spirit of San Pedro" to activate its power.

Born in 1959, Vicky had begun watching the curing ceremonies of her mother and father from a very early age. That was how she learned the profession. Her brother also became a *curandero,* but, unlike Vicky, he had come to specialize in the dark side of the magic and had become a powerful *brujo.* Now, the two of them rarely talked, and Vicky sees him as a hindrance, rather than an ally, to her work.

Despite their obvious influence over her development as a healer, her mother and her father had not wanted Vicki to follow in their footsteps. They feared the repercussions she might face with disgruntled clients should she ever fail to cure a patient. They were also practical people, who emphasized the business aspects of their profession and the risks involved. She recalled how they counseled her, saying, "As a *curandero,* one makes money without working hard for it, but if one makes a mistake, the patients quit coming and then how is one to survive? . . . Remember, too, people are envious. . . . This Peru is very small but tongues are big."

Since her parents did not want her exposed to the perils of the profession, after she had completed primary school they had sent her to a vocational boarding school in Túcume, so that she would become a seamstress. She was thirteen years old at the time, but she didn't like to sew and began to cure instead. Her schoolmates did all her sewing projects for her in exchange for the love magic which she performed for them. Eventually, the director became suspicious—since at every recess the girls would crowd around Vicky as she smoked her cigarettes and invoked her black magic to "tame," and "tie" their boyfriends. When the ruse was discovered, she was dismissed from the school.

So, at age fourteen she returned home and began to cure for real. Her first cure was of a young man who was eighteen years old. After her success with this young man, her clientele grew. Then, when she was sixteen, she suffered from a *daño,* which manifested itself as a cystlike growth accompanied by excruciating stomach pain. By then, her father had died, so her mother took her to her maternal grandfather to be healed, and he discovered that she had been done *daño* by means of a magically prepared and poisoned banana. He was a spiritist, and after he had cured her of the *daño,* he encouraged her to open herself up to the spirit world so that she might learn to become a spiritist as well.

Vicky's parents were both *curanderos hierbateros,* and both had pacts with the spirit powers of the local *huacas* and those of the far-off mountains and lagoons of Huancabamba. From her parents, Vicky had learned how to conduct the all-night *mesa.* She had learned how to manage and propitiate the magical power of these charmed places. She had learned how to pray over the San Pedro and how to dominate the *artes* of the *mesa.* From them, she had also learned the healing properties of many herbs, because from the time that she was eight years old, she had been sent to market to buy the herbs which they used to heal their patients. People tell her that she is a great *curandera,* but she claims that if that is true, it is because she knows her herbs. And this, she reiterated, she learned from her parents.

Her vocation as a spiritist, on the other hand—including her knowledge of the souls of her ancestors—was given to her by the spirits themselves. As she expressed it, "One can decide to become a *curandero* [with ties to the *encantos* of the natural world], but spiritism chooses you. Strange things have to happen to you, mysterious things, if you are to become a spiritist." Unlike the *curandero hierbatero,* the spiritist is apprenticed to the spirits alone. As Vicky told me, "One goes deeply into communication with them [to learn], but one must have a very strong character, so as to dominate the spirits, or they may lie about the cause of illness." The spirits who taught Vicky to cure were those of her dead relatives, and especially that of her father, as well as the spirit of the Virgin of Túcume.

When Vicki married, her new husband had also objected to her profession, although for different reasons than those of her parents. Like many husbands, he was a jealous man, and concerned about her activities with the patients who sought her out at all hours of the day and night. Once, her husband had refused to allow a family from Lima speak to her, even though they had driven for almost twelve hours to seek her advice. She had rebuked him then, saying that this was her work and her calling in life.

She told him if he didn't allow her to practice, she would leave him. So they reconciled, and he had become her assistant, to "keep an eye on her" during the all-night ceremonies. During these, she treats him as a subordinate, an assistant, rather than as a husband. "To get back at him [for his jealousy], I would give him [*tabaco*] to raise which made him choke," she laughed. At this point Vicki's husband, who had been present for most of our conversation, joined in the laughter, adding "Now that life is so expensive, I wish she would work every day. Thanks be to God that He has given her this gift because, as I tell her, 'You have a gift, and I can't take this away from you.' "

Clorinda

I met Clorinda in July of 1989 in the town of Huancabamba. That year, I had accompanied Isabel and Olinda to the Black Lagoon, one of the sacred Huaringa lagoons where healers and patients alike travel to bathe in the icy waters to cleanse and renew themselves. Although there are also highland lagoons in the Department of Cajamarca, Huancabamba and the lagoons of Las Huaringas are much more famous and are the most frequent destination of the obligatory pilgrimage of northern *curanderos*. Thus, I was especially anxious to meet a *curandera* who lived and worked in the shadow of these power places.

My friend Olinda, originally from the town of Huancabamba herself, had a cousin who counted Clorinda as a relative. After Olinda explained the purpose of my study and my interest in meeting Clorinda to her cousin, she agreed to take us to Clorinda's farmhouse seven or eight miles out of town on the shores of one of the tributaries of the Huancabamba River. The three of us walked the distance in about three hours, and I could barely contain my enthusiasm as we approached the farmhouse. Unfortunately, when we arrived, Clorinda wasn't home. Her mother told us she had gone into Huancabamba earlier in the day, and she was not sure when her daughter would return. Disappointed, we headed back and I turned my mind toward the other tasks I wanted to accomplish in the few remaining days that we planned to spend in the area.

Two days later, as we were preparing for the return journey to Chiclayo,

Clorinda arrived at the house where I was staying in downtown Huancabamba and invited me to accompany her to her home. We spent the next
twenty-four hours together, a very short time compared to the weeks and
months that I spent with some of the other women who collaborated in
my research. But in that short time, Clorinda told and showed me much.

Clorinda was born November 23, 1957. The second of eleven children
she still lived with her mother and other siblings on the land where she
had been born and raised. She had been to school through the fifth grade,
but did not continue her education, at least in part because there was no
secondary school near her home. To continue past the fifth grade, she
would have had to walk the seven miles to Huancabamba. Another reason
that her education stopped was that she became ill when she was ten years
old with an affliction that produced deep wounds on her legs, "so deep
that the bones were exposed." This made walking difficult for her and was
extremely painful. She suffered for eleven years, until she was finally
cured at the age of twenty-one. The illness was the result of a *daño* which
had been directed at her father, but which she had acquired because she
had been working as his assistant when he was attacked.

Her father had been a famous *curandero,* and she had been apprenticed
to him from the age of five. She assisted him until he died when she was
twenty-two. Yet, despite the fact that he was very powerful, her father had
never been able to cure her of the illness. So, during her adolescence, she
had gone to many other *maestros.* Her cure had finally come, but only
after she had dreamt the name of the *maestro* who would help her. She
went to him and he took her to bathe in the Laguna del Rey Inga. It was
this man, Clorinda told me, who "gave me the power to be able to cure
like I do now."

It was only after her father had died that Clorinda began working on
her own. As she explained, she had foreseen her father's death at a *mesa* in
which she saw a man being put into a coffin. (At the time, she hadn't
realized that the vision foretold the death of her own father; rather, she had
thought that the vision had to do with the patient they were curing.) Soon
after her father's death, her sister had become ill with a *daño* by which, as
Clorinda described it, "her legs stuck out behind her." Since their father
had died, Clorinda went to ask another *curandero* to ask him to heal her

sister. He declined because he was in mourning.[5] So, Clorinda explained, she cooked and drank some San Pedro herself and saw that she was the one who needed to cure her sister. Soon after, she did successfully cure her sister, and she also cured an aunt of a *daño.* After this, she began curing strangers who also suffered from *daño,* such as those who suffered from "head problems" like epilepsy.

During the years that she had been practicing her craft, Clorinda told me, she had cured many foreigners.[6] And as we sat talking on the verandah, she brought out the pictures and postcards that she has received from some of her international clientele, thanking her for curing them of their afflictions. Now, Clorinda is the chief "breadwinner" in the family. The money that she receives from the cures that she performs feeds and clothes her mother and younger siblings and helps them receive the education which she never had.

When I met her, Clorinda was single. She told me that she does not believe that it is possible for a woman to be a *curandera* if she is married. According to Clorinda, *curanderas* must be strong, because if they are not, they are vulnerable to possession by many spirits. Married women cannot cure, she told me, because they are weak. She did not specify exactly why this might be so, but she assured me that this weakness precludes married women from becoming powerful healers. Female *maestras,* however, are very powerful. As she told me: "The work done by a [female] *maestra* can only be undone by God with his power."

On a more practical side, she told me that it is difficult to be a *maestra* if one is married because married life conflicts with the demands of the profession. A married woman must attend to her husband, but a *maestra* works all night and therefore must rest during the day. Also, she said, married men tend to be jealous of their wives and do not look favorably on the healer's need to engage in private consultations with male as well as female patients.

When I asked Clorinda if anyone could learn to divine and cure as she had done, she told me that that power was God-given and not just anyone could learn it. Her ability to command as well as to interpret had also come from God. But, "Just as God imparts His power to the *maestro,* it is the *maestro* who 'imparts' the ability to see to whomever he or she wants and also imparts power to the *artes*. This is a gift from God." When one has a "good heart," and when the *maestro* "imparts" this power, only then does the San Pedro gives visions—or it may speak to those who are under its influence. But even though the vocation of curing is given by God, Clorinda went on, the sixth sense that aids divination and the ability to predict events based on dreams tends to be inherited. "It is in the blood," she explained. "It is of the descendants."

iii *Diagnosis and Prognosis*

*S*unday, October 9, 1988, First *mesa* with Isabel. Field notes.

I arrived at Isabel's house about 9 o'clock last evening with the bottle of champagne and the perfumes that Isabel said I should have for the *mesa*. When I arrived, it was raining but the brown wooden door was standing open. Oil lanterns lighted the room. There were already several people waiting in the living room and a few were gathered under the eaves around the doorway commenting on the strange weather. The resonating and infectious laughter of one of them seemed to be animating the entire group. She was a deeply tanned woman with short-kinky hair and a square, solid build. She welcomed me and introduced herself to me as Olinda—Isabel's housemate, friend, and assistant. I entered the house and greeted Isabel, as well as the small crowd gathered there. An older woman in a house-dress, sweater, and sweatpants commented that it would be difficult to have the *mesa* in the open-air corral if this rain kept up. Isabel replied that she would set up the *mesa* in the house if she had to, but that it would probably not be necessary—she had some secrets that would take care of the rain.

After a while, Isabel and Olinda excused themselves from the chatter of the waiting patients and went out to the open-air chicken corral behind the house. The rest of us—eleven in all—continued talking, more quietly now, as we waited. When we were called to join them to begin the ceremony about 10:30 p.m. the *mesa* had already been set into place. We were invited to sit on the benches at either side of Isabel, and at about 10:30 p.m., Isabel told us to kneel beside her and pray. Then she served the San Pedro and invited us to sit once more. One of the men—a trucker whose job often took him from the coast to Cajamarca and back began—asked me where I was from and commented on my excellent command of Spanish. He began recalling other foreigners he had met who were less proficient in his language. We laughed and chatted amiably. The atmosphere was one of relaxed cordiality, as when spectators gathering before a performance await the opening curtain.

After about half an hour, Isabel stood and took a steel knife and some *yonque* [cane alcohol] from the *mesa*. Stretching and shaking off the lethargy of the late evening, she took the bottle of *yonque* with her as she walked to the left around the eastern end of the *mesa* and over to the auxiliary *mesa*, blowing some of the liquid on it. Then she blew some liquid on the staffs and into the air above her head in the four different directions. She returned to the *mesa* from the west, then raised a toast to Olinda, who took the bottle and made the same circuit, blowing the liquid on the *mesa* and the staffs, and finally handing the bottle off to the first patient. The rest of us stood as we waited to receive the bottle in order to drink a toast with our neighbors, then drink and blow some of the *yonque* on the *mesa*. After drinking, we received the mesa staffs which Olinda handed us, and we were told to face the south end of the corral and to rub ourselves briskly with the sticks from head to toe. It seemed the ceremony had begun.

Isabel's tone changed from one of relaxed jocularity to one of complete authority. A few moments before, her words had been those of a companion or friend—polite, social, and congenial. Now, they commanded: "Cleanse yourselves, cleanse yourselves like you really want to, please." No longer one of a group of expectant spectators, we had become participants in a drama that she directed. She stood at one side of the *mesa*, her gaze turned inward. As the San Pedro took hold, her own movements slowed and became more awkward. While she directed the movements of those around her, she seemed removed from the action. The sword she carried hung free from the leather thong which held it to her wrist. Her voice commanded, but the directions seemed to come through her from another source. Olinda's role, on the other hand, seemed to have become one of a production assistant or stage manager. Isabel asked Olinda to hand her a bottle from the *mesa*, which she put to her lips, once again blowing the liquid toward the sky. As Olinda began moving among the patients, cleansing them with one of the staffs which she had removed from the *mesa,* Isabel complained of the cold—and of the pains that the patients had brought with them, which she now felt.

I yawned from where I stood at the south end of the corral. With a scolding voice, Isabel asked who among us was yawning. "*Yo,*" I replied, and she sharply told me I must resist. Yawning once the *mesa* begins, she explained, was not an indication of normal sleepiness but of a *daño,* which I must fight off. A little later, she asked who it was whose stomach was hurting. When she received no response, she scolded us, as one would scold a small child. Speak the truth, she said, how could we expect her to help us if we didn't?

At this point, a baby began crying somewhere in the distance. Isabel asked who among us had a baby that had died. No one responded. The baby, she told us, was crying because it had not been given a proper burial. It had died and never been baptized. Still, no one responded. She took some liquid, blew it in the direction of the sound, and said, "God willing, it will be born." The crying stopped. Then, after asking us to return to our seats, she told us that the *hierba* was asking her to inquire whether or not we believed in reincarnation, and why or why not. Like a teacher administering an oral examination to a roomful of students, she stood before us and heard our answers as we spoke. She seemed, by turns, a counselor, a mother, or a teacher—scolding one moment, advising the next. In all her roles, she spoke with authority and commanded obedience. All present said that they believed in reincarnation, but I told her that I did not. "You will," she said. "Remember what I say. Someday soon you will find this very important."

After a while, Isabel turned her attention toward me, calling me to her side. "What is your full name?" she asked. I told her. She turned to me, swaying a little, and spoke, her speech slightly slurred:

You are a good woman. I have looked within you and have seen the beating of your heart. But—there is a "but" here—so many years studying for your degree, just a piece of paper. And yet, you take nothing with you. . . . You walk around empty. . . . For all that you have studied and all that you have seen, you have actually experienced very little. You

83

must create something which is yours. You must find your own road, your life, yourself, your don [gift, talent].

   You don't know what this is yet. You have come looking for it. You have come to Peru and decided not to leave until you find truth, but you have not found it. Up to now you have found nothing, nothing, nothing. You have taken nothing. You have an entire life studying and you have nothing. You are worth nothing. You have come looking for something, but you haven't found that something. You have been studying to find that don. You . . . are poor, very poor. You are a very poor woman and you are in much need of our help. Who would have thought that you need help more than any of the other patients? You are poor, very poor. Nobody has told you that, have they? Nobody has told you that. You didn't marry for love but out of some other reason, something like convenience, I don't know. Yes, you married for convenience. You are very long-suffering. You have suffered much. All think of you as a great woman, but not you. You are poor. Your husband is greater than you. He married you for something, I don't know, he saw you, he fell in love. . . . I will help you because you are worth the effort. . . . All look for their lives, all want to be the owners of their life, no? They want to create something for themselves, but you, I don't know, you still don't know . . .

   I will help you, because you are worth the effort . . . not only to get your degree, but to own your life, to experience your own life, to discover your reality. . . . You have come to this country, to my country, to search . . . because in your land, you are worth nothing, you are worth nothing. Here you are worth a little more. But, I want you to go back to your country, to take this don, to take that something to your country. Help me to help you. I will help you take your own experience, to say that red is red and green is green and why it is red and why it is green. With truth. Because for all that you have traveled, you have experienced little, you have very little experience. . . . You have to create something which is yours, your own life's road, and I will help you. One day soon, not today, but soon, I will ask you to come back to my mesa in order to remove the evils [males] which have frustrated your search, which have frustrated your path, because you are suffering from [males] aire of the air, tierra of the

earth, and mar *of the ocean. You are with all three* males. *Now, I need*
you to help me with the others.

As she spoke to me, I was transfixed by her words. She seemed to have
looked into my soul and beyond it. When she called me "poor," I immediately thought of the spiritual and emotional poverty and of the emptiness that I had felt for so long. She was right: I had come to Peru in hopes
of finding myself, and I realized that I was drawn to return again and
again because of the extra attention and recognition I received for being
different. I was drawn to the attention and the strokes and had somehow
equated that external validation with self-worth.

She was right about my marriage also. Dan and I had married at the
end of our senior year of college. He had won a fellowship to do graduate
work in English literature from a school in California. I didn't know what
I wanted to do with my life, and I was afraid of making the wrong decision. I saw many options, but I felt paralyzed to act. I didn't feel ready to
get married, but I wanted to be with him. Living together was an option,
but I didn't want to disappoint my parents, whose values did not include
that possibility. Rather than confront them with a choice which I knew
would not be acceptable, we decided to marry. But I still had vague notions
about my Peruvian sweetheart, and ideas of settling in Peru.

At one point during Isabel's *rastreo* [divination], I began crying and the
tears began flowing down her face as well. "Cry, if you want," she told me.
"Come, cry with me. You have cried too much in your life. You are a good
woman, frank, with a pure heart. You don't like lies, you don't like hypoc-
risy. I will help you. Tell me what you want me to do." She asked me to
give the group a *tarea* [assignment] according to what the San Pedro indicated, and I asked that I be allowed to cleanse the entire group, one by
one, with the sword that I was carrying, which was my personal *arte*. It
seemed that if I was to gain experience, I must start here. I wanted to act
instead of waiting, instead of suffering any longer.

The rest of the night, I participated, like all the others present, as she
directed. Each of the patients was called before the *mesa*—a fifteen-year-
old girl who had suffered from a *daño* because of a jealous classmate; a

young teacher from Chota who was suffering from a *daño* effected in order to separate her from her boyfriend; a *comadre* of Isabel who was suffering from joint pains and needed to be cleansed with slices of the San Pedro to counteract their feverish heat; a patient's family member who had arrived drunk on too much *chicha* and whom Isabel sent off to gargle San Pedro in order to cleanse his system. When not taking their turn before the *mesa,* each patient joined the chorus of those who vigorously cleansed the one before the *mesa* and shook out the illness according to Isabel's direction. By the end of the night, my mouth was raw with the taste of the rubbing alcohol and vinegar that we used to "dispatch" the *daños.*

With the arrival of the dawn, Isabel completed the ceremony, calling us again to pray as we gathered around the *mesa:* "Thank you, God, for having accompanied us this night. Accompany us always wherever we are, and wherever we may go . . . " Then, we all shared in orally spraying the *mesa* to end the ceremony. A rooster pecked across the corral, reminding us that the long night was, indeed, over. In her closing prayer, Isabel mentioned the date, October 9, 1988. All of a sudden, I remembered. My miscarriage had occurred exactly one year earlier on the night of October 8th and into the early morning hours of October 9th. I remembered the baby that she had heard crying and commented on this fact. "Of course," she told me. "It was your baby who was crying. Its soul was trying to speak with us on the anniversary of its death."

Lima, October 22, 1988, Journal

Today was the last day of the workshop at the Academy of Physicians [where I had been invited to make a presentation about my work with traditional healers]. The conference began well. My presentation was well received, and I was designated to lead a discussion group with several physicians to respond to their concerns. As the discussion opened, one of the participants suggested that I, as a champion of traditional healers, represented a viewpoint which was both imperialistic and detrimental to the economic and social development of his country. I was encouraging backwardness and ignorance because of my romanticized view of peasants and my country's wish to keep Peru underdeveloped. It was an ad hominem attack, and it took me by surprise. I hadn't anticipated the political angle of the argument, and I had never expected to be accused of being bourgeois by a member of the physician class!

But there it was. I was a foreigner, supported by foreign money, meddling in internal affairs. There was nothing I could say in my defense, the way he had structured the argument. Luckily, a young Peruvian anthropologist came to my rescue. He assured the physician that no one in the room was more anti-imperialist than he was. He had been born of impoverished, Quechua-speaking parents in a highland village near Cuzco. He had fought for land reform, for peasant's rights, and against the exploitation of the bourgeoisie for as long as he could remember. Traditional forms of healing were of, for, and by the people and not some romanticized notion imported from our North American neighbors. That they are the only ones who have taken an interest in studying the "people's medicine" should make the physicians feel shame. It was time they claimed this birthright as their own, instead of fomenting argument and discord within the nation! The young anthropologist's vehemence, and the political correctness of his argument, silenced the first speaker.

I felt awful walking back to the hotel, as if I had been in a deep fog and had suddenly been hit by a truck emerging from nowhere. In that moment, with an intensity of realization that shook me to the core, I recognized how I had been mistaking "red" for "green" (to use Isabel's words). I had constructed a personal and a cultural identity tied to the illusion of being accepted as Peruvian. I knew, of course, that I could never *be* Peruvian, but I also knew that I had become an anthropologist so as to have a legitimate claim to living here. Now, I saw that because I was white, I had lost legitimacy even as an anthropologist. My North American and European origins made it impossible for me to participate in the political agenda of indigenous Peruvians.

First, I felt angry. But now, as I write these words, a feeling of utter demoralization has begun to rise within me. I have built my own personal identity around my cultural belonging in Peru. Without that, who am I? An immense void. Will I find inner direction to fill it? If I don't pass through this confrontation and come out the other side, will I go mad? There is no "I" within me—only the internalization of external stimuli.

This lack of "self" has been unmasked and I am disintegrating—imploding into nothingness. I feel completely alone and desperate.

88   Chiclayo, December 14, 1988, *mesa* with Isabel. Field notes.

Dan and I went to a *mesa* together last night for the first time. Isabel told me it was time to begin curing me of the specific *daños* from which I was suffering, and that Dan should come with me, so we arranged the ceremony. Early on in the ceremony, as Dan was being cleansed by Olinda with the San Cipriano staff, Isabel asked us, "Are you two of the same religion?" I answered that I had been raised as a Lutheran and Dan told her that his family background was Quaker. She asked us each about our religious heritage and the importance that religion had played in each of our lives. She asked us about our relationships with our families. She encouraged us to keep talking as she reflected on all that we told her. She seemed to be waiting for a sign. All of a sudden, she pointed to a barn owl which flew silently through the night sky above us and said:

> Look at that. That is not a normal animal. Its [appearance] is like saying you are flying through the air, you are in the void, . . . that there is nothing. It comes as though your spirit . . . has nowhere to land.

After asking me about the origin of this feeling of emptiness and about my feelings toward Dan when we were married, Isabel told me that she "saw" a photograph with two people—a couple—depicted in it. Someone was ripping the photograph in half and throwing each half to the winds. She concluded, "The emptiness comes from there, from a love magic, a separation that really harmed you both, you as well as him." She asked if I had once been in love with someone from Peru? I told her about Carlos, about my return to the States and our subsequent breakup. "No, the separation comes from earlier, a family member it seems—on his mother's side—broke the bonds . . . so he would forget, so you would separate, so your love would die. Her idea was that only in that way would her son be able to focus on his studies. There was no harm intended, but harm was done." Carlos's mother had taken the picture to a spiritist who had "cut it apart and thrown the pieces to the winds." Isabel explained it:

> *The problem is that when it is truly love and somebody forces you apart . . .*
> *this is a very sad case. Not only is the love destroyed, but also your luck*
> *and future. . . . Both of you were left empty. . . . That is why you wander*
> *as though flying . . . like a whirlwind. . . . This was a* jugada *[a*
> *manipulation] of the winds. It wasn't intended to harm you, as a daño,*
> *but it took from you that which is most essential. I would rather suffer*
> *from a daño in which I am hit with a bullet, I die, and that is that, than*
> *to live like that, that is to say, to wander as an air without having*
> *anything inside. That is the saddest thing.*

Both Carlos and I had apparently lost our centering, our grounding, at that moment. It had been impossible to make a future for myself because, from that moment, our spirits had been thrown to the wind. Our "steps left no imprints on the Earth," and we had both been wandering aimlessly since that thoughtless moment when the picture had been torn.

Isabel instructed Olinda to "cut the cords of the love magic with the scissors" that stood behind the Mesa San Cipriano. I felt cold and she admonished me, "Don't you want the ties of that *daño* to be cut? Do you want to remain the way you are, without any triumph in your life?" No, of course I wanted to get on with my life. "Then you must not feel that chill; it must leave your body." Like the advice I had heard her give to other patients on previous occasions, the import of her words was twofold. The past was not my fault. I had suffered from a *daño* which I had been powerless to combat. I should not blame myself. I should not feel victimized. I had been powerless to combat my problems on my own. The future, however, was my domain. I had to take responsibility for my choices, and I had to want to break the cycles of pain and of despair. She could not help me as long as I insisted on clinging to the past.

I told her I wanted to put the past behind me and look toward the future. Olinda began by cleansing both Dan and me with rocks from the *mesa*. Next, we put the rocks in a sling in order to hurl them over the corral wall and into the fields beyond. Our marriage would be fuller, our love for one another stronger, and—in my case—I would finally be able to begin to find my path, to choose my future, without the illusions which had clouded my vision in the past. But, when it was my turn to hurl the sling, I couldn't make it fly. I tried several times, but the rocks dribbled out of the sling a few feet in front of me. Isabel told Dan to try, on my behalf. As he hurled the sling, he let go of it by mistake, and the rocks, sling and all, went sailing into the night! It was a bad sign, Isabel told us. Perhaps I wasn't really decided after all.

Next, Isabel asked Olinda to cleanse us with various items from her *mesa* to help us in the construction of good roads. She told Olinda to concentrate on my head, in particular, since I had been confused, unable to focus on my destiny, reacting to the moment instead of taking a stand toward life. "Pull them up, up so that the indecision is carried away by the mountain air, by the stars. . . . You have no reason to cry anymore. . . . You have already cried too much in your life. . . . Get close to God. There you will find the answer. . . . Believe in Him and He will help you."

As she spoke, the intensity of light in the star-studded night sky suddenly dimmed, as though a giant switch had been thrown. I had seen this before, but it was especially frightening as a sign that related to my circumstances. My heart began to pound. Isabel called us before the *mesa* and told us that we must "commend . . . [our]selves to God. . . . Having God in your heart, in your mind, you have the wonders of the truth within you. Ask it of Him, that all your paths be clarified, your projects." She told us to kneel before the *mesa,* and she began to lead us in the following prayer, saying:

> *God, we have faith in you. If perhaps sometime these two have strayed, forgive them. Help us, illuminate us, guide us. But don't let us fall into an evil hour, into an evil moment. You are here in my heart, here in my spirit, here in my mind. You are the owner of my life. . . . Help me in this mesa curandera . . . so that the emptiness is left in the past . . . so that my head is cleared, my heart, my faith in you. I have to believe with greater strength, with more faith . . .*

As she prayed, the sky began to clear and the brilliance returned to the stars that had dimmed. But now the stars seemed to have bunched together in a single band, forming a kind of road above the *mesa*. To the south end of the corral, the sky remained black. Isabel interpreted this new sign for us, saying:

> *Wherever you walk anywhere in the world, wherever you go, because the path is yours to choose, you will have to confront that which is reality. Many times as children we are told what is right, what is wrong, what we should think, but we are not made to confront life. . . . That is why often we think we know, but we do not. . . . You have been living in darkness, and darkness is emptiness. Living in darkness is the same as being empty. You touch no one. You can't see. You only know that at any moment you will trip and fall. You may run into something good or something bad . . . but if you believe in Him you will have happiness and your own power. You will explore the richness of life, of yourselves, of things which you create. . . . You won't be lonely. You won't be sad. . . . You will always have His gift to do many great things upon the earth . . . and if anyone wants to do you* daño, *God is first. He puts out his hand and the* daño *ceases to exist.*
>
> *Illness is not just feeling pain, it is also feeling [that you are] empty, feeling [that you are] nothing. . . . But if you cure yourself by going to [a* curandero], *. . . you are made to see reality, your mind is cleared, and you are left healed, which is how it should be.*
>
> *God is a Spirit . . . a Spirit which you feel inside of you. . . . [Denying this] is the worst error! . . . [Those that say the Bible is just a book don't realize that its lasting lesson] is really one's life experience. . . . And that experience has to be lived by each one of us. I'm not going to live the same experience that another lived! Each one has to live his own experience, each one has to live his own life as it should be. . . . There it is.*

She turned her attention back to Dan and me, still kneeling before the *mesa*. She admonished us then, "You have been given this sign from God, and yet you still don't believe it. But think about this, about that which

I tell you, and little by little you will say that I am right, that this is truth. . . . As you two begin seeing the reality, seeing things the way they are, then you will face everything and you will also create something new."

As the sky brightened and as she spoke, a deep feeling of surrender came over me. I had spent so much effort seeking meaning, seeking explanation, seeking a reason for living over the years that my mind was indeed confused and tired. During this night, I had been confronted with an emptiness that came from a time when my actions had been motivated by a desire for external validation. In my haste to reassure myself that Carlos still loved me, I had asked for him to validate the relationship. When he refused, I felt rejected, hurt, and confused. But instead of risking further rejection by insisting that I still loved him, I had slunk away in defeat. Ironically, it seems, he had done the same, because his fear of rejection also overcame desire. In the sense that our misfortune had been orchestrated by a spiritist at the behest of his family, what happened was not my fault and Isabel had given me permission to forgive myself for the misunderstanding that had broken both our hearts.

But Isabel did hold me responsible for my stubborn refusal to accept reality. As long as I refused to forgive myself, as long as I refused to let go of the past, as long as I would not accept that the hands of time could never be turned back and yesterday's choices could never be relived, I would be rejecting, not living, the gift of life which God had given me. I had told Isabel that I was decided and determined to change, but here she was presenting me with the hardest of all choices. To take control of my destiny, I had to give up the fantasy which had sustained me for so many years. I had to surrender my hold on the mind-sapping "what ifs" that kept me from fully engaging my current life as a wife, as an anthropologist, as an American. Like a doubting Thomas, even when faced with the sign from God, I found myself clinging to the false security of what could have been rather than abandon myself to the risk of fully engaging my present life. Isabel entreated me to believe in a power greater than myself and told me that my cure depended upon it, but I found myself resisting. Perhaps if I had not resisted, my cure would have come much more swiftly . . .

4 ▊ Healers at Work

In this chapter I describe the ritual healing practices of the five women who were introduced in chapter 3. Each of the five healers is presented by means of a ritual ceremony they performed to diagnose and/or cure a specific patient of specific ailments. The stories told here are merely a representative sample of the activities in the thirty or so ritual healings I participated in with the five women in this study. These case studies are intentionally presented without much of the analytical framework that so easily boils important particularities down in the search for generalities. Instead, such analysis is presented in chapters 5 and 6, where it can be dealt with more comprehensively.

Yolanda

This story is about Rolando Vargas, the highly educated political functionary, and a long-time friend of mine, whose illness initially led me to Yolanda (see chapter 3).[1] The symptoms of Rolando's illness manifested themselves one Saturday toward the end of March. He had been trying to relax at a friend's house when he was overcome by pain in his abdomen. He struggled home and called his family doctor, who came over to the house and gave him intravenous and intramuscular injections for the pain. Having rested all day Sunday, Rolando insisted upon returning to work the following day since he had to make a public appearance in a neighboring village. He reported feeling "tied to the bed" and was concerned because he seemed unable to get out of bed and fight the illness. The symptoms continued, but he did not give in. By Wednesday, however, he could no longer function at work and was forced to leave the office. Immediately, rumors began circulating that he was very ill. This concerned him because the last thing he wanted his political enemies to think was that he might be forced to step down from his post due to bad health.

The next day, Rolando was flown to Lima and hospitalized. Just leaving Cajamarca, he said, made him feel better, as he "felt a kind of freedom" surround him. Although he endured several painful examinations in the hospital in Lima, what most distressed him was not his physical condition but the loss of control over his daily routine. Even his "legendary" will power did not seem to help in this situation. After a week in Lima, Rolando returned to work in Cajamarca, but now his sense of panic increased. He had terrible headaches and felt "heavy" and completely drained of energy. Where he had been accustomed to working twelve- to fourteen-hour days, now he felt exhausted after half a day. He also began sighing uncontrollably, overcome by "deep exhalations that seemed as though they were tearing out my heart." During the next few nights he began to have nightmares about his political enemies. "Figures, scenes, attitudes, scenes of people in Cajamarca all came at me," Rolando reported. He began to feel desperate enough "to go to the hilltops and throw myself off." He was unable to get out of bed yet felt afraid of being bedridden. After two more days of this, Rolando reported that he experienced a "crisis." He felt flushed and his head pounded. He begged a cousin who was caring for him to "bring all the *brujos* in Cajamarca" because he couldn't take it any more. He concluded by saying that he felt completely "vanquished in the fight against his illness."

Yolanda came to see him and did the preliminary diagnosis that afternoon. She looked at Rolando with such a steady gaze that he felt uncomfortable. Then she began to turn slowly to the right, all the while uttering prayers from the Catholic Mass with her arms raised toward the ceiling. After a while, she stopped suddenly and began to ask Rolando questions, to which he was instructed to simply answer yes or no. He insisted that she knew nothing about his political position, only that he was ill and needed a diagnosis. He recounted their conversation as follows:

Y: You manage many documents?
R: Yes.
Y: There is a tall, balding man in a jacket who wants to do daño *to you.*

There is a tall, good-looking female lawyer who wants to harm you.
There is a mustached man from a ministry that also wants to harm
you. There are two men that you helped rise-up, and now they want to
do you in. . . . There is also a woman, who to your face is very sweet,
but who stabs you in the back. . . . These people want to bind you, they
want to tie you up, they want to rob your soul, and they have your life in
the palm of their hands. The only thing left is to close their hands over it
to kill you.

Yolanda also told him that the reason he had been so ill on Wednesday
was that in various places around Cajamarca he had been hexed the night
before in various sessions by various *brujos*, all of whom were trying to
call his soul away from him.

Rolando's reaction to Yolanda's diagnosis was immediate:

I was very surprised by so much coincidence and so much detail with
which she precisely divined these things. I didn't know if those people had
such power to bring me to my current state. . . . She told me she could
cure me and I told her . . . that she should cure me, if she could help me
that she should help me. After she left, I felt different . . . more at peace.

That night, Rolando said, he slept well for the first time and determined
to undergo the prescribed treatment. The price was negotiated. The cure
would cost 8000 intis (about $70) for as many sessions as needed.

Yolanda and her partner, José, arrived at Rolando's house for his first
healing *mesa*. Contrary to most others I'd participated in, this *mesa* would
be held during the day. Although Yolanda and José had conducted *mesas*
at night in previous years, their respective health problems and the rigors
of operating their small store now convinced them to hold the *mesas* during the day. Besides, as José noted, *brujos* work at night, but he and
Yolanda—because they are God's servants—cure in the light of day.

They set up the healing altar, covering a small table with a white cloth
and placing upon it a two-foot-high crucifix, several smaller wooden
crosses, a small statue of the Virgin of Lourdes, and a large bowl to hold
the warm infusion of San Pedro after it had been prepared on the stove.

Each participant—Rolando, another friend whom he had asked to accompany him, myself, and the two healers—was given one of the wooden crosses to defend against the Devil. José stood behind the small table with Yolanda at his right. The rest of us stood in a semicircle facing them, holding the crosses in our right hands. After an opening prayer in which José called upon God, the Virgin, all the saints of the Heavenly Court, and the Holy Cross to forgive our errors and our sins and to cure, untie, disabuse, protect, bless, and support us day and night, both he and Yolanda led us in the Our Father, the Hail Mary, the Apostle's Creed, the Hail Holy Queen, and other prayers from the Catholic Mass. After this, we crossed ourselves and were led in the precommunion song entitled "Receiving God" in preparation for receiving the San Pedro. As we were each called before the altar to receive our two glassfuls of the warm liquid, José prayed over the San Pedro as the priest prays over the communion wine, reiterating his opening invocation and then adding a prayer that the San Pedro might come to our aid, "conversing all things clearly."

As each person in the room received their portions of the brew, the others were instructed to repeat the words "by God and the Holy Virgin" while raising their arms in the direction of the recipient from floor to ceiling. Each person receiving the San Pedro was instructed to make a complete circle to the right, so as to untie, to unravel, all his errors, all the twistings of his spirit, and the rest of us were instructed to help the recipient in this task by also turning toward the right.

After this first portion of the ceremony, Yolanda led us in the song, "Come, Holy Spirit," which is also sung in the Mass to entreat the Holy Spirit to illuminate those who receive communion. As we sang this and other songs from the Mass, we were instructed to keep turning to the right to "shake out" our arms and legs so that the San Pedro would begin to work in our bodies, and to protect ourselves with the cross as a way of collaborating with the patient. Yolanda began pointing out shapes and figures which appeared in the dust that our shuffling and turning kicked around on the floor. She indicated that these figures represented the *daño* and those who had effected the *daño*. Rolando was instructed to step on and stamp out these manifestations of the evil which had been done against him. The rest of us were told to collaborate, stamping out any figures that appeared in our area of the room, and we were also invited to help him rub out the figures which appeared around him. Occasionally, Yolanda interrupted her singing and shuffling to interpret the meaning of the figures and to ask questions.

As we continued shuffling, stomping, and turning, the San Pedro took effect and we all began focusing on the dusty floor beneath our feet. Like the figures that appear when one concentrates on the clouds in a summer sky, the floor seemed to be covered with figures and shapes, each scuff-mark and swirl of dust transformed under Yolanda's guidance. She noted that although she guided and watched over us, it was our faith, our sincerity, and our participation which was at the core of Rolando's cure. Without faith, she said, and without, "attention to a spiritual state in which one is completely with God, there is nothing; everything has to be dedicated to God and to the Holy Virgin. . . . We have to concentrate with all our hearts to be able to help others, and in this way to liberate them."

The figures that Yolanda interpreted for Rolando seemed to coincide with her original diagnosis. She noted a dark figure on the floor in the shape of an eagle with many people under its wings, which Rolando interpreted as a manifestation of his enemies who had been publicly trying to undermine his position as a government leader. He recalled Yolanda's warning that these enemies had tied him up like a sheep being led to the slaughter. She also made reference to a bomb-fuse in his doorway, which he related to a recent attempt on his life. Yolanda also pointed out a number of women amongst the figures of his enemies.

After about an hour and a half, the ceremony ended with a benediction and a closing prayer. Yolanda told Rolando to bathe with the rest of the San Pedro liquid and then to get into bed to get warm. The bath caused him to sweat profusely, so completely did it warm him. Although his teeth chattered from the cold when he poured the liquid over his body and climbed into bed, "within ten minutes my body began warming up, but in such a way that I said, 'Well, this is going to cure me,' . . . because in my head I got the idea that I was like a fierce beast and I was shaking from the heat of my body. I said, 'I will be cured; this will cure me. . . . ' Then, naturally, I fell asleep."

Rolando attended two additional *mesas* that clarified for him the nature of his illness. Privately, Yolanda had admitted to me after the first *mesa* that Rolando's illicit involvement with other women had played a larger role in his illness than she had thus far acknowledged to him. She was choosing to withhold the information until she felt he was ready to accept it. But after the second and the third curing sessions, Rolando began sharing with me how many of the women whose names Yolanda had mentioned had personal reasons, as well as political ones, for wanting him to suffer. His first girlfriend, whom he had been forced to abandon when his father discovered the relationship, now worked with the cadre of competitors who were eyeing his job. He told of how a friend of hers had come to his room and had inquired about his health, offering him an herbal remedy, which he had drunk. She disappeared after that, never asking after him again. He wondered aloud to me if she might not have been sent by the jilted lover. Another woman who was currently a lover of one of his political enemies had been his brother's girlfriend, and Rolando had also dated her. He associated one name that Yolanda mentioned with his wife's cousin—also a former girlfriend—who was crushed when he abandoned her to marry his wife. Finally, there were problems at home because his wife had recently ascertained that he was having an affair with one of his secretaries.

Earlier in our friendship, Rolando had told me that although he loved his wife and his three children, he wished that he had never married. He told me that all he had wanted out of life was to be free, to not be tied down, depended upon, or controlled by a woman. He felt that the responsibility to provide for his family's needs had limited his freedom, and he resented this intrusion on his life. Now, Yolanda was echoing his conclusion that the main threats to his life were women, particularly those with whom he had become embroiled in romantic liaisons. During the second session, when Rolando's wife's face appeared again and again among the dust-figures on the floor, Yolanda asked him what had happened in his marriage, and he responded that something had died and that he felt responsible. She warned him to beware of temptation and to put his life in order. Only then, she said, would he be able to come close to God and regain the strength he would need to vanquish the Evil of those who wished him harm.

By the end of his third *mesa,* Rolando was able to tell me that the pressures in his job were beginning to subside. Some of those who had publicly defamed him in the previous weeks and months had, since he began the cure, begun to publicly show their support for his policies. He now also felt recommitted to his marriage and to his family and noted that Laura, who only a few weeks before had threatened to leave him on account of his secretary, seemed less bitter. He was somewhat surprised at his own attitude toward Yolanda and her abilities. He had understood the meaning of the faces and figures that had appeared on the floor "as though I had lived (their meaning) all my life. . . . I don't know how to explain it to you, [but] I see those faces as dragged down, chained, tied up because of their bad feelings, their hatred, their bitterness—all those feelings which imprison us all and with which we hurt one another." I was struck by the relationship between the letting go of these bad feelings and Rolando's own interpretation of his cure, which did, indeed, seem to involve self-reflection and rehabilitation.

In subsequent weeks, Laura also came to Cajamarca and I took her to see Yolanda, who had said to us that she had also been the victim of *daño.* Although I didn't participate in Yolanda's diagnosis of Laura, they both recounted the conversation to me later. Laura insisted that Yolanda had not said it was necessary for her to be cured, whereas Yolanda told me she had clearly indicated quite the opposite. According to Laura, the problem was that her husband was having an affair with his secretary. If he would just break it off, things would return to normal. Yolanda's assessment was that Laura was even worse off than Rolando because of her closure, bitterness, and unwillingness to forgive the affair. She told me that this was also the result of *brujería* which was aimed at destroying Rolando's life by "destroying his home from the inside." At one point, Yolanda commented that "until [Laura] receives spiritual help," no amount of counseling would help the situation.

When Laura finally did consent to be cured, the price was negotiated at 6000 intis (about $52) for as many sessions as would be needed to complete the cure. Laura participated in a total of three *mesas,* and she asked me to accompany her during each of them. During the first *mesa,* Yolanda reproached Laura for her stubbornness and counseled her to forgive her husband, comparing his affair to one that her brother had been involved in which she had been able to forgive. Again, I was struck by the need for letting go of the bad feelings in order to be healed. Acceptance seemed to be the critical component of spiritual rehabilitation.

Rolando attended Laura's last two *mesas*. Yolanda didn't participate because of her health, so José brought two elderly women to help. Laura and Rolando seemed skeptical and threatened to cancel the sessions since Yolanda would be absent, but they were informed that these women had a "clean spiritual conscience"—that they were strong and could help Rolando and Laura because their spiritual lives were healthy. At the end of the second session, Laura and Rolando stood together, arm in arm. They discussed the figures they had seen, comparing notes. They seemed to be working together to fight the Evil.

But later that day Laura told me, half-jokingly, that she wanted me to take her kids and raise them while she ran off alone. Still, she decided to attend the third and final session the next day. I assumed that afterward she would tell me that the sessions had been for naught. Instead, she reported that she wanted to come back in a couple of months for more.

The sessions completed and Yolanda too sick to see me, there seemed little reason to stay in Cajamarca, so I left the next day for Trujillo. On the bus ride home, I tried to make sense of the previous month. Had there been a positive outcome to this story? Between the two of them, Rolando and Laura had spent over $120 on their cures. They both had incomes: Rolando's salary as a political functionary provided the bulk of the family income, but Laura's work as a schoolteacher in Lima also gave her a measure of independence and allowed their three children to attend a prestigious private school. Although the cost of the cures stretched their monthly budget somewhat, it did not pose an overwhelming financial hardship. Rolando's health had improved during the course of his treatment, but his marriage was still in jeopardy. Laura was more convinced than ever of his philandering since conversing with Rolando's assistant who had accompanied us during Rolando's first session. I also realized I had become too involved to be able to lay any claim to objectivity. But my close friendship with both Laura and Rolando had also given me insights about how a belief in sorcery can often be intertwined with acts of sexual indiscretion.

These "temptations," as Yolanda calls them, keep us chained to an impure state in which we are vulnerable to attacks of envy, jealousy, and acts of sorcery. On the other hand, when our spiritual consciences are clean, when we resist the temptations associated with impure action, even while accepting the imperfections of those we love, we are defended against the envy, the resentment, and the retribution which are the breeding grounds for sorcery.

Isabel

In January 1989 I was introduced to Violeta by a mutual friend, who knew of my work with Isabel and Olinda. Violeta, convinced she was suffering from *daño,* asked me if I would please introduce her to the *curanderas.* This thirty-four-year-old woman of medium stature suffered from headaches, numbness in her limbs, coughing fits that had been diagnosed by one physician as tuberculosis, fatigue, and rapid weight loss. In the previous two years, her weight had dropped from sixty-six kilos, which she described as her normal weight, to forty-four kilos, but she also reported that in the previous two weeks, her lack of appetite had intensified because of a *bola que camina,* a "ball," or "knot" that had "walked" from her stomach to her throat and which made her vomit whenever she tried to eat. Her illness was also affecting her ability, and interest, in attending to her husband and their nine-year-old daughter. She had begun neglecting her appearance, often snapped at her daughter for no reason, and was surly with her husband. She was having trouble sleeping and had frequent nightmares of a naked woman in bed with her husband—a woman she recognized as a "cousin" of her husband's who had lived with them during previous years.

Violeta described economic problems in the household as well. Her husband had once been a trucker who made a handsome profit selling the merchandise that he transported. He had once had so much money, she recalled, that he would go off drinking with his friends for a week at a time, always leaving her enough money to run the household before he left. During these excursions, she reported, he was so generous that he would buy all the beer and even pay his buddies the wages they had lost because of drinking with him instead of going off to work. Now, he was lucky to get day jobs unloading cargo trucks.

Her illness also prohibited her from making the frequent trips between Chiclayo and her childhood home in the jungle that had previously given her some financial independence. On these trips, she would carry and distribute commodities native to each region. Her cargo on trips to the jungle might include plastic tubs and kitchenwares bought directly from the factories near Chiclayo; her return cargo might include semiprocessed chocolate and coffee from the plantations to the east. She would then sell these to friends and family. Even through her prices were only slightly lower than what these commodities might cost at the local markets, she could still turn a handsome profit with each trip.

In addition, Violeta reported that the flock of ducks, chickens, and geese she raised at home to provide for her family's protein needs had been drastically reduced during the previous months. A mysterious disease had swept through the flock, killing a number of her finest birds. Egg production was also down, so she had fewer chicks to replace the lost animals. And a number of *compromisos* (social engagements) during recent months had required the slaughter of many of her remaining animals so as to feed the guests she was obliged to entertain.

When I met her, Violeta was convinced that she was not suffering from any naturally caused illness. She had reached this conclusion after the laboratory work on her blood, sputum, and feces had turned up nothing to explain her impaired physical condition. In addition, she had been to an herbalist knowledgeable about *daño,* and she had informed her that sorcery was the cause of her affliction. Violeta attributed the cause of her physical, economic, and domestic problems to a *daño* orchestrated by the woman in her nightmares—who wasn't really a "cousin" at all but her husband's lover. Violeta was convinced that this woman's agenda was to steal her husband away from her, either by killing her outright or by causing her husband to simply tire of the economic and domestic stress and leave.

According to Violeta, her problems had started almost exactly two years before our first interview. She had been pregnant at the time with what would have been their second child, a little boy. After she had begun showing signs of labor around one o'clock one afternoon, her husband had taken her to a nearby hospital. Instead of admitting her, the hospital told her that there were no beds available and that she would have to go to the nearby town of Lambayeque for the delivery. When Violeta and her husband arrived in Lambayeque, once again she was told there were no beds and they were sent back to the hospital in Chiclayo. She was refused admission at the hospital in Chiclayo and sent, this time, to a clinic on the other side of town. There, for the fourth time that day, she had been told there was no room and the two of them were sent back to the hospital in Chiclayo. for the third time, where her husband insisted that she be admitted, or left to die at the hospital door. Her son had been stillborn at ten o'clock that evening. In addition to the mental anguish she had suffered because of losing her son, she told me, her postpartum bleeding had gone on for an entire year. "Every time I got my period," Violeta reported, "water came out of me like a hemorrhage." It was at this time that she had sought out the woman who had prescribed herbs to stop the bleeding and who had told her she was most likely suffering from a *daño*.

I asked Violeta how she thought the *daño* had been done. She reported that in the early months of that last pregnancy, a turkey she had been raising suddenly disappeared. When she went to the corral to look for it, she had come across a bunch of flowers and, almost immediately, had began to show the early signs of miscarriage. Her husband had then suggested that she visit a *curandero* to prevent loss of the baby, and the man he had recommended turned out to be the "other woman's" cousin. The *curandero* had given her things to drink, and he also instructed her to lie down at a crossroads. She had taken his advice, thinking her health would improve. But instead it had just gotten worse. About this time, she reported, a pair of underpants had disappeared from her drawer and she had begun feeling stabbing pains around her genitals. Now, she believes the cousin and the "healer" worked the *daño* together so that she would lose the baby and die.

I took her to see Isabel, who used a tarot-card reading to discover that Violeta had been the victim of *daño por boca,* which was the reason the doctors could find nothing wrong with her. According to Isabel, *daño por boca* manifests itself without any perceivable cause. *Daño por aire,* on the other hand, will often be diagnosed as any number of illnesses, none of which reflect the "real," magical cause. If a doctor follows up on the false diagnosis and treats the symptoms of *daño* with ingested, or especially, injected medicines, these medicines will have an adverse effect on the victim, poisoning instead of curing him.

Isabel told Violeta about the tumor that "walked around" in her stomach and about how she had been done unto so that she would remain incredulous instead of seeking a *curandero* to help her before it was too late. Isabel suggested that she come to a *mesa* the following Saturday, where, under the influence of the San Pedro, more about her illness would be revealed and Isabel would learn what action was needed in order to cure it.

The next Saturday, Violeta, her husband, and I arrived at Isabel and Olinda's house and took our places in the living room while the *mesa* was being set up in the courtyard. Violeta seemed nervous, and her husband seemed a little angry that she would not be the only patient scheduled for the evening. In addition to we three, a young man who had lost the use of his legs because of a *daño* intended to keep him from earning a living, and another young man with mysterious boils on his hands and arms, were among those waiting for the *mesa* to begin.

Shortly before nine o'clock that evening, we were invited to take our places on the adobe benches which line the three walls of the courtyard facing the *mesa*. Isabel had us kneel in a semicircle around the *mesa*, and she began praying to God, the Virgin, the spirit powers of nature and of dead Christian souls, and the blessed San Pedro, to help and guide her throughout the night. Then, one by one, she served everyone present two glasses of San Pedro, beginning with the person to her immediate left. When Violeta was served the San Pedro, she vomited—a sure sign, said Isabel, that she was very ill indeed. After this, Isabel invited all present to sit once more and wait with her until the spirit of San Pedro arrived.

After about forty-five minutes Isabel stood, stretched, and began the mesa ceremony as on previous occasions. She took the steel knife that was her personal *arte* from its place at the *mesa,* as well as a bottle of cane alcohol and walked clockwise around the corral, orally spraying the contents of the bottle on her *mesa*.[2] At the south end of the corral, she made her offerings to the lagoons and mountains, to the golden *mesa* of her great-grandfather, and to the silver *mesa* of her grandfather, and then she made her offerings to the "four winds" and the "four roads" as she turned first north, then east, then south, then west. Finally, she returned to the Mesa Novata and made her offerings to it as she finished her left-to-right circuit of the corral.

After Olinda had also completed this initial circuit around the corral, and after all present had drunk a toast to each other and to the *mesa,* Olinda handed each of us a staff which would be our personal defense *arte* for the duration of the ritual. We were told to cleanse ourselves with the staff and to orally spray it with rubbing alcohol when we were finished, so as to "dispatch" any traces of illness it might have captured during the cleansing.

During the self-cleansing process, Olinda circulated among the patients and their families and cleansed each of them in turn with a staff taken from the line of staffs that stood to the south of the Mesa Novata. After vigorously rubbing all four sides of their bodies from their heads to their feet with the staff, the patients were sprayed with rubbing alcohol so as to "dispatch" the residue of this cleansing toward the west side of the corral, in the direction of the nearby ocean. During the cleansing, Isabel stood behind or beside the Mesa Novata, rocking or swaying, as the San Pedro began revealing the problems of the patients to her.

Isabel called Violeta before the *mesa* to begin her diagnosis. She asked us to help cleanse Violeta even further using the particular staffs she pointed out, so that she might better see where Violeta's shadow had been delivered by the *brujo* who had effected the *daño*. Violeta began to cry and Isabel admonished her, "Be strong, be strong. . . . Only ask God that He help you. . . . If you cry, your shadow becomes weaker. It is worse for you and for me." She implored Violeta to concentrate on the *mesa* and on her cure, or it would be impossible for Isabel to follow the path her shadow had taken when it had been called from her body back to the *brujo's mesa* and then turned over to the spirit force presently holding it. As Violeta still vacillated, Isabel admonished her sharply:

Right now, forget about your illness, forget about it. Leave it with the mesa *and leave it with God so that I can get to the bottom of it. In other words,*

> *give yourself over to God. Maybe I am a human being who can lie to you, but God won't lie to you. He is. He exists. He is a spirit in your heart and in your thoughts. Only He is there. And He, in your subconscience, is going to tell you: yes, yes, yes, you are going to be cured.*

When Violeta regained her composure, Isabel described the cause of her illness. There were multiple *daños* here, she said. Because Violeta had *daño por boca,* the doctors could find nothing wrong when they examined her. But she also had *daño por aire* because of the stolen underpants. These had been fashioned into a package and buried in one of four cemeteries somewhere north of Chiclayo.

Isabel told us to do cleansings with staffs from the *mesa* to determine which of the cemeteries contained Violeta's soul. As we rubbed her body with the staffs, we were to invoke the names of various possible locations. When we mentioned the cemetery in the town of Morrope, a cold wind suddenly blew across the corral. Isabel recognized this as a sign that the package had been buried there.

Isabel told Violeta that it would take time to cure her and that she would have to return for another *mesa* very soon. To hold back the progression of the illness, she told Violeta to turn her sweater inside out. To address the immediate symptoms of Violeta's debility, she also prescribed a vitamin-rich vegetable tonic (to be made at home) and serum (to be bought at the pharmacy). Since the *daño* had caused a ulcerlike lesion to form in Violeta's stomach, she told Violeta to avoid all hot and greasy foods, especially hot peppers and duck, and to increase her consumption of foods with cooling properties. To begin expelling the *daño por boca,* Isabel prescribed an enema. To begin the process of reclaiming Violeta's soul, Isabel told her to cut her hair and leave it as an offering in four churches in various parts of the city.

After the first *mesa,* Violeta told me, she felt much better. Some of her appetite had returned and the ball in her stomach was less a knotted mass than before. The enema had had a positive effect, as had the vitamin tonic. Unlike her experience with the "other woman's" cousin, who, she was even more sure than before, had orchestrated the *daño,* she had been reassured by Isabel's approach to healing because of her reliance on

Catholic saints and crucifixes as well as her obvious faith in God. For the first time in many months she had had a pleasant dream, one which added to her conviction that Isabel healed with the permission and power of God.

Violeta returned the next Saturday for her second *mesa,* but the large number of patients precluded Isabel from spending much time discussing Violeta's illness directly. Rather, Isabel told Violeta to bring a black guinea pig to the house for a cleansing, as well as an extra pair of underpants, since the pair she wore on the day of the treatment would be burned. Isabel explained that this next phase of her treatment would help break the bonds any sorcerer or evil spirit had over Violeta's soul.

The guinea pig cleansing revealed symptoms Violeta had complained of as well as a new problem. When Isabel completed the cleansing and cut open the animal, she found its insides full of blood, a sure reflection of the hemorrhaging Violeta had suffered. She also found evidence of the *daño* that had been placed in Violeta's stomach, problems with an ovary, and stones in both of the guinea pig's kidneys. "Have your kidneys hurt?" she asked Violeta. When Violeta responded that they hadn't, Isabel noted, "Until now, you've been in so much pain you haven't noticed specific spots that hurt. But you will." While Isabel finished the cleansing, Olinda burned Violeta's underpants in the back part of the corral. The flame ignited as though sulfur had been thrown on the fire. Olinda said the *daño* caused this reaction.

Although Violeta now began gaining weight, the cure was not yet complete. Isabel suggested that Violeta have a personal *mesa.* To prepare, Isabel told Violeta to bring a black guinea pig and a white guinea pig to the house to be blessed. Once dedicated to the mission at hand—the recovery of Violeta's soul—the two guinea pigs would be placed in each of four different crossroads north of Chiclayo from twelve noon to six o'clock in the evening. This action would hurry the return of Violeta's soul by acting as an offering to whatever spirit held it. Violeta was instructed to say aloud as she placed the guinea pigs in each crossroad, "Return my shadow. Here, I offer you this guinea pig instead."

The night of Violeta's personal *mesa,* the moon was full and scattered clouds skated across the sky. Violeta's first cleansing was done with the steel sword, the chonta wood sword, and the staff of San Cipriano. Olinda, Elena (a neighbor who often attended and helped out at Isabel's *mesas*), and I performed the cleansing. As we worked, Isabel instructed us to say, "We go untangling so that we may see her shadow . . . lighting the paths." We were then given white bandannas and rattles and told to run around the corral calling back the soul while repeating the following: "Un-charming your shadow, your spirit, your footprints from wherever it has been enchanted. I am Violeta R., I come calling and pulling my shadow from any *daño,* any evil, any earth, any cemetery, any whirlwind which holds it. I go depositing it here in this holy *mesa* where I find my cure, where I raise myself up, where I stand tall, where my health is." Over and over again, we ran to the four corners of the corral and began waving the bandanna and rattling the rattle.

As we ran, I looked up into the sky and the clouds had shaped themselves into the form of a doll which had been formed in Violeta's likeness. It had a pug face and shortish hair and was very thin, just like Violeta, and was perfectly visible in the clouds above. After it vanished, I saw an impression of a foot in the clouds. I asked Isabel what it meant, and she told me it was evidence that Violeta's footprint had been gathered up and used to perform the sorcery. Then I saw a whirlwind shape, and Isabel said this was a sure sign Violeta was suffering from *daño por aire.* Isabel called us back to the *mesa.* We continued pulling Violeta's shadow into the bandannas, periodically shaking it out over the *mesa artes* so that the shadow would come back alone, leaving all evil behind. At another point, Elena seemed suddenly gripped with fear. When Isabel demanded she recount her vision, she said that she had seen a ghost and thought it meant that Violeta was dying. Not so, counseled Isabel. Rather, she explained, this vision had been inspired because Violeta's shadow had been placed beneath a dead soul.

After this extended period of calling to Violeta's soul, we stood while Isabel prescribed more remedies for Violeta. In addition to a poultice which should be applied to her legs and feet, she would need another enema and would need to return to still another *mesa* in three weeks, where Isabel would give Violeta her final cleansings. In anticipation of this final *mesa,* Isabel prescribed a kind of tea as one last treatment: for the next two and one half months, Violeta was to drink the prescribed tea every Tuesday and Friday.

By the time of the last *mesa,* Violeta had begun to feel much better, but true to Isabel's warning, her kidneys had begun to hurt. Now that other symptoms had subsided, the kidney stones had become more of an issue. After she had completed the prescribed treatment, I visited with Violeta again. She told me her kidneys still hurt, but that Isabel had said this wasn't connected to the *daño.* She wasn't worried either, so convinced was she that Isabel's cure had had its desired effect. When I asked her why, she told me that she had dreamt of Isabel, Olinda, and the *mesa* several times on the nights when she had drunk the prescribed tea. In one dream, Isabel had told her to buy something that looked like starch. When she woke up, she had vomited a similar substance and she realized it was the *daño* that had been given to her. Another time she dreamt that Olinda was giving her a glass of milk to be drunk "with all faith that you will be healed. Your faith will heal you." At that moment, the dream changed, and Violeta said she saw the image of San Martín at her side. She remembered that Isabel had said to her, "Black dissolves black," at the last *mesa.* She hadn't understood what that meant at the time, but she now realized that this referred to the black saint, who appeared before her now in her dream. On the final night of the treatment she had dreamt that Isabel and Olinda stood at her feet with two fingers raised, healing her, lighting her way, caring for her.

One year after I left Peru, I received news about Violeta from Isabel when we spoke on the phone. Violeta had returned to her normal weight and had conceived another child, which she delivered normally nine months later.

Flor

Flor recounted to me many stories about the people she had cured before I met her, but I only witnessed one curing ceremony in the four months that I worked with her. Although many of the stories she told involved her use of a *mesa* and ingestion of San Pedro, the curing ceremony I witnessed did not. In part, this was because Flor no longer possesses her own *mesa*. She is afraid that the police will imprison her, as they have in the past, if they were to find a *mesa* in her house.

One afternoon in April, while we were talking together at her house, two women came to request her services. Both were dressed in housedresses and flat shoes, and both looked very concerned. The first, a neighbor who had known Flor for a long time, introduced the second woman, whose name was Maruja. Maruja's only grandchild, just twenty-two days old, had not slept in two days. The little boy didn't have a fever, or diarrhea, or the vomiting that would indicate he suffered from the syndrome which most affects young children—the evil eye. Even so, the women were worried that he might be suffering from soul-loss or another magical illness since he didn't respond to any of the standard remedies for colic or other natural illnesses. They asked Flor to perform a tarot-card reading to determine what was wrong with the child. I asked if I might watch and learn, and they agreed.

Flor first asked some basic questions: how old was the baby, what was his name, and what exactly did they want to know. Their main concern, they informed her, was to discover whether the baby's illness was a magical illness that would require a *curandera's* treatment or whether they should take him to a medical doctor. She pondered their questions and chose cards from the deck to represent the baby, the mother, the house, herself as a *curandera,* the medical doctor, and the baby's "path." She asked Maruja to blow on the cards three times. Then she laid them down in a circle, arranging and rearranging them until she was convinced the order was correct. Next, she put down six cards in the shape of a cross, prayed over these, then picked up all the cards and began to expertly shuffle them. She directed Maruja to divide the shuffled pile into four parts and to lay these down from left to right. Then, she took these piles and laid them face-down in the form of a cross. She prayed over each pile of cards. She directed her prayers to God, the Virgin, the Heavenly Father, and the young patient, respectively. She then drew the top card from each of the four piles. One of the four cards was the card she had earlier chosen to represent the "house," and another was the card she had earlier chosen to represent the "mother." "Look how God answers my prayers," she told the women. Next, she gathered all the cards and spread them, still face-down, in a single line. She asked Maruja to pick up three cards and with these she began the reading.

The baby was suffering from an evil-air, which had been sent by a shadow-soul and had entered the baby through its feet a few days before when he had been left alone in the house. Maruja protested that she had left a rosary and an image of the Sacred Heart of Jesus to guard over her grandson while she was out of the house. Flor countered that "when the illness is not of God, to have such images for protection means nothing." The illness was not "for the doctor," she said. Rather, it had been caused by a sorcerer. After this determination, she repeated the reading to learn if she was the person best suited to cure the baby. The cards did not immediately give her an answer, but after three more readings, and her fervent prayer, "in the name of Lord Jesus . . . for the last time, will this baby get better or worse, Mother of God with your wisdom and intelligence, help me Heavenly Father," she seemed satisfied that she could cure the child. Since the death card had appeared, she cautioned that it would be very difficult to cure the baby but that it could be done because the *curandera* card could be made to cover the death card. She also said that she saw a house full of tears and that there were many obstacles ahead. But, she asserted, she could do the cure with herbs and special baths. She would begin that afternoon if they liked. Her charges would total 21,000 intis (about $14). Of that total, 10,000 intis would be used to buy the needed materials, 10,000 intis would be for the cure itself, and 1,000 intis would pay for the cost of the reading.

We all left Flor's house about five o'clock that afternoon to go to the child's house. It was a one-story, brick house with a staircase leading to what would one day become the second floor. The living room was sparsely furnished with a dining table and chairs, an electronic sewing machine, and a black-and-white television. Behind the living room stood the kitchen, plumbed with running water but still unfinished—it was open to the corral beyond. At the far side of the walled-in, but open-air corral was a bathroom, also plumbed. Three additional rooms provided sleeping quarters for the child's grandmother, her three daughters, including the child's mother, and, of course, the baby. The child's father had recently left for the mountains to try and add to the family income, and Maruja had left her own husband fourteen years earlier so, except for the baby, this was a household entirely composed of women.

Into every corner of the living space had been stuffed large boxes of detergent, toilet paper, and other bulk items whose contents were hidden from view by their wholesale packaging. A knock at the door soon after our arrival heralded the appearance of a young man riding a three-wheeled cart with more boxes for delivery. The grandmother explained that she and her daughters were working informally as wholesalers to make ends meet. Since these were highly inflationary times, the women could always expect to turn a profit on drygoods and other items that had an indefinite shelf life. Of course, hoarding basic necessities until the next official announcement of higher prices was technically illegal because it created artificial scarcity in the marketplace. But the risk was worth the danger since monthly inflation rates had averaged more than 30 percent since the previous September. In addition to this income, Maruja ran a condiment stand in the public market at Pimentel, about ten miles west of the city. The child's thirty-one-year-old mother also had a stand at the market in Chongoyape, an hour's journey by bus toward the mountains from Chiclayo. Although her baby had been born by cesarean section less than a month before, she was already making the daily trek to market when we met. Her twenty-four-year-old sister suffered severe hearing and speech impediments, so she worked at home as a seamstress. Her youngest sister, though still in high school, spent most evenings preparing and packaging her sister's and mother's condiments for sale at the markets where they worked.

Maruja told me, "There is so much envy and so much anger here, especially from merchants who are just starting out and feel they're competing with the more well-established merchants for clients." The baby's mother asked us about the card reading and about Flor's interpretation of the illness. When she learned that Flor blamed an evil-air, a spirit-power sent to harm the baby by a sorcerer, for her son's illness, she told me about her own experience with such things. As a young girl, she said, she had been pursued by a shadow-soul. She supposed it belonged to a male sor-

cerer who had come to her in her dreams to try and rape her. The first time
he came to her, she said, she had felt him slap her hard, but she had been
able to resist his advances. Still, she did not believe she had rid herself of
him even though he had not bothered her for several years. Then, just
seven days before, he had come to her again. She had once again resisted
his carnal advances, and he had left her alone. But now she wondered if
he had attacked her baby instead.

Flor excused herself and went to the market to buy some things she
would need for the ceremony. When she returned, she made a doll out of
red cloth, carbon, salt, and some leaves of rue. She named the doll White
Lily and proclaimed it to be the baby's fiancée. She fashioned carbon eyes,
a mouth, shoes, and even female genitalia so that the doll would look "just
like a woman." Flor said the doll would "replace the baby's spirit so that
the evil spirit would give up the baby's soul and take the fiancée instead
when the evil-air came to be with the baby again at midnight. Next, Flor
called for the child and gave it a small teaspoonful of liquid to drink so
that the child would sleep soundly that evening. She held the doll close to
the baby's mouth and had the baby breathe on it so that it could stand in
for the baby and fool the evil spirit. Then, Flor cleansed the baby with the
doll, rubbing the doll over the child's body and saying the following prayer
as she did so:

> *Wherever you be found, you will be let go, you will be turned over, so
> that . . . these evil airs release you. Your fiancée will be turned over so that
> you . . . will return to your parents.*
>
> *Leave him all you airs, leave him all you evils, leave him all you airs,
> all you evils. . . . Go in his stead. . . . the fiancée called white lily with the
> green dress, with the green crown, with the white habit, with the black
> eyes.*
>
> *You will enter, with God's benediction, so that this child will return
> here, before God, in the name of God . . . Heart of God. Entering for the
> baby, releasing the evils, the bad luck, the bad blows of the evil airs, of
> colic . . . evil shadows, by night and by day.*
>
> *That the sustos be taken away, that the crying be taken away, that the*

fevers be taken away, that all of the pain that he might have be taken away. In the name of God, before God.

114   Afterward, Flor tucked the doll into the baby's waist and sent him off to bed. She cautioned that he must be put down in the bedroom that bordered the corral, with his feet facing the outside wall. She then put a cross of rue under the baby's bed in order to protect it during the night ahead.

Next, she placed a mixing bowl on the floor in the hallway, near the entrance to the corral and in front of an image of El Señor de los Milagros. Into the bowl she put some leaves of rue, some medicinal vinegar, some *agua florida,* and *agua de kananga.* She also added some garlic, a rose-colored carnation, and two other liquids which she called *agua desatadora* (untying water) and *agua de la contra* (the counterhexing water). This mixture was to steep in front of the sacred image using a lighted candle between the hours of midnight and four o'clock in the morning. Then the baby was to be awakened and bathed in this mixture, which was designed to pull out or suck out the illness. Afterward, the child should be wrapped snugly and kept out of the sunlight until the afternoon of the following day.

After she had put the herbs to steep, Flor and I went outside to the corral to build a fire pit. The flames of the fire that would be built in the pit would engulf and destroy the evil spirit when Flor called to it to trade the baby's fiancée for the spirit it had already captured. A channel to one side of the fire pit would allow the baby's spirit to escape the purifying and destroying flame. Flor took a piece of saltpeter and sprayed it with scented water, from the bottom to the top, to raise the baby's luck, and from the top to the bottom, to "send to hell all evil temptation." As she worked, she invoked God to help her. As she looked into the sky, she reminded me that she cures only with the light of God and never in darkness. Then, she went into the house to cleanse the baby with the saltpeter. When she was finished, she buried the saltpeter under the coals in the fire she had built in the pit.

As we sat around the fire, she told me how evil airs, such as the one that had attacked the baby and stolen its soul, can also suck the blood from children. This can cause the body to twist and contort, and when that happens, it is a sure indication that an evil air is to blame. Out of earshot of the baby's mother and grandmother, she admitted that the baby had already begun to show signs of this twisting. If the cure were not completed soon, she told me, the baby would continue contorting until its little neck broke from the strain.

After keeping vigil by the fire until midnight, Flor and I went in to sleep, and she waited for the evil spirit to appear to her in her dreams so that she could combat it. The next morning, she told me about her dream. The spirit had come in by one door, and then by another, trying to get at the baby. It came disguised as a man—beautiful, passionate as a lover, and dark-skinned, with tremendous teeth which he bared as he came. The spirit had asked Flor's name and she had replied, "My first name is running water and my last name is the wind." She had asked the spirit's name and he had told her that he was called *hombre tragadero* (swallowing man) and that he had come to swallow up the baby. I asked Flor why he had come for the baby and Flor told me, "Spirits don't attack just anybody. It is because of an immoral act committed by the baby's mother." In her dream, Flor fought with the spirit and she prevailed: he was not able to get the baby. She had been able to defeat its evil intent because of all the preparations she had taken and because God protected and guided her actions. In the morning, when we went to look at the saltpeter that she had buried under the hot coals of the fire, it had taken on the shape of a man with a large hole between his legs.

After the baby had been bathed in the steeped herbal mixture, and Flor had gathered up the saltpeter, we took our leave. Later in the week, Flor and I went to the seashore to deliver the piece of saltpeter, which now contained the evil spirit, to the sea. Only then would the illness be completely destroyed. As she threw the saltpeter into the sea, she said:

For the child [name] who is twenty-two days old. He has a shadow who grabs him. He has a shadow who torments him, who torments him as well as his mother. I want to give you it, dear sea, so that you will destroy that shadow who comes to offend the little baby. I also work with you, sea, always with this beautiful mermaid who always answers me. Dear sea, I

give you this bundle, so that you will eliminate this evil shadow.
Good-bye, you [the shadow] pass within forever . . . and you will never
return. Good-bye.

As we walked back to her home, Flor told me that the evil spirit had actually been sent to afflict the baby's mother, but it had attacked the baby instead, because the mother had an amulet which protected her from such attacks. The night after the cure, Flor said, she had seen this clearly when she again called to the baby's spirit in her dreams. She had wanted to see if the child was completely liberated from the evil air. The spirit had indeed accepted the fiancée in place of the child. They had married, and the child was now free. But in that dream, she had seen that things were not well with the mother.

According to Flor, the evil spirit which had afflicted the child had again appeared before the child's mother, trying to rape her. This time he had been successful, laying with her not as God intended, but cohabiting with her "from the left," which was a sure sign of Evil. In Flor's dream, a woman had presented herself with a yellow cloth and a cord, saying, "It is not right that you intervene in this, but if you have decided to get involved, look at the stain." The stain referred to a sin that had been committed by the mother. This sin would have to be destroyed and the mother purified, Flor explained, in order for the mother to be liberated from the spirit which had attacked her baby but which now afflicted her.

Vicky

One afternoon as I arrived to continue my interviews with Vicky, I found her just beginning a cure. The patient, Javier S., was a forty-three-year-old man who had come to her after consulting several doctors in the Chiclayo area for what they diagnosed as a punctured lung. Even after checking into a hospital, his condition hadn't improved, so he began to think it might be a problem more suited to a *curandero* than to a doctor. Vicky had cured his wife, so his family knew of her, and they had all come to see her two days earlier. Vicky had done a guinea-pig cleansing and had determined that Javier had a "swollen heart" as well as a "swollen bladder." The cause of his problems was an evil air—an "air of the dead" that he had sustained some days before when he had gone to a relative's house to drink the home-brewed *chicha* for which the entire region is famous. This relative lives near a *huaca* and in passing too close to the *huaca*, Javier had been infected by the evil air.

Today was Javier's second visit and his second *mesa*. Between the two sessions, Vicky had given him an herbal remedy to allay the symptoms, but his cure was not yet complete. Vicky invited me to a small room off the kitchen, where she had set up her spiritist *mesa*. It contained rocks, shells, skulls, a crucifix, staffs, religious images, a *seguro,* and perfumed waters—the most powerful subset of objects from her larger "sorcery *mesa,*" with which she cures patients during all-night ceremonies. She had named this small spiritist *mesa,* Reina del Páramo Blanco.

The cure that I witnessed lasted just under two hours and was marked by stages. As Vicky told me, "First, I commend myself to God so that He will open the doors for me, and I give myself and my patients a blessing so that God will illuminate me and will clear my mind and my intelligence." Then, she calls the spirit power into her *mesa* objects and commends these to help her patients, after which she does her divination. Today, she told Javier that he was suffering from headaches, brain-aches, "agitation" in his eyes, palpitations of his heart, cold feet, weakness in the knees, numbness on the right side of his face and in his right hand, fevers that come to him "from the inside," and a ringing in the ears. As she enumerated each of these symptoms, Javier responded affirmatively, sometimes mumbling, sometimes giving Vicky a quizzical look, and sometimes strongly agreeing. She also told him that as he lay sleeping in the middle of the night, he might wake suddenly, as though someone were attempting to rouse him, and that he was suffering from a deep sadness, and that he sometimes felt faint, as though he were about to lose consciousness.

The curing ritual that afternoon involved "raising" Javier to pull out the illness. Vicky's husband and assistant, Emilio, did this repeatedly, with the fragrant liquids that Vicky indicated, using one of the shells from the *mesa*. During this second *mesa*, only fragrant colognes were necessary since most of the Evil had already been "dominated." As Emilio raised the liquid, Vicky prayed, chanted, and sang her power-songs. One of these, roughly translated, went like this:

> *Walking with my staff, I "play" you and invoke [your shadow], and thus I go working you,*
> *And thus he [Emilio] goes raising you, taking away all your pain,*
> · *From the air as from the* huaca, *from great whirlwinds as from spells,*
> *And thus I go uninvoking you, and thus I go taking it [the evil air from you] with my great herbs . . .*

> *And thus I unwind you from this whirlwind from this great* encanto,
> *There from that* huaca *I come taking out your shadow, which is enchanted,*
> *Your shadow which is "played" and your shadow which is named [and thus captured in the enchanted* huaca].
> *I invoke you, I name you, I call you[r shadow].*

Next, Vicky asked Javier if he felt when he walked that he was "going to fall, like a drunk man?" She also asked him about a specific person, who had come toward him and then turned away before he had had a chance to greet her. Vicky told him that he feels as though people are calling him, but when he goes to the place where he hears their voices there is no one there, and also that he had put off coming to see her, even though he had every intention of going to her for help. After this, she asked her husband Emilio to get her cigarettes and she began smoking. Between each drag she invoked her prayers and the *artes* of her *mesa* to bring the patient's shadow to her *mesa*, to liberate it of all sorcery, and to take out all the evils from his body. After finishing the cigarette, she continued chanting, accompanied by her rattle:

> *. . . With my good fragrances, with my good perfumes, with my water from the lagoons,*

With my herbs of the huaringas, from inside the huaringas, from my
good ravines,
And thus I go accounting you, and walking with my huaringas . . .

From inside Huancabamba, thus I go putting you in, and there I go
accounting³ your name, your shadow, inside the lagoon,
So you will come recovering, so you will come refreshing, with my white
lagoon, with my great lagoon, powerful lagoon,
And with the black lagoon, thus I go naming you, from my great ravines I
go playing you, where I go accounting you . . .
Hurrying my good lords, my good medicines, my good herbs so that they
come circulating within your body, within your organism,
In good hours, I go accounting you and playing you . . .

As she sang, Vicky directed Emilio to cleanse Javier with the *artes* and spirits from her *mesa*.⁴ Next, she told Javier to repeat after her as he held a shell from her *mesa* to his nostrils, ready to "raise" himself with the perfumes which she gave him. As he prepared to nasally imbibe the liquid, he repeated the words, invoking the power of the prayers, the power of the chonta wood of the Aguaruna, and the power of San Antonio, and of the Virgin of Túcume to help him.

Vicky continued singing, invoking the *artes* and her *mesa*, her *seguros*, the spirits of her mother, of Ricardo Palma, and of all her Blessed Souls. As she sang, she placed the patient's name, his shadow, and his spirit within her *seguro* and within her *encantos*. By the magical connection with these forces, he would be raised up and cured; he would be well appreciated, well esteemed, well "flowered," and well thought of in his work and in his home. Each of the magical herbs of her *seguro*, according to their names—gold, silver, carpenter, and fortune—were named so that they would bring him riches, work, and good fortune. As she finished her "flowering," she told Emilio to blow the perfumed waters on Javier and also on her, to empower the invocation.

Finally, she sang another power-song to close her *mesa*, gathering up the powers which had been laid out during the course of the ritual and putting them away, refreshing and calming them, singing them to inactivity and rest, as she had sung them to life. She reminded Javier of the diet that he must follow and told him to stand before her for the final, formulaic benediction: "Up with your name, and down with your evils, up with your shadow, and down with your pains, with my good fragrances I perfume you." With this, the *mesa* was officially over.

120

Clorinda

On a clear, cold evening in Huancabamba in late July 1989, Clorinda planned a *mesa* ceremony for me, my friend Bernardo, a professional photographer who had accompanied me on my trip to the lagoons, and a local man. Clorinda and I had spent the afternoon talking about her life story and her introduction to healing on the verandah of the country home she shared with her mother and younger siblings. While we talked, the San Pedro cactus she had taken from her garden, blessed, cut, and put on the stove, boiled gently in the adjoining kitchen. Now the sun was low in the sky and the evening chill was noticeable, but her patient had not yet arrived for the cure. Since her home was a seven-mile walk from the center of Huancabamba and darkness was quickly settling over the trail, she began to wonder if her patient would arrive at all. If he didn't arrive by eight o'clock, she would do the *mesa* anyway, she told us. The San Pedro had already been prepared and it shouldn't be wasted. Besides, she reasoned, even though we did not really come to her as patients, perhaps we would learn some things by simply participating in the ritual.

Around eight o'clock, she invited us to accompany her outside, to a courtyard sheltered on two sides from the chill of the high mountain air. Against an outside wall of the house, she had set up the handsome *mesa* she had inherited from her father. While about the same size as some of the larger *mesas* I had seen previously, Clorinda's *mesa* contained fewer overtly Christian images than either Vicky's, Isabel's, or Yolanda's *mesas*.

After Bernardo finished taking pictures of the *mesa*, Clorinda began the ceremony. She led us in the Lord's Prayer and the Hail Mary—prayers from the Catholic Mass. Then, she prayed in the names of all present that we might "see, and know, and be lifted up and be cured, and grow, and bloom," both this evening and when we returned to our homes. She prayed that her *mesa* would "open a good road, a good future . . . a good dialogue, a good conversation, in this place, and back in their homes." She prayed that we might carry with us the "good winds and good *encantos*," and that if anyone wanted to harm us, work evil against us, or send an evil wind our way, that they would be stopped, dominated, and defeated by her good *mesa* and by her good San Antonios. She prayed that any enemies we might have be dominated and dumbfounded, and that any *brujos* working evil against us be struck down and stepped on. She prayed that we might be good, healthy, virtuous, and powerful. She invoked the great spirits, forces, and great healers to help her in her task, as well as God and the Holy Virgin. She prayed to the accompanying beat of her rattle and the music of her harmonica.

After this initial invocation, she raised her *mesa* and her *artes* with *tabaco* (tobacco leaves macerated in cane alcohol) as she asked God to help her defend against human enemies as well as evil spirit forces. She chose her words carefully, and rhyming was an important part of her speech (although it isn't obvious in the translation):

> *Thus we go remembering with my good* tabaco. *Any evil blindfold, any evil obstacle, any evil bonds, any evil attack, any evil air, any evil wind, any evil storm, any evil desire. We go dominating and we go raising . . . to be able to dominate, to be able to give over those evil winds, those evil hours, those evil pains to these airs, to these* encantos *of these mountains, of these* compactos *[contracts] . . . and we go dominating all evil air, all evil envy, all evil desire, all evil stepping, all evil failure, all evil temptation, all evil treason, all evil devotion.*

After the raising, Clorinda prayed to God the Trinity, to the Virgin, and to all of the dead Christian souls, including the soul of her father, for permission and support of her endeavors. As she prayed to the *encantos* of the sacred lagoons with whom she works, it began to rain, even though it simultaneously remained a bright, starlit night. It rained because she invoked the *encantos,* she told us, reminding us that she had been born with the power, granted by God, to be a healer. After this, she served us the San Pedro, admonishing us to take it in our right hands, giving us each two glasses. She began to cleanse herself with her staff as we waited for the herb to take effect. "Hopefully, it will arrive strongly," she said.

In a few minutes, Clorinda began her *rastreo.* She divined by repeatedly tossing two seashells onto the *mesa* and examining the position in which they fell. When she told me that many people envied me, we heard the sound of an owl screeching somewhere nearby. She told me, "There, that is the envy, when the bird that you are hearing screams, that is the shadow of an enemy. We call that bird *Cortapelo* [haircutter]. When it comes and screeches near the person with whom I am working, it's because they are envious of him, because they want to take his hair [to use to effect a *daño*]." Clorinda complained that we had not brought alcohol or *vinagre bully* [medicinal vinegar] with us, which she needed to spray so as to counteract the power of the visiting shadow.

As she divined, several fireflies approached the *mesa.* Clorinda said that these were other shadows arriving at the site of her ritual. Those which gave off a reddish glow were evil shadows, and those which glowed white were good shadows, she told us. The shadows of all those who bore malice or envied us presented themselves, including any *brujos* who had worked *daño* against us. The shadows of patients who would come seeking her services in the days ahead also came through the night as points of light to her *mesa.* As she continued to divine, she interpreted the sounds of woodpeckers, crickets, dogs, and even bulls braying in the cold, clear night. All sounds and sights seemed impregnated with meaning as the night progressed and her work continued.

After she completed her *rastreo,* she picked up a metal rattle and began chanting and singing as she sat in front of her *mesa.* By now, it was almost midnight. She told us that the evil hour was at its peak, the hour of the night in which "the evil spirit is working, in which the Devil is working, in which those who work with 'the other side' are working." To dominate and defend against this evil, it was time for us to "raise" the black tobacco through our nostrils. She began another song, invoking the *tabaco:*

*We go remembering, we go playing, in these hours, in these moments my
good herb, my good* tabaco.
Tabaco *bull, bull* tabaco, *rise up, grow, convalesce, cover up, strip away,
tie, break the tie, undo the* shuca *[magical attack], undo the* jaca.
*To be able to cut, to defend, to be able to raise up, to be able to grow, to be
able to dominate all wind, all air.
All* shuco, *all* jaco,[5] *all* daño, *all prejudice, by means of my places.
Clorinda C. G. is my name, my paternal and maternal last names since
the day I was born . . . to go playing, to go raising up . . .*

As we raised the *tabaco,* coughing, spluttering and retching, she chided
us, saying that we should accept that one must "suffer a little to get to
Heaven." She told us that the *tabaco* would help us dominate and defend,
especially if we had any "enemy who wanted to interfere with our lives,
because the Devil is great, because the Devil is there tempting, he wants
an entry, he wants to tempt." The *tabaco* would also act as a purgative,
should we be suffering from any *daño* that a *brujo* had effected against us.
It would be a tonic for our heads and a tonic for our bodies. And if any
brujos had prepared a *daño por boca* for us, the *tabaco* would help us expel
it: "From the tail I cast it out." As we raised the mixture of black tobacco
and cane alcohol, served first to the left nostril and then to the right, we
said:

I am raising myself with my good tabaco, *I am raising myself and I am
curing myself, I am dominating, down with my enemies, down with
robbers, and I am raising myself up, and I am curing myself, I am
laughing, I am convalescing.*

Clorinda led us in the Lord's Prayer as we raised the *tabaco* and continued invoking the *tabaco* to cure us and let us dominate any temptations,
any treasons, any bad living, any bad conversations, any misfortunes, any
evil wind, any *daño* that might be plaguing us.

Afterward, she called us over, one by one, to stand in front of her Mesa
Negra. She intoned a *tarjo* [power song] to call out the *brujos* which she
had seen working evil against us. In my case, Clorinda had discovered, in

the course of her *rastreo,* that I suffered from a previous contact with a *brujo espiritista* who lived on the coast. When I had been working with him, she told me, he had wanted to take advantage and abuse me sexually.

I remembered an incident that had occurred several years before, in which I had been invited to dinner in Trujillo by a male informant, who was, indeed, an *espiritisto.* My understanding was that his wife would accompany us and that the three of us would talk about my research interests. When he arrived in his car, he made some excuse about his wife not being able to join us and then drove me to a restaurant some miles away in a fishing village renowned for assaults and robberies, especially after dark. I was very frightened, and I felt extremely foolish for having trusted him. When he ordered a bottle of rum and tried to get me drunk, I became even more frightened. Thankfully, at the end of the evening, he drove me back to my house and let me out of the car, as though nothing were out of the ordinary. A few days later, however, when I telephoned his home to set up our next interview, he screamed and swore at me and said he never wanted me to set foot in his office again. Stunned, I later learned that he had not told his wife of our dinner and that she had learned of it and had assumed that he was having an affair with me. His outburst over the telephone was for her benefit. My working relationship with him was ruined.

As I stood in front of the Mesa Negra, Clorinda had me hold some cane alcohol in my mouth as she spoke an invocation. I was to then spray it in her face when she finished speaking. Then we changed places, and she did the same to me. Finally, she had me take an *arte* from the Mesa Negra and beat on one of the rocks that formed part of the Mesa Negra. As I beat the rock, I began to shake and cry, whether in frustration, anger, or relief, I cannot say. She told me, "These bad men have wanted to hurt you." Afterward, I was directed to spray in the direction of a bush which stood behind the *mesa* toward the river, and then to the Mesa Negra itself, saying, "I go entrusting all this evil." Then Clorinda asked that I shake out the evil, leave an offering of an amount of money of my choosing on the main *mesa,* and return to my seat.

After I sat down, she put the Mesa Negra back in its place, at the left side of her main *mesa,* and asked each of us to stand again as she cleansed

us with one of the *artes* of her *mesa*. As I took my turn, she recited the
following:

> *We go taking out, we go taking away an evil air, an evil wind,*
> *An evil odor, an evil flavor, an evil liquor, an evil friend's love,*
> *We go taking out, we go taking away . . . an evil humor, an evil*
> *obstruction.*

Clorinda told me to repeat after her that I was entrusting all evil that
had been done to me to the staffs, to the *encantos,* and to the weapons
of her *mesa,* and to assert that "with this *maestra,* I am raising myself up.
. . . I am throwing away all envy, all obstacles, all *daño,* all prejudice, all
misfortune, all blindfolds, all the obstacles (put up by) evil *brujos* who
have wanted to deceive me."

Afterward, she sat at her *mesa,* took up her rattle, and began singing
another *tarjo,* in which she explained how she was resolving my problem
with her San Pedro and her *encantos.* Her *tarjo* was long and complex, and
it was clear from the words that these were pronounced as a kind of powerful mediation on my behalf. She commanded the rooster to crow (a sign
of good fortune and luck) and the bull to bray (a sign of her power as a
healer). As the words were pronounced, the sound of the roosters in the
corral and, more surprisingly, the sound of a bull from somewhere across
the river, filled the early morning air.

Clorinda continued singing for her mind to be cleared and to receive
understanding and embodied power. She called on all of her *encantos* and
her *compactos,* on the magical herbs which filled her *seguro* and which
were imbued with the power of the lagoons and of the hills where they
grew wild. She called on her *mesa,* and her seats of power, on her prayers,
and on her profession to cure me. She continued, saying, "Just as the sun
shines in the sky, you must grow, you must flower, you must raise up, and
cure, and smile . . . wherever you go. . . . You must be loved and appreciated."

Clorinda sang other *tarjos,* to the morning which was arriving, and to
the "hen in her henhouse"—which was a sign of luck and good relations
within the household, of family and of children, which she hoped were in

my future. The evil hour had passed, she said, and with the arrival of the morning and the new day the ceremony would turn from defending against evil forces to *floreciendo,* to the cultivation of the forces of luck and good fortune.

About three o'clock in the morning, we were called again to stand in front of Clorinda's main *mesa,* and there we raised white tobacco (*Nicotiana tabacum*) which had been mixed with honey for our luck, good health, and good fortune. She told me to repeat after her: "For my studies, for my health, for my work, for my thesis, for my household, for my family, I am *floreciendo,* and I am raising up." Then she stood in front of each of us and repeated our names, as well as the names of our spouses, and blew sweet lime, sugar, scented waters, and perfumes onto our heads, hands, and chests. My photographer friend, since he was a man, was given a white rose to eat, and if there had been any white carnations, I would have been given one of these, she told me. She gave us sweet lime with sugar to spray onto our chests, as well as onto her *mesa* and in the direction of the mountain across the river and the lagoons beyond. She then took a mixture of water and white corn meal and drenched us in spray (making us all laugh), and then told us to drink as much as we wanted of the mixture. This was the *arranque,* the completion of the *mesa,* and with a final prayer the ceremony was officially over. We were told to follow the prescribed diet for the rest of the day and were invited to stay and chat until it was light enough to make our way back over the footpath that led from Clorinda's house up the river valley and back into the city.

*C*hiclayo, February 12, 1988, Journal.

   Last night's *mesa* may have been a turning point in my career and in
my life. Maybe for the first time ever, I realized what personal responsibility means. As a result of last night's lesson, I know my life's failures have
been the result of my inattention, my stubbornness, and—most of all—
my action or inaction. I have not been the victim of an imposed destiny,
even if I claim that this is so. Valuing my life according to external valida-
tions has kept me empty and vulnerable to the avarice of others, but it does
not relieve me of responsibility. I have succumbed to the temptation of
abdication long enough. It is time I took responsibility for my actions . . .
they really do have consequences. Last night, they almost killed Isabel.

Chiclayo, February 12, 1988, *Mesa* field notes

   The *mesa* started out normally enough. Seventeen people present, including Isabel and Olinda. Only one new patient, a woman from a rural
district in the mountains. She has been sick a year; she says the lower half
of her body is slowly dying. Her legs and feet are numb and swollen, and
she finds it difficult to walk and gather the firewood she needs for fuel.
Also, she's often dizzy and everything aches—especially her stomach,
bladder, ovaries, and head. She went to a doctor in Huamachuco, who gave
her pills and shots but found nothing wrong and said it was her age. The
injections made her kidneys burn, so she began taking "fresh" or "cool"
herbs for the pain. But these made her legs and feet colder and more numb.
Her husband agreed that they should see a *curandero,* so they came to
Chiclayo to find Isabel.

As the woman stood before the *mesa* for her diagnosis, Isabel told her not to turn around. "Don't turn back, for anything. Turning around is like looking back to yesterday, which will never return." Isabel called upon the woman's husband: "Stand back-to-back with your wife. You must help her because you are her helpmate. Stand together and be as one; you are her shadow double." She called upon four of us present—Olinda, Olinda's nephew Caesar, another long-time friend, and me—to help cleanse the patient, to help "clarify," so that Isabel could see how her shadow had been stolen and where it had been imprisoned. She told us to take four staffs from the *mesa* to cleanse the patient. One should be a staff made of quince wood. This wood has the power to pull out sorcery from the body and to drive off evil spirits and winds. One should be a staff made of *ajos jiro* ("garlic wood"), which works against sorcerers, destroying any *daños* they have caused and keeping them from sending the smell of garlic, which inactivates the San Pedro, to foil Isabel's psychic vision. The third staff should be the scissors, used to "cut the ties of *daño* that bind the victim." The fourth should be the Cripples' Cane—the Bastón de los Inválidos—which cures the kind of crippling paralysis that was afflicting this patient. Always before, Olinda had handed me the proper objects from the *mesa*. But tonight Isabel trusted me to know which staff to take. She trusted me because she had already taught me the names of all her staffs and the use to which each was put. I grabbed the *bastón* as she had instructed. But I forgot that two staffs carry that name. She had asked me to get the Cripples' Cane. Instead, I had grabbed the Bastón San Hilarión—St. Hillary's Cane—and had begun cleansing the patient with this staff.

It was some time before Isabel realized the error. I thought it strange that she seemed so disoriented. She became so dizzy she could hardly stand. She seemed quite drunk—her speech slurred, her instructions increasingly without meaning. She began to doze and seemed not to care about the *mesa* anymore. Then, she turned to Olinda and with labored words said, "I don't know, San Pedro is telling me to just put my neck on the chopping block. Which of you would turn over your spirit to another. Better it would be for you to destroy yourself than destroy the healer who can save you. It's the cane . . . " And then Olinda saw it. I had been cleansing the patient with Isabel's personal tool, her alter ego, St. Hillary's Cane.

The one from the garden where her great-grandfather's golden *mesa* still stands. The one that bears the *encanto* of that place and protects her with that power. It is never used for cleansing patients. I had forgotten what she told me. I had written it in my notes but not internalized the significance. By taking this cane instead of the other, I had put her in great danger, even giving her over to be destroyed by the same sorcerer who had hexed her patient.

There was penance to be paid. All four of us would walk on our knees ten times around the corral where her *mesa* stood. Then we would "raise" the cane which had been so misused four separate times with *tabaco*. As we began our rounds, Caesar hissed, "Because of you, we do this. Why did you grab the wrong staff—how could you be so stupid?" Isabel also chided me:

Why did you choose anthropology? Anthropologists stick their noses where they don't belong. Better it would have been to stick it elsewhere. Already thirty-one years old and only your thesis to show for it. You've lost so much time. You would already be somebody, otherwise. So you'll write a thesis, fine; you'll get it done. But that is not what's important. Ay, Bonnie, what a pity.

Afterward, she bade me stand before the *mesa*:

I'm talking about your personal problem now. You've been in Peru all these years and you still don't know us? Peruvians are proud: there is no love without self-interest; we are interested in ourselves. Ay, Bonnie, you should know Peruvians by now! You go to Trujillo because of "family" commitment. When they call you to help, you go. But who will help you when you are sick? Form your own household with your husband and your children. They are the ones who will help you. Why do you give so much to this supposed family when they give nothing in return? You thought you would give them the chance to return your love? They will never give it, not now, not ever. Their affection has always been motivated by self-interest. Learn already about my people. Ay, Bonnie, you have always played the victim. But you have been fooled: you are the fool in this.

During the rest of the night she made veiled references to my stupidity, about not doing my "homework" even when she shared the meaning of her *mesa* with me. I felt the sting of her words and realized how much time I had spent obsessed with my personal problems, obsessed with Carlos and his family, to the exclusion of the work I had come to do with her. When they treated me well, I felt lovable and loved. When they treated me poorly, I felt the victim of ill will. In both cases, I defined and valued myself based on external opinion. Because of that error, I had not been wholly present at the *mesa,* nor at any time during my work with Isabel. My spirit had been absent. And at last night's *mesa,* that lack of presence had cost her dearly.

A wandering spirit, a fantasy-filled mind, can also hurt the ones you love. As I contemplated the lesson, I felt terrible, but also wiser than last night. It was time to begin taking responsibility and to be wholly present. It was time to start living responsibly, in this world, and to leave Bonnie-the-victim behind.

Chiclayo, February 22, 1989, *Mesa* field notes

An amazing thing happened at the *mesa* last night. Isabel was using St. Hillary's Cane (the staff I defiled on the 11th) instead of the dagger she usually carries. At one point, she began singing a *tarjo*—a power-song. Although quite common among other *curanderos,* I have never before heard her sing like this. Isabel appeared possessed. Olinda told me it was the spirit of God speaking through her, something that used to happen frequently but that hasn't occurred in a long time. The voice called me to the *mesa.* It said: "I have heard there are foreigners here, that's why I've come. Why else would I come here. First time I've met foreigners. Ay, but you've always denied the existence of God. Why is that so?"

"I've repented," I replied.

"Of what have you repented?" the spirit demanded. "Of having a child? Oh, that boy child, the little man in the family. You are poor, perhaps poorer than I. . . . Why didn't you bury the child you lost?"

I explained that the doctor had requested the fetus and had not returned it to me.

The voice continued reproaching, "Why have you done all these things? You need to be cured here at this *mesa*. If you are not cured here, you will never be cured. You will never have a child but will always be sterile. . . . Think about the parents who bore you and the God who cre-ated you."

"Please cure me, help me be cured in this mesa," I pleaded.

Once again I found myself walking around the *mesa* on my knees, while the spirit that spoke through Isabel intoned: "In the name of God—Father, Son, and Holy Spirit—we will walk where you tell us, in grace and in dis-grace. When we have our children, we will have to live so it isn't in dis-grace. In the name of God. . . . Thank God on your knees, thank the lagoons, thank the Holy Spirit. . . . Oh, Black Lagoon, Black Lagoon, she will triumph beyond this place, beyond that place. There! There is the cemetery that carries her shadow away."

After the singing and the trips around the *mesa*, the spirit began speak-ing again.

"Your efforts up till now have only served to make you feel better, but you have changed nothing. All is dark behind the communion host. Up to now you have learned nothing, but from here forward you will learn much. You will learn 'this is what they mean by real.' "

This last phrase was spoken in English, without any trace of an accent. I pondered how this was possible and thought about the spirit's words.

I had not suspected a connection between my miscarriage and my illness until then. But as the spirit spoke through Isabel, it all made so much sense. I had, at some level, always associated having Dan's child with the end of my fantasy about Carlos, with the end of my fantasy about being a true member of his family and a "real" Peruvian. Since my first meeting with Isabel, she had insisted that my future was in the United States, not here. She said I needed to face reality and begin distancing myself from my supposed family in Peru. She said I needed to build a life, renew ties with my natal family, and put down roots far to the north, in my native land.

Recently, I had become conscious that the comfort of a fantasy is a false comfort: it cannot cure the loneliness or fill the emptiness within. All the energy put into constructing worlds from "if only" and "it might have been" cannot change the facts. Yesterday can never be relived. As Isabel had told me, "Of all that 'supposed' family, Carlos is the only one who ever loved you. He still loves you, in fact. But destiny, for whatever reason, has come between you. That is life. It can't be changed. Accept it and move on."

Coupled with this was the issue of my borrowed identity. I was like a ship lost on dizzying waters, tossed about by the validation, or rejection, of others. I was poor because I was empty within. And I would remain so, incapable of creating life or love until I truly accepted my own destiny. Isabel's analogy of the empty womb and the empty host—the body—seemed suddenly clear. Both need energy or spirit to survive. When a sorcerer calls the spirit away from the body, the victim eventually dries up and dies. "God is a spirit, a spirit you have deep within you . . . and rejecting that is the worst error," Isabel had once told me. The spirit that animates the body thus comes not from without, but from deep within. It is this spark of Divinity within each one of us that is the true gift of life—*el don de la vida,* as Isabel called it. But this gift cannot grow untended. If too much energy is devoted to keeping alive the fantasy, this gift of life, of accepting and rejoicing in what is, will wither. Instead of creating something new and wonderful, the host will be empty, sterile, and, eventually, abandoned.

As I thought about all these things, Isabel touched St. Hillary's Cane to my belly and the spirit speaking from within her said, "That you might become a mother."

May 5, 1989, *Mesa* field notes

At last night's *mesa,* although Isabel's attentions were fixed on her other patients, it seemed that everything she told them had special significance for me as well. In one case, a young girl who had suffered a *daño* was told that she must learn to have a stronger character, in order to not be so malleable (and vulnerable) to deception. A couple was also present at the *mesa.* Isabel admonished the wife to live up to her obligations as a good wife and mother and to leave her childish, self-indulgent behavior behind. Then she called me before the *mesa* and asked me again if I wanted to end my feelings for Carlos and to move on with my life. I told her that I did, and she asked me, "for the first time, the second time, or the last time," with a bite to her words that clearly communicated the difference between contrition and repentance. I had been contrite before, but now I must really repent and work to change my behavior in the future. This time, I had to be sure of what I wanted, and I had to be unfailing in my conviction. I told her that I wanted to forget but that the wound was deep. She admonished me that the wound was an old one which I must decide to let heal over. I had been picking at the scabs for years and had kept the sore inflamed. Now I had to concentrate on mending it.

As I reasserted my desire to change, she told the others to cleanse me with the deer foot. This fleet-footed animal has the power to drive all that is unwanted away forever. She told me that the strong feelings for Carlos would subside and that he would also become more indifferent to me. She told the others to repeat the words, "You will be a stranger to me, and I will treat you as a stranger." She told one of the men cleansing me to concentrate on cleansing my head, "because this woman has been without a brain in her head since the start." As he continued the cleansing, she told him to counsel me on what a good wife should be. "She should not be jealous, she should appreciate her husband and not take him for granted, she should be faithful," he told me.

With this action, Isabel seemed to have set in motion a new element of the cure. Acceptance of my own powerlessness, surrender to God, even confession wasn't enough. I also had to undergo the penance and the purification of one who must make amends for their past sins. As I listened to her counsel, I realized that in many ways I had not been a good wife at all. Dan had loved me from the beginning, but I had not responded in kind. I had withheld my affection and my love from him for years, wishing it instead upon a man who didn't want it.

Isabel directed her counsel to the young wife who had not been sure of her love for her husband either, and the words might as well have been directed right at me: "I will not be your accomplice," Isabel said to the young woman. "I will not protect you if you are not a good wife and mother. To destroy the evil in your household, you have to be very sure of something. It has to be your *yo personal* that wants to be cured. You must repent, but you must not confuse this with feeling persecuted and being the victim. You have no one to blame but yourself."

Isabel continued speaking to the young woman: "You have to take responsibility from here on out. God can help you. His work within you can move mountains, but you must also recognize your faults, be repentant and willing to change. You have to repent, and you have to make amends." The words seemed aimed at my forehead. As I listened, I wondered how I might find the strength to take full responsibility for my future. I felt frustrated because I had blundered before, more than once. My intent to change always seemed strong at first, but then the old feelings would come back. As these thoughts crossed my mind, Isabel spoke once again to the young wife who stood before the *mesa*. She told her:

> When you are strong, it will not be so easy for anyone to capture your shadow. Pray to God. Repent. Tell him, "I want to be closer to you. Forgive me. Maybe I have doubted before that you exist, but I know now that you do and that you are in me." When you are with God's Grace, they can't call your shadow away.

May 7, 1989, *Mesa* field notes

At last night's *mesa*, Isabel laid a question before a man who was suffering from a *daño* that had affected his kidneys and that had been done to him by an employee so that the man would eventually die. Like all of the questions which she posed, Isabel expected a response from all present. The questions were whispered to her by the San Pedro and contained clues about the nature of the *daño* and the means that she must use to cure it. They were never straightforward but were laden with symbolic meaning that never seemed immediately apparent. Last night she asked, "What is the *contra* of salt?" Before last night, her parables had always terrified me. The obvious answers were never right. Now, she had asked me again and she demanded an answer, so I began:

Sugar? I thought. No, it is not the *contra* because if you put sugar in salt, it still tastes like salt. Air? No, even though you are scientifically correct that salt water becomes sweet to the taste through the process of evaporation, this has nothing to do with solving the problem of the *daño* at hand. Then, the answer came. It was like feeling someone speak without hearing the words. I said, "Faith is the opposite of salt. Faith in God who has the power to make and unmake everything, to turn around bad luck and to make too much salt palatable. Faith is the key." Yes, Isabel now told me, that was an adequate response. While the others continued working on the answers to their questions, she sent me behind the *mesa* to watch over the *artes* and to be alert for any dangers.

As I stood behind the *mesa,* while Isabel continued her interrogation of Olinda and the other two, I began to feel the *mesa* come alive. It seemed that the greater my faith in God, the greater my faith in his power to inhabit the images of the *mesa,* the more in tune with the night I became. At one point, I knelt, asking the *mesa* to help me by telling me what it needed in order to work better. I felt more than saw an intimate relationship between the ceiling of stars above us, as "the eyes of God," and their reflection in the *mesa* itself. I could "see" much: all is connected, the *mesa* images to their points of origin and to the *encantos* which empower them, the *mesa* as a whole to the sky above and the earth below. Faith gives the power to understand, and it is this power which keeps the channel open so that the spirit essence—part of the creative potential of the universe— can flow into and empower the *mesa* objects. This essence flows through me as well.

My body seemed to open, and pinpricks of light seemed to flow in and out in an exchange of energy with every star in the sky, every earthly *encanto,* and every object on the *mesa.* The flow of energy is all. I am a fulcrum between these places, between the stars in the sky, the lagoons and the mountains of the earth, and the *mesa* images. As the *mesa* reflects and embodies this circulating power, it is Reality. To deny Reality is to turn one's face away from the *mesa,* to the world of emptiness, fantasy, and illusion which Isabel calls Evil. This is utter darkness and utter desolation, but the *mesa* is filled with Spirit—the Spirit of God, the Spirit of the Ancestors, the Spirit of the Cosmos, and it is Good.

Next, I saw crosses on the *mesa,* as the shadows transfigured the forms of the *mesa* objects before me. At one point, the *seguro* opened as a seashell before me. The pictures and the crucifix became much brighter and easier to identify than the seemingly dim night should permit. I began to see small pinpoints of light alighting on the *mesa,* and I recognized these as Spirits. Later, I saw the staff that Isabel calls the king which sits on the Mesa San Cipriano with a full-sized crown sitting on top of a king's head. I began to catch snatches of holographic images . . . ; they were like subliminal frames interspersed in a movie reel. There were animals and people, but they disappeared from my vision too quickly for me to be able to identify them. They seemed to disappear because of my fear, which still takes over as soon as I begin to let myself experience the effects of the San Pedro.

Chiclayo, May 10, 1989, Journal

I dreamt of Isabel last night. She was sitting at a table and telling me, "Now you will begin to see." I saw her turn into a very old white-haired woman. Then she said, "But you have to be stronger . . . not let your fear dominate you." This was still a problem for my emerging vision, it seemed. As I jerked back into wakefulness a few minutes later, I wondered if I would ever really be able to let go of my need for control and accept whatever the future held for me.

Chiclayo, June 30, 1989, *Mesa* field notes

Last night, Isabel and Olinda celebrated the tenth anniversary of their *compacto* with the *mesa* in a ceremony in which I hoped to be allowed to participate. As the time grew near to lay the *mesa,* however, Isabel told me that she was sorry but that I could not be a part of it. She invited me to stay the night, however, and to sleep at their house. During the middle of the night, Olinda burst through the door of the bedroom, waking me and telling me to walk, on my knees, from the door of the bedroom where I was sleeping, through the house and the corral, and to continue until I reached the *mesa.* While I walked on my knees, I was to assume an attitude of reverence and contemplation and to ponder the question, "Why did I have to experience this contrast in my religious beliefs?"

I began this journey with some trepidation. I knew that Isabel would demand an answer, and I knew that if the answer was not to her liking, things would not go well for me during the ensuing minutes or hours. I tried to focus on the question and forget the fear of giving a wrong answer. I thought and prayed and when I reached the *mesa,* I responded, "I had to experience this contrast in order to learn to live, to love, and to adore God." Her gaze was level and calm. "What else?" she asked. "And to adore the Saints," I responded. Calmly, she added the key that I had neglected: "You had to experience this contrast in order to respect yourself, so that you can triumph."

Learning to love and to respect myself had meant accepting that each of us is given a gift or a talent by God. Our impact on the world is one of creation rather than destruction only when we utilize and celebrate that gift. Isabel's is the gift of curing. I am still in search of mine. But each of us in our own way will change the world according to our experience. And, as I was reminded last night, a part of experience is an engagement with others. This engagement brings with it an awesome moral responsibility.

One day last November I had asked Isabel whether it would be okay to photograph the *mesa* during the daytime? She responded that she didn't know, because she had never before tried it, but that we should go ahead and do it. As she set up the *mesa* against the wall of her corral that day, a small, brown-tinted bottle broke. She said nothing at the time. Later, while documenting the *mesa,* I learned that this had been one of her central *artes,* and that God Himself had told her that any patient who received Holy Water from this flask would be healed. When I asked what its breaking had meant, she told me she did not know. But last night at the *mesa,* I learned, San Pedro had revealed to her that the breaking of that flask had shortened her lifespan by one-third. Chagrined, I had asked her if there was anything that could be done to restore that which had been lost. She replied, "You must not pay me back poorly but must make something of your life: serve others, give something, be somebody."

Then she had Olinda cleanse me once again with the staffs from her *mesa,* and with a heavy rock which she called Cerro Guitiligún, so that I might become a woman of substance, like the weighty rock. Then Isabel continued: "Wherever you go and wherever you are, only you and your husband are for each other. Think on God. The *jugada* that was done to you by Carlos's family is over." She told me to walk on my knees around the corral as Olinda followed me, spraying Holy Water at my back. As I

walked, she directed me to say:

> *Carlos's family will not beat me. They put obstacles in my way so that I would marry someone else, and I did. But now I am well married to my mate. Now they have erred in their attempts to harm me because Dan is a good husband and I am a good wife. Everything else has passed into history.*

Next, Isabel asked me to think about what I wanted to do when I finished my thesis:

> *I want your life to be a success. You have to make something of your life. You have to be something, a writer or something. . . . You have to live, not just observe the lives of others. Make an offering to this* mesa, *so that you will be something. . . . God gives us each a road. . . . [If you do write] will you write dreams or write reality? You must write what you have thought or what you have lived. . . . Until now, you have not known how to live. You have known illusion and disillusion, but you haven't known how to live, you haven't stepped firmly, you haven't left footprints. Now you must find your path and leave your mark.*

Sorcery "Packages" and Sympathetic Magic in Peru
The picture shows a "package" in which a sorcery victim's clothing and photograph were intentionally wrapped together with human bones in Chiclayo's main cemetery. This action is part of the magic that "binds" the victim's soul to that of the *ánima* or soul of the deceased.

(Photograph by Bonnie Glass-Coffin.)

Ceramic Vessel, Lambayeque Tradition (Northern Peru)
This one thousand-year-old ceramic vessel depicts a veiled (female) shaman with a piece of San Pedro cactus in her hands. Her expression may be one of shamanic "ecstasy" or of the *mocha* (similar to the act of blowing a kiss), which was a pre-Columbian gesture of reverence and offering and is still used by northern *curanderos* today.

(Collection of the Rafael Larco Herrera museum, Lima. Photograph by Bonnie Glass-Coffin.)

The *Mesa* of a Contemporary *Curandera*

Like most *mesas* of northern *curanderos,* this one, which belongs to Isabel, has
pre-Columbian and Christian artifacts as well as rocks,
shells, knives, swords, and staffs. The brewed San
Pedro is in the pot at the far right. At the left is a
portion of Isabel's second *mesa,* which she
uses for defense and for "cleansing" only.

(Photograph by Bonnie Glass-Coffin.)

Ceramic Vessel, Moche Tradition (Peru)

The veiled (female) shaman in this ceramic vessel of the Moche tradition (ca. 100 B.C.–A.D. 700) is using what appear to be rocks to cleanse a prostrate patient lying in front of her. Rocks are key *mesa* artifacts used to cleanse the patients of contemporary northern shamans.

(Collection of the Museo Nacional de Arqueologia y Antropologia, Lima, catalogue #C-54571. Photograph by Bonnie Glass-Coffin.)

Ceramic Vessel, Chimu Tradition

The veiled woman in this ceramic vessel of the Chimu tradition (ca. A.D. 700–1475) is *mochando* (blowing an offering to the Gods). Standing at her side (just out of the picture) is a young child suggesting that, in addition to her ministerial role, the woman depicted in this ceramic was also a mother.

(Collection of the Museo Nacional de Arqueologia y Antropologia, Lima, catalogue #C-54581. Photograph by Bonnie Glass-Coffin.)

Peruvian Shamans with Their Curing Altar
Yolanda and her common-law husband José hold crosses
and stand before their curing altar, which they do not
call by the usual name *mesa* because of their association
of pre-Columbian healing arts with the work of the
Devil. They do use San Pedro as part of their healing
ceremony, and they call on the spirit of God (the Holy
Spirit) to help them "see" the origins of sorcery from
which their patients suffer.

(Photograph by Bonnie Glass-Coffin.)

Cruz de Motupe

Isabel, Olinda, and Isabel's two children pose for a picture at the
shrine of the Cross of Mount Chalpón, sometimes called the *Cruz
de Motupe* after the nearby town of the same name. The cross is
revered throughout northern Peru for its miraculous power to
heal and it attracts up to half a million petitioners each August.
Isabel and Olinda are devotees of the cross; a representation of
the *Cruz de Motupe* figures prominently on Isabel's *mesa*.

(*Photograph by Bonnie Glass-Coffin.*)

Flormira and Her Offerings

Although Flormira had a *mesa* hidden on her property,
she rarely brought it out or used it to heal patients
during the time I knew her. But, like the other women
in this study, she used *agua florida, agua de kanaga,*
holy water, and something called *Agua de las siete
espíritus* to cleanse and "flower" patients as well
as to make offerings to *encantos* and *ánimas.*

(Photograph by Bonnie Glass-Coffin.)

Clorinda with San Pedro Cactus

Clorinda poses next to a San Pedro cactus growing in her garden.
In addition to providing the *vista* needed to see into other worlds,
according to Clorinda, the San Pedro cactus was blessed by Jesus
Christ and Jesus later adopted the cactus as his personal staff.

(Photograph by Bonnie Glass-Coffin.)

Isabel and Her *Mesa*

Isabel poses next to the indoor altar where all her *mesa* artifacts "rest" between sessions. She has bought some artifacts, some have been given her by grateful patients, and she has found others. Not all artifacts are used during her all-night ceremonies—she considers some more powerful than others—but all have special significance and meaning.

(Photograph by Bonnie Glass-Coffin.)

Setting up the *Mesa*

Isabel sets up her *mesa* as patients look on just before
beginning her all-night ritual. Patients (and the family
members/friends they have brought with them to the
ceremony) will actively participate in all aspects of the
mesa once it begins and will not be allowed to sit or
rest until sometime near dawn.

(Photograph by Bonnie Glass-Coffin.)

Patient Cleansed with Staffs

Cleansings (*limpias*) with staffs and power objects from the *mesa* help "draw out" the sorcery and also help the healer "see" the cause of affliction. At Isabel's *mesa*, this cleansing is done not only by the healer's assistants, but also by other patients and family members.

(Photograph by Bonnie Glass-Coffin.)

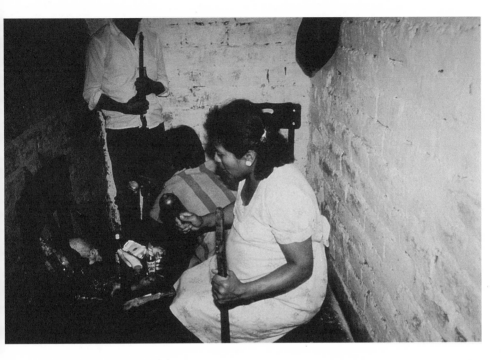

Vicky Blowing an Offering

Pregnant women are not excluded from participating in healing ceremonies. In this picture, Vicky is in the act of blowing an offering to the power objects on her *mesa*. In the background, her husband is "raising" the patient's luck.

(Photograph by Bonnie Glass-Coffin.)

Clorinda Seated at *Mesa*

Moments before the beginning of her all-night
ceremony, Clorinda poses with the handsome *mesa*
she inherited from her father.

(Photograph by Bernardo Rojas.)

Pilgrimage to Las Huaringas Lagoons (Peru)
Pilgrims walk and ride mules for the last four-hour
leg of the pilgrimage from Chiclayo to the sacred
Las Huaringas lagoons near Huancabamba.

(Photograph by Bernardo Rojas.)

Peruvian Shaman and Patients

Isabel and her patients stand on the shore of the sacred
Laguna Negra (Black Lagoon) as Isabel sets up her
mesa for a ceremony.

(*Photograph by Bernardo Rojas.*)

Relaxing After a *Mesa*
The author and author's husband pose with Isabel, Olinda,
and other patients after one of her all-night
sessions in 1989.

(Photograph by Bonnie Glass-Coffin.)

5 ▪ The Spiritual Tools of Healing

As previous chapters indicate, a tradition of shamanic healing—practiced by women as well as men—flourishes in contemporary northern Peru. Both men and women use *mesas* and conduct all-night ceremonies to heal their patients of sorcery. Both men and women utilize the psychoactive San Pedro cactus to see and travel into realms beyond the boundaries of ordinary reality. Both experience the kind of ecstatic trance that makes this soul-travel possible. In other words, both men and women perform similar roles as shamans (in accord with Eliade's classic definition) in this region of the world. In this chapter, I further explore the differences between male and female healing in this region, with a particular emphasis on differences in healing philosophies and in therapeutic strategies.

The relationship between the gender of the practitioner and trance type is well discussed in the literature of shamanism and healing. It has been noted that, among those traditions in which the possession by spirits predominates and shamans receive their wisdom passively, women are conspicuously present as both healers and participants. By contrast, male practitioners predominate in traditions where the shaman actively engages the spirit-world by sending his own soul on a magical flight. Many classic investigations of shamanism differentiate between true (male) and degraded (female) shamanic traditions in terms of trance type (Shirokogoroff 1935; Eliade 1964; Lewis 1971). As Atkinson summarized current thinking in this regard, "The classic model of the shaman in non state societies [is] charismatic, masterful, and male" (1992, 317).

In part, this assumption follows from the observation that where shamanic traditions coexist with state-sanctioned, institutionalized religions, these shamanic traditions also tend to be dominated by women. Declining prestige, marginalization and peripheralization of women, and reactive rather than progressive ideologies, are given as reasons for this phenomenon. In sum, women are associated with marginal, peripheral, degraded, passive, or reactive forms of shamanism.

Lewis's now classic arguments provide one example of these gendered assumptions. According to Lewis, female-dominated shamanic traditions are "thinly disguised protest movements" which function to ameliorate socially structured gender inequalities (1971; 1986; 1989). While his arguments have been challenged, revised, and problematized of late (see Boddy 1994, 415–27 and Atkinson 1992, 317–19 for excellent summaries of this literature), the impact of gender on cultural constructions of meaning is still emphasized. In these reworkings, the female participants in these "cults of affliction" actively engage the complex processes which shape cultural meanings—both resisting and accommodating the patriarchal structures that oppress them. The focus has shifted to what women do, rather than what they are kept from doing "on behalf of themselves, their families, households, or communities. . . . [Women's work within the spiritual realm] is about morality, social identity . . . [and about] wider social discourses and practices of power" (Boddy 1994, 416).

But for all of this emphasis on gender and shamanism, most discussions of these relationships (and the relationship between shamanic traditions and social process or cultural meaning) focus only on traditions in which women predominate as healers, that is, traditions where shamans are possessed.[1] In northern Peru, by contrast, male practitioners predominate and the shaman's ecstatic trance is better defined as soul-travel or magical-flight than possession.[2] Thus, a discussion of how shamanic traditions are engendered, and of how gender provides a local context for emergent meaning in this region of the world, is neither redundant nor insignificant.

In writing this book, the urge to compare female shamans against a male standard has at times been overpowering. With over fifty years of inquiry into the shamanic traditions of northern Peru—by male investigators about male healers—this is not surprising. These studies have provided tools for understanding how perceptions about life and death, illness and healing, relate to the dynamics of self, family, and society in this region of the world. But if gender provides a local context for under-

standing these dynamics, it is particularly important to problematize the
measurer as well as what is measured. Since the use of ecstatic trance has
been posited as fundamental both to shamanic identity and the construction of cultural meaning, I shall begin with a discussion of the elements
of the classic "shamanic journey" and show how these correspond to the
mesa ceremonies as performed by the male healers documented to date.

The Classic Shamanic Journey

In a seminal article describing the phases and elements of the shamanic journey, Barbara Myerhoff recounted the following:

> *The shamanic journey is in three phases. The shaman sets forth from the*
> *realm of the mundane; he then journeys to the supernatural and returns.*
> *Always the passage involves these three destinations or locations. . . . The*
> *shaman travels to the edge of the social order each time he undertakes*
> *these journeys. He enters non-form, the underlying chaos of the*
> *unconceptualized domain which has not yet been made a part of the*
> *cosmos by the cultural activity of naming and defining. With each*
> *crossing over, he gains power, as do all persons who travel to the edges of*
> *order, for . . . such contacts with the boundaries of conceptualization are*
> *sources of power as well as danger. Shamans are liminal people, at the*
> *thresholds of form, forever betwixt and between (Joralemon and Sharon*
> *1993, 166).*[3]

In this journey, the shaman travels from the domain of the defined, the
named, and the ordered world of social customs to the chaotic, unconcep-
tualized, ambiguous, and murky realm beyond human conception and
back again. This account of the shamanic journey emphasizes the dichotomous nature of these categories, the transcendent nature of the shaman's
journey, and his active role in transforming the suffering of others. His
power comes from transcending the primordial struggle between the
knowable and the inchoate, and from mastering both sides of this dialectic. In the classical shamanic journey, power is achieved through "trans-
porting a man beyond the boundaries of himself" (Sharon 1978, 49) and

transcending both physical and natural worlds. The shaman gains power through mastering the perils of the journey itself and by successfully returning to this world. In other words, the shaman's journey parallels the

142   crises and reintegration of his own path to healing. Just as learning to place oneself above worldly oppositions (e.g., life/death, goodness/evil, social obligations/individual desires) so as to master or transcend them is key to becoming a shaman, these same stages of separation, transcendence, and return are often expressed in the symbols of the shaman's trance—and in the healing philosophy which he communicates to his patients.

The Shamanic Voyage, Transcendence, and Male Models of Healing

The *mesa* serves as a kind of focal point for the shamanic voyage among male healers in northern Peru. It opens the lines of communication between worlds because the objects on the *mesa* contain the power of the *encantos* from which they have been taken. These objects embody the forces of the universe that are involved in causing and curing sorcery. Thus, when a healer (or sorcerer) dominates the powers contained within the *mesa* objects, he is acting upon the forces responsible for the patient's suffering and his actions have direct consequences for the lives of his patients. In other words, by "acting on the object-symbols [contained within the *mesa*], one can analogically act on the universal forces that are condensed in them and [in which] they find correspondence" (Polía 1988a, 27–28).

The forces represented on the *mesa,* like the elements of the classical shamanic trance, are represented in dualistic and oppositional terms. Pre-Columbian artifacts associated with worship of the ancestors and the forces of nature are most often grouped on the left side of the altar. Images of saints, crucifixes, and other Christian elements are often grouped on the right. Often, there is a center section of the *mesa* consisting of objects that help the healer dominate the *mesa* as a whole (Giese 1989, 151) or to mediate and "balance" the divergent powers of right and left (Sharon 1978, 1979; Joralemon 1983, 1984).

The ritual manipulation of these *mesa* forces during the all-night ceremony is also patterned: the healer invokes the powers of the right, then the left, then the right sides of his *mesa* in a way that "replicates a shamanic journey in the classical sense" (Joralemon and Sharon 1993, 166). He transcends the primordial struggle between the knowable and the inchoate and transforms it into passage for his patients.

As suggested in chapter 2, Andean cosmology was full of oppositional dialectics long before the arrival of the Spaniards, male/female, sky/earth, llacuaz/huari, and virility/fecundity are just a few examples of these. As reported by the first chroniclers after the Spaniards' arrival in 1532, the Andean cosmos consisted of three worlds. The under-world (Hurin Pacha, or Ukhu Pacha) and the upper-world (Hanan Pacha) embodied opposite but complementary powers symbolized by dualities like earth/sky, darkness/light, female/male, fecund/fertile, innate power/extrinsic power, left/right. In between the chthonic and the celestial was the world of human relations and discourse. Called simply "this world" (Kay Pacha), it was here that the dialectical forces came together (sometimes violently) to create new life, biological as well as social. It was here, on the surface of the Earth, that the sun's light and the damp soil created an environment in which the implanted seed could grow. It was here that the encounter between male and female engendered a new generation. It was here also that *forasteros* (outsiders) and natives met and confronted the changes produced by their meeting. This encounter was called *tinku,* the dialectical and generative power of creation.

Summarizing work by Giese (1989, 152–57) and Polía (1990, 109), Sharon notes that in the *mesas* of at least some contemporary *curanderos,* the oppositions of Hurin Pacha and Hanan Pacha are explicitly associated with the left and right sides of the *mesa,* respectively. The center portion of the *mesa* correlates with the earth's surface and is often associated with the healer's power.

> *The left side contains objects from below the surface of the earth (e.g.,*
> *pre-Columbian artifacts from ancient burial grounds), or from the bottom*
> *of the ocean (e.g., shells)—all associated with "down," hurin. On the*
> *other hand, the right side contains materials from highland lagoons (e.g.,*
> *herbs), or objects linked to the sky (e.g., saints' images)—all associated*

> with "up," hanan. . . . *The central section of the mesa, like the earth's surface, is the place where these dualistic forces are expressed in human life, in this case through the instructions of the* curandero *as he receives information from the right and left (or up and down) and then directs the concentrated forces of the mesa.*" (Joralemon and Sharon 1993, 179)

The chthonic and celestial forces represented on the left and right sides of the healer's *mesa*—and corresponding forces in the world at large—have very specific meanings and uses for patient and healer alike. A clue to these can first be found in the etymology of the *mesa* itself. The right side of the *mesa* is frequently called *banco curandero* (curing bench, or bank), while the left side of the *mesa* is frequently called the *banco ganadero* (Joralemon and Sharon 1993, 5–6). *Ganadero* has several meanings in Spanish, including the occupational name given to those who herd livestock (*ganado*) and the nominative reference given to "one who wins or dominates" (from the verb *ganar*). While these two meanings seem to have little correspondence, Sharon gives several possible interpretations that link both meanings (Joralemon and Sharon 1993, 273n. 2). For example, "given the many animal and natural referents of the left side of the *mesa,* 'herder' could be taken to indicate the ability of the curer to control or manage 'animalistic' or subhuman forces." Similarly, *ganadero* may be associated with the power of the colonial overlord (the Spanish brought cattle and other European livestock to the New World) and may represent the "domination" of the European oppressor with the occupation of "herder." Additionally, the conflation of *ganadero* (as "herder" and as "one who dominates") may reflect the post-conquest demonization of all things pre-Colombian. When asked to explain the term *ganadero,* many contemporary healers correlate that which "dominates" with Satan, and that which "is dominated" with the human soul.

In any case, many healers interrogated by colonial officials and ecclesiastic judges reported their profession as *ganadero.* During the colonial period, itinerant merchants and livestock-herders were among the few Indians who could legitimately live and travel outside the villages where Catholic indoctrination was strongest. Since *ganaderos* and itinerant merchants lived more at the margins of Catholic influence than those whose presence or absence could quickly be noted at Mass and catechism, they were regarded with suspicion as carriers and progenitors of pagan ritual and practice (Gareis 1994).

In chapter 2, I outlined the impact of Catholic campaigns to "extirpate idolatries" on ecclesiastic and popular perceptions of *curanderas*. This overlay onto Andean dualisms of Christian moralism, expressed as the struggle of good against evil, also had a tremendous impact on indigenous world views. The dualisms of Andean cosmologies were reciprocal and complementary forces, and both were necessary for engendering life. But the Christian perspective

> . . . divided the universe into two clearly defined and opposing spheres: the world of virtue and the world of vice. On the one hand Christians—the servants of God—were upholding a moral order of goodness against onslaughts made by the servants of the Prince of Darkness. Within this conception of the world, the devil, the incarnation of evil, was ever-energetic in his perpetual attempts to overthrow God's kingdom. (Silverblatt 1983, 415)

One result of this Christian absolutism was the demonization of all that was non-Christian. Since Christians believed that one of Satan's key roles on this Earth was to win over souls by tempting humans with Faustian pacts (see Glass-Coffin 1992b), the veneration of Andean deities and ancestors became essentialized and was transformed into simple Devil worship (Gareis 1995; Millones 1994). Serving the animating essence of these deities was reinterpreted by priests as having a "pact with the Devil." For Andeans unfortunate enough to be questioned about their beliefs and ritual practices, this confusion over conflicting explanations often resulted in labels of nonrepentant and recalcitrant (as well as torture and prolonged seclusion). Sometimes, though, healers used the new associations to their advantage, embracing their role as Satan's followers to contest the Spanish intrusion into their lives or to increase their power and prestige as shamans (Silverblatt 1987, 159–210; Duriols 1986, lxxvi; Gareis 1995; Griffiths 1996; Mills 1997, 285).

At any rate, because of the missionizing influence of the Catholic church, Joralemon and Sharon suggest that the *curandero* and the *gana-dero*, the celestial and the chthonic, and the right and left sides of the *mesa*

146

> . . . *frequently translate into Christian versus pagan, that is, good versus evil, or to put it in society terms, order and stability versus chaos and disruption. In effect, a ritual movement from the right, with its predominantly Christian icons and healing herbs, to the dangerous left, with its pagan, antisocial overtones, can be perceived as a journey beyond the status quo, or natural order, into the supernatural. The elaborate battles with spirits and ritual "cleansings" aimed at "throwing away" or "turning around" sorcery signal the incredible power being marshaled in this murky realm inhabited by ill-defined forces and beings associated with . . . the ambiguity prevalent on the left (Joralemon and Sharon 1993:166). . . . Thus it should come as no surprise that in most* mesas *encountered in this study pre-Columbian artifacts are identified with sorcery/witchcraft and placed in the Ganadero zone [the left side of the* mesa *also associated with the underworld], the side of the devil, while Christian icons and artifacts associated with the triumph of good over evil are placed in the Curandero sector [the right side of the* mesa *also associated with the upper or celestial world], also called Gloria, the side of God. . . . Thus far it appears that our informants' verbalized interpretations of their* mesas *are directly inspired by Catholic colonial moralism—that is, the battle between God's servants and the agents of the devil. . . . Within this structural framework the good/evil dichotomy is assimilated along with a host of other pairs: Curandero/Ganadero, Christian/pagan, curandero/ brujo, saint/sorcerer, Christ/Satan, health/ sickness, right/left, white/black, life/death, up/down, and so forth.* (Joralemon and Sharon 1993, 174–75)

To this dichotomy of left/sorcery/pagan/downward versus right/curing/Catholic/upward, Joralemon adds a discussion of the referential and performative metaphors used by contemporary healers—and their patients—to further illuminate the associations of sorcery and healing with chthonic and celestial spheres. According to Joralemon,

Patients in our sample expressed their suffering with metaphors of
contamination and entrapment. . . . They frequently used the following
words to describe their condition: cochinado *(made filthy, pig-like), [and]*
podrido *(rotten). . . . Expressing the idea of entrapment, patients referred* 147
to being agarrado *(caught, seized),* amarrado *(tied up),* jalado *(pulled in),*
trancado *(bolted in). . . . Those patients who indicated satisfaction with*
their treatment . . . used metaphors of purification and liberation to
describe their transformed condition [in addition to metaphors] of
spiritual restoration and tranquillity . . . expressed via upward
directional metaphors, as in patient references to being levantado
(raised), parado *(stood up),* elevado *(elevated) or* alzado *(lifted)*
(Joarelmon and Sharon 1993: 249–50).

Furthermore, as Joralemon continues, the scent of sorcery becomes
associated with the fetid or putrefying smells of cemeteries, death, and
the underworld. By contrast, the scents associated with purification and
healing utilize olfactory metaphors like "sweeten" *(endulzar)* and "flower"
(florecer), which connote above-ground associations with growth, light,
and life. These references are commonly used by *curanderos* as well, suggesting that the associations of sorcery/down/dark/fetid and healing/up/
light/flowering are shared by patients and healers alike (Joralemon and
Sharon 1993, 250). As Joralemon concludes,

The suffering associated with daño *and the healing process [are phrased]*
in terms of a metaphorical transformation from contaminated to
cleansed, entrapped to liberated, demoralized to enheartened, and from
agitated to tranquil. A comprehensive directional metaphor, from down to
up, is layered on top of these other associations. (Joralemon and Sharon
1993).

Celestial and Chthonic Metaphors in Cajamarcan Folklore

These logical juxtapositions of entrapped or entangled/down/chthonic
and liberated or untangled/up/celestial correlate exactly with the meta-

phors used to describe their world by children and adults in the Quechua-speaking community of Kilish in rural Cajamarca. According to the cognitive domains elicited and described by Ana De la Torre for this agricultural community in the northern highlands of Peru, the physical, spatial, and temporal characteristics of the world in which the Cajamarcans live are governed by the dualistic principles of God and the Devil, glossed as Amito and Shapi. In the Quechua dialect of this region, the former signifies God, Lord, Father, or Master (Amo), and Amito is the diminutive. Shapi is synonymous with Awqa and Shapinku (which translate as Devil, enemy, incestuous, cat, and fool) (1986, 146–47).

Shapi's world mirrors Amito's world, but there are fundamental distinctions between the two. Amito's world is above ground; Shapi's world is below ground. The first is warm, the second is cold. The first is filled with the light of the sun, while the second is always dark. The water that nourishes comes from the sky in Amito's world, but it comes from underground springs, lagoons, and rivers in Shapi's world. Humans live in Amito's world, but other entities—maleficient entities—inhabit Shapi's world. Both worlds contain cultivated and wild plants and animals, as well as food for the inhabitants who live there. But these foods, also, are quite distinct. The prepared foods of Amito's world are flavorful and well condimented. Salt, garlic, and hot peppers are all used to season these foods. But the prepared foods of Shapi's world are bland, and sugar is the only additive allowed.

The cultigens of Amito's world are dependent on human care, are good to eat, have a morphology that emphasizes symmetry, and (if they need to be planted by humans in order to thrive) they are planted in an ordered fashion in straight rows or terraces. Shapi's cultigens, on the other hand, grow "where they will," in complete disorder and disarray. They may be climbing vines or ground plants that grow in tangled thickets, and they catch on clothing, are hairy or full of spines, and are generally asymmetrical in shape. They are not good to eat, but are often used for magical purposes. When children were asked to draw pictures of Shapi's cultigens, their drawings emphasized this tangled-up disorder (De la Torre 1986, 15–41).

Similarly, the animals of Amito's world live above ground or fly through the air. The untamed animals of Amito's world do not sting or bite but are "friendly" toward humans. And all domesticated animals belong to Amito's world, with three exceptions: the cat, the mule, and the pig. When De la Torre asked her informants why these animals belonged in Shapi's world, a common denominator emerged. All three animals are "unnatural," in the sense that they disrupt the social order by breaking up nuclear families, which constitute a fundamental Andean opposition, the male/female pair. The cat, sometimes identified as a manifestation of Shapi because of its whiskers, claws, and bristly body, figures prominently in local tales of marital discord. In these stories, Cat is the one who breaks up couples, thereby disrupting this necessary and complementary dyad (see also Allen 1988). Mule—the product of an unnatural and sterile cross between species—also represents the disruption of "natural" reproduction and the necessary union of male and female. Finally, Pig appears as the star character in a folktale in which Amito and his pregnant wife are denied lodging by a wealthy *hacienda* owner during a time when Shapi stalks them. A poor servant hides them in the kitchen and they escape. The next morning, Amito turns the landowners into pigs and makes the servant their master. Pig is thus associated with the unwillingness to share and the lack of hospitality—two highly regarded aspects of moral and social behavior throughout the Andes (De la Torre 1986, 50–56).

Applying a structural analysis to the categorizations described by her informants, De la Torre concludes that the fundamental opposition between Amito's and Shapi's world is that of order versus chaos. While Amito's world is one of logical categories and straight furrows—a world which distinguishes social and moral rules of conduct from those which are unacceptable, Shapi's world is one of chaos—a world of complete indistinction and lack of categories (1986, 148). Using the structural concepts of Culture and Nature, Amito's world is one that has been imprinted with the biological, moral, and social order of human society. Shapi's world, on the other hand, is untamed, immoral, inhumane, and non-human. According to De la Torre, Order and Chaos thus exist in a complementary relationship to one another and both are integral parts of the world view she documents. But within this classificatory scheme (of Order/Chaos), all humanity is ascribed to that group of beings associated with the cosmic principle of order and is therefore subject to difference in every aspect of life. In biology, this difference appears as sexual distinction; in society, it is manifested as norms which are differentially appropriate for discrete categories of people; in subsistence, it is seen as precise lines (furrows) which are distinguished from uncultivated lands; in foodstuffs, it is flavor (which, itself, is defined by difference); and in cosmology, it is the presence of oppositional categories for Sun/Moon, light/dark, and Amito/Shapi (1986, 152).

Cosmological Dualisms and Shamanic World View

Joralemon and Sharon argue that the dualisms expressed on the *mesa* both reflect and influence world view. The binary oppositions of celestial/chthonic, straight/tangled, orderly/chaotic, and culture/nature that permeate cosmological beliefs like those described for Kilish find close correspondence in *mesa* symbolism. Additionally, this emphasis on dualism and opposition seems to influence and reflect the healer's conceptualization of the harm that threatens his patients. In Sharon's words, "There is an adversarial quality found in the accounts of *curanderos'* lives and therapeutic philosophies . . . [They] express an oppositional view of the world they live in, a black-and-white struggle between forces of good and evil." (1993, 166). The healer's task is to dominate, resolve, or transcend these oppositional forces in order to effect a cure. In other words, the resolution of opposites that occurs on the *mesa* is a kind of "symbolic cipher for the resolution of conflicts in the lives of the healer's patients" (Skillman 1990, 14).

Several of the male healers summarized in Joralemon and Sharon's work (1993) explicitly use metaphors of combat. For Victor Neyra, "curing sessions were battles between the negative forces of evil, death, and destruction . . . and the positive forces of goodness, life, and growth marshaled by the shaman" (1993, 30). The left side of his *mesa* contained knives, stone mace-heads, swords, and even a pistol (1993, 33). On Roberto Rojas's *mesa,* "The largest cluster of objects on the left side . . . consists of eighteen pre-Columbian 'Warrior' Ceramics that form Roberto's 'army' of spirits, helping him to cure curses and ailments associated with pre-Hispanic ruins. The next largest group includes stones from pre-Columbian sites used to 'counter-arrest' the attacks of sorcerers" (1993, 83).

In Rojas's ceremony, as well as those of other male shamans documented and discussed by Joralemon and Sharon, the symbolic emphasis on combat was also made manifest in ritual action. As Sharon describes it,

> *During the cleansing of patients in the early morning hours, Roberto frequently performed the delivering of a golpe [blow] against the sorcerer responsible for a particularly strong curse. Grabbing his iron serpent from the head of the mesa and the skull from the Ganadero, Roberto would charge into the open and engage in an aggressive spirit battle with his adversary. He would curse, yell, and throw the skull and serpent staff at the enemy, unseen except by him. . . . This dramatic battle, performed for difficult cases, also is found among other shamans, although the specific techniques employed vary according to the personality and style of the healer (1993, 84).*

In these battles, the healer reconfigures the patient's suffering in terms of these oppositions and moves the patient from affliction to relief. The patient's participation "is not much different from his participation in orthodox religion: It is activated when expedient and experienced vicariously."[4] (Sharon 1978, 147)

How do these ideas of opposition and mediated dualism, as well as the role of the healer vis-à-vis the patient, compare to what I found while working with the five women of my sample? As the following paragraphs suggest, I found similarities and differences, both between the women and their male counterparts and among the five women themselves, in both *mesa* symbolism and in the cultural meanings ascribed to *mesa* objects.

How Mediated Dualism Is Expressed (Or Not) on Mesas *of Female Healers*

Clorinda inherited her handsome *mesa* from her father. It includes an assortment of staffs, both wooden and metal, which she leans against the wall of her house rather than standing these up in the ground. In front of the staffs lie her *mesa* objects, which include a large collection of conch shells, as well as stones, rattles, a few wooden crosses, and statues of Catholic saints. A small bowl of black tobacco, steeped in cane alcohol, occupies a spot in the center of the *mesa*. On the right, half a dozen bottles contain *agua florida, agua de kananga,* and fragrant seeds in a tincture of fragrant liquid, water from the lagoons, and cane alcohol. Two *seguros* also sit on the right side of the *mesa*.

Among the five women, Clorinda's *mesa* most closely resembles that of the male healers documented, in the sense that it has a left, a right, and a center. Although Clorinda denied having separate names for these, she did assert that her one *mesa* is actually three: "One is for raising luck, one is for curing, and the other is to hit or strike but for justice's sake. . . . This is the Mesa Negra." The objects contained in this *mesa* are a subset of her main *mesa* objects. In the ritual that she did for me, when it was time to deliver blows to sorcerers, she placed these objects behind where she sat facing the *mesa,* and to her left. In addition, Clorinda clearly distinguishes between the cleansing, striking, and flowering/purifying portions of her ceremony. The left-to-right/down-to-up/contaminated-to-purified movement, summarized by Joralemon and Sharon (1993, 6–9, 168–73, 246–56) for northern healers, was clearly evident on Clorinda's *mesa*.

The association of curing with good and sorcery with evil is also apparent in Clorinda's explanation of her *mesa*. Describing herself as a *curandera hierbatera,* she explained that the main difference between the two is that spiritists work with the souls of the dead instead of highland *encantos*. The spiritist's powers are naturally antithetical to those of the *encantos* of mountains, lagoons, and other power places. Furthermore, although herbalists may work for good or evil, depending upon how they use the power of the *encantos,* spiritists always work for evil. They kill their victims instantly, obtaining their power from renegade souls called *malas muertes*. These are the souls of people who have died evil deaths. They have passed over to the "other world" because in life they committed either an act of murder or of incest. Both are crimes against humanity and belong to the realm of chaos because both violate the prescriptions, categories, and fundamental behaviors expected of people as members of society. Such spirits fly through the night and transform into animals. They have Faustian pacts with the Devil.

By contrast, even though some might argue they are part of the underworld, the *encantos* with whom Clorinda works were created by God. They are part of an ordered world, as are those people who have a good heart and are opposed to the evil forces commanded by the spiritist. Good spirits are associated with light, with the upper-world, and with God's Kingdom on Earth. As Clorinda told me, "All of us who have been born on this earth have our star." Part of her healing gift includes the ability to correlate the individual stars in the sky with her patients on Earth and to read her patients' luck and future by examining the stars above. By way of illustration, she described the counsel she had recently given a patient.

> *Look at [that star], it is [the name of the patient's girlfriend]. If you should marry her, it will shine brightly and will throw off sparks like diamonds, like gold, like flowers in the star. And if a cloud comes and covers it, it is because she isn't for you. And if it clears up, she is [to be] your wife.*

Vicky's *mesa* is similar to Clorinda's in that it contains rocks, shells, skulls, a crucifix, staffs, religious images, a *seguro,* and scented water. Actually, the *mesa* I saw is only a subset of her *mesa,* some of whose objects Vicky also inherited from her father. Despite its small size, Vicky asserted that her *mesa* has two sides. The *artes* of the left side, which she calls the *ganadero,* are used for defense and are nourished or fed with cane alcohol and tobacco to strengthen their power. The *artes* of the right side, which she calls the *curandero,* are used for curing and for raising the patient's luck, and these are fed with perfumes and other sweet things like sugar. There are specific tasks associated with each of these libations as well. Vicky employs *agua de kananga* to lift out the *daño* afflicting her patients, and cane alcohol to cure. Name-brand perfumes like Ramillete de Novia, Tabu, Macizo Negro, and Maja, as well as scented water (*agua florida*), are for flowering the patient. *Tabaco,* on the other hand, is used for chasing away evil spirits, and for dominating.

Like Clorinda's, Vicky's ritual also has three distinct phases that emphasize the movement from cleansing to curing to flowering. First, the powers of the *mesa* are activated; then comes the diagnosis, or *rastreo*. This is followed by the curing portion of the ceremony, which includes both cleansings and raisings. Following this, the patient and the *mesa* are "flowered" and sweetened. Finally, the *mesa* powers are deactivated with holy water and white corn meal. These substances refresh and calm the *mesa* spirits, while also cutting the effects of the San Pedro on all present.

But, unlike Clorinda, Vicky does not dichotomize the work of spiritists and herbalists or assign these categories of healers to Evil and Good, respectively. This difference is not surprising, considering that Vicky describes herself as a spiritist and claims allegiance to both spiritists and herbalists within her own healing heritage. What defines her as a spiritist, according to Vicky, is that she commends herself to the Blessed Souls or *ánimas* when she works. Vicky distinguishes between the rituals of the herbalist and the spiritist, noting that the former utilizes the power of the *encantos* of lagoons, plants, and mountains resident in the talismans on the *mesa,* whereas the latter utilizes the power of these *ánimas.* Herbalist healing ceremonies must be performed at night, but spritists can conduct their ceremonies during the daytime. Another difference, according to Vicky, is that San Pedro is a mandatory part of an herbalist cure, but does not enter into the ritual of the spiritist. Instead, the spiritist's *mesa* requires that she smoke black tobacco as she commends herself to the souls of her dead relatives.

For Vicky, the spirits invoked by the spiritist-healer include those of Jesus and the Virgin, both of whom once walked the earth. Unlike the *malas muertes,* which are alienated from the social order of humanity, these spirits belong to the world of God, of light, and of human morality.

One of these *ánimas* is the spirit of the Virgin of Túcume. According to Vicky, this Virgin is an *ánima* because she was at one time also a living being—the daughter of a poor coastal peasant who became enchanted by the mountain known as Cerro de Túcume, which is near the town of the same name.

As Vicky explained it, the Virgin of Túcume had two other sisters who were also enchanted. They are now worshipped as the Virgin of

Guadalupe and the Virgin of Mochumí, respectively. Vicky is most familiar with the Virgin of Túcume's story, and she described it as follows:

> The story goes that there were three sisters, the Virgin of Túcume, the
> Virgin of Mochumí, and the Virgin of Guadalupe. It happened that they
> were herders, campesinas; their mother was a poor, honest woman who
> sent out her daughters to herd their sheep. She sent them out all dirty and
> her [one] daughter arrived clean, with her hair combed. Her mother
> asked her, "Little daughter, who has washed you, who has combed your
> hair?" "An old woman," [the daughter answered]. . . . The story goes on:
> Well, . . . day by day the girl went growing more, she became prettier, the
> best of all the other daughters of the woman; the girl was very pretty. And
> it is said that whereas the girl used to arrive [back home] at twelve o'clock
> noon, now the child didn't arrive at twelve o'clock noon but rather at six
> o'clock in the afternoon. . . . [Then, one day,] the sheep returned home
> but the daughter didn't return. She remained. . . . the sheep arrived but
> [she didn't]. That girl is the Virgin. . . .
>
> She remained up on the peak [of the mountain of Túcume]. There is her
> cross, everything. . . . Then, what happened is that the Virgin of Túcume
> was taken to the church. Look, they took her down to the church, and the
> next day they found her back on the mountain where she became enchanted.
> She returned there. That is how they discovered that it was an
> encanto. . . . Many times the priest . . . conducted his masses, his
> novenas to the Virgin. [She would be in the church at] eight, nine, ten
> and eleven [o'clock] at night. [But] at four or five in the morning, [she was
> gone]. They saw the Virgin up on the mountain, dressed with her crown of
> gold and everything. And so they brought the Virgin down and gave her
> Mass, they commissioned her mass . . . and they chained her [to the
> golden chair where she sits in the church]. She is chained there by her
> hands and by her feet, chained by her hands and feet so that she won't
> move.

When Vicky "commends" herself to the Virgin, the *encanto* opens so
that Vicky can see her and converse with her about her patients' problems
and the source of their suffering. As Vicky asserted, "The Virgin does

miracles for me; she never deceives me. I commend myself to her and she helps me very much. I converse with her, and it is as though I were seeing how it is."

At first glance, Isabel's *mesa* is quite similar to both Vicky's and Clorinda's—although it is quite a bit larger. Actually, during my time with her Isabel had two separate *mesas*, the Mesa Novata which she sets up at the north end of the corral looking toward the south, and the Mesa San Cipriano, which is set up to the left of the Mesa Novata, against the east wall of the corral. The Mesa Novata was the first *mesa* that she acquired and is her curing *mesa*. It actually extends the entire length of the corral, from north to south. The objects of the *mesa* itself are set up on top of a white canvas ground cloth, the color of which allows Isabel to better "see" the source of the *daño* from which the patient is suffering. About ten feet south of the ground cloth, a row of staffs stands facing the north wall of the corral. These, as well as the two lone heavy/weighty staffs which stand at the south end of the corral, are all part of the Mesa Novata.

The objects and staffs of Isabel's Mesa Novata are used to protect and defend the *mesa* as a whole, as well as to cleanse patients when directed by Isabel. Her second *mesa*, the Mesa San Cipriano, is a defending rather than a curing *mesa*. It sits, as previously mentioned, against the east wall of the corral, to the left of the Mesa Novata. Its objects are laid out upon a black ground cloth so that any sorcerer who attacks either Isabel or Olinda will not see how they defend against the attacks. The objects which sit upon the black ground cloth of this *mesa* are used infrequently, but the staffs are the exact counterparts of those on the Mesa Novata. They are used to cleanse Isabel and Olinda from any evil-air which they might absorb from a patient every time they work. No patient is cleansed with the staffs of this *mesa*.

It is no accident that this *mesa* sits to the left of the curing *mesa*, for Isabel is fully aware that sorcerers traditionally effect *daño* by invoking objects from the left half, or *campo ganadero*, of their *mesas*. She places her own defense objects to her left, in order to protect herself and her patients from these leftward attacks.

According to Isabel, the Mesa Novata has a center field, although the Mesa San Cipriano does not. This is composed of the two crosses, the two *seguros* (which belong to her and to her assistant Olinda), the crucifix, the bottle of plain brown glass from which patients are given holy water to drink, and the framed picture of El Ojo de Dios. These occupy positions in the center of the Mesa Novata and are the first objects set up (and the first to be removed) when the *mesa* is laid. In the line of staffs which correspond to the Mesa Novata, the Santa Isabel staff also corresponds to this center section of the *mesa*. At the south end of the corral, the two weighty staffs also belong to this center grouping.

Unlike the *mesas* previously described, Yolanda's *mesa* contains only crosses and religious images, including a crucifix approximately twenty-four inches high, several smaller wooden crosses, and a small statue of the Virgin of Lourdes. Yolanda's *mesa* is completely devoid of the staffs, skulls, rocks, herb-filled *seguros,* and other objects, which Yolanda and José associate with "the Devil's work."

In spite of this deviation, there are other parallels between Yolanda and the other healers, particularly in the way they use their *mesa* objects. During the ceremony itself, Yolanda and José give the wooden crosses from their altar to the patient as his "defense against Evil." These are used to cleanse the patient's body in the same up-to-down fashion described by Flor, and witnessed with Isabel's, Clorinda's, and Vicky's patients. Also, at each ceremony all present were admonished to shake out the evil by vigorously shaking their arms and legs throughout the ritual.

Although Yolanda's altar has neither right or left sides, she does associate the right side with Good and the left side with Evil during the course of her ritual. As described in chapter 4, Yolanda and José see the representation of Evil on the floor beneath the patient's feet and stamp out these figures as the cure progresses. During this process, they insisted that the patient turn to the right to untangle, unwind, and untwist the Evil. As Yolanda told me: "Turning to the left, like driving a car on the wrong side of the road, is dangerous. It only adds to the twisting. Instead, one must turn always to the right to untie, to unravel all their errors." Whereas the twistings of our errors and sins against God are unwound by turning to the right, a leftward turn will create yet another knot to untie before the patient can be completely cured. This language clearly associates sickness with that which is tangled, wound, tied, and bound, while it associates healing with that which is untangled, unwound, untied, and unbound. The worlds of Amito and Shapi come once again to mind.

Although Yolanda was the only one of the women who clearly associated tangling up with the left, and straightening out with the right, this language of tangling/sickness, and untangling/health, was very common among the five women in my study. *Cruzar, anudar, enredar, atar, enroscar, amarrar* (to cross, to knot, to roll, to tie, to coil, to bind) were among the many synonyms for *daño* utilized by these women. Conversely, health involved uncrossing, unknotting, unrolling, untying, uncoiling, and unbinding, as well as putting oneself on the "right path" and "straightening out."

According to Isabel, a direct relationship exists between the degree of "winding" and the difficulty of the cure. To cure a *daño,* one must be able to see how the victim's soul was captured and commended to the *encanto* or the *ánima* who keeps it at bay. One must cut the ties that continue to bind the victim's soul to this entity in order for the soul to return home. Isabel told me that when a victim is very wound up, the cure is difficult precisely because it is impossible to see through the tangle of threads that surrounds the victim. This entanglement serves as a screen, which has the effect of blindfolding the healer. It is through ritual acts of cleansing that this tangled weave begins to unravel and that Isabel begins to see how the victim's soul was captured. One of the objects that she uses for this purpose is the scissors, which cuts through the tangled threads and clarifies the actions Isabel must prescribe to complete the cure. When describing the power of a sorcerer to effect harm against one of her patients, Isabel used other terms like *tapar* (to cover), *vendar* (to blindfold), *oscurecer las vistas* (to darken one's sight), and *cegar* (to blind). And just as sorcery and darkness are aligned for her, curing requires the ability to see, and this requires light. In her prayers to San Pedro, Isabel asks her herbs to *iluminar* (illuminate), *revelar* (reveal), *despejar* (clear up), and *aclarar* (clarify) so she can recover the victim's soul.

Isabel, like all the women I studied, associates curing with being close to God. She also associates sorcery with the Devil. Spatially, God inhabits and rules over the world above, whereas the Devil rules over the world below, the world of *encantos* and the world of buried souls. Isabel once told me that all buried treasure is associated with *encantos* and belongs to the realm of the Devil. Even if the treasure was buried by one who was pure of heart, over time it passes into the Devil's realm because it is buried deep within the earth.

For these women, too, the light of the night sky is always associated with God and humankind. As Isabel told me, stars are the eyes of God. Just as she must see to heal her victims of the evil from which they suffer, God will guide her *mesa* ceremonies so long as He can see. She never begins her ritual until she can see at least one star in the sky above and know that God is watching over her actions. Any sudden dimming of the stars in the night sky (as happened during my own cure) means that her patients need to get closer to God. Sometimes the stars illuminating one side of the corral where she works seem dimmer than the stars directly over her *mesa*. When this happens, Isabel interprets it as a sign from God that those of us who believe most powerfully in the *mesa* are also closest to God.

As previously noted, Clorinda believes that "all of us born on this earth have our star" and all humans are reflected in the stars above. Flor also shares this view: as we kept watch over the fire on the night Flor cleansed the baby, she pointed out that only three stars were visible in the night sky. "There we are in the sky up there," she told me. "The little star over there is the baby's, and those two next to each other are the two of us." When I asked which was which, she responded playfully that mine was the star highest up in the sky, "because you are the tallest." Even Vicky associates the world above-ground with God and Christian images. Recall that when the Virgin of Túcume became enchanted, she lived at the top of a mountain and kept returning there, even after the faithful brought her down and chained her to a chair in the Church. In summary, for all five of the women with whom I worked, the dichotomous relationship between light/dark, up/down, good/evil, God/the Devil, and straight/tangled correlates well with De la Torre's summary of the ways in which the world of Amito and Shapi are characterized in the rural highlands of Cajamarca.

There are other parallels between De la Torre's analysis and the philosophies of these women. As previously discussed, Shapi's world is a chaotic world. It lacks the biological, social, and cosmological categories necessary for human survival. Recall that one distinction between the worlds of Amito and Shapi is the inversion of social obligations and mores. In Amito's world, as De la Torre summarizes it, Amito requires that his children recognize social norms and distinguish social groups to maintain group harmony, especially that of respect between *compadres*. By contrast, Shapi tempts humankind to turn their backs on these norms and to rip apart collaborative relationships between social groups. Thus, [in Shapi's world] incest between *compadres* is euphorically celebrated" (1986, 153). Incestuous relationships, whether between *compadres* or biologically related family members, certainly disrupts social harmony. The evil of this type of "unnatural sexual relation" so permeates Shapi's world that, in one Quechua/Spanish dictionary (Quezada 1976), the translation of the term Shapi is simply incest.

Also recall the juxtaposition of sickness, moral turpitude, spiritual rape, unnatural sexual relations, the left side, and the underworld in Flor's discussions of the baby's illness recounted in chapter 4. In one of the prayers offered to God during the cleansing of that child, Flor intoned,

> *In the name of Lord Jesus I cleanse [name of patient]. Here before God, in the name of God, who is magnified and glorified, I offer my soul and my love to the Lord of Heaven and Earth who is Creator of all things so that this evil temptation . . . will leave here, . . . so that it will go to the depths . . . deep into the sea and so that [the patient] will be left sound and healthy . . . in the Lord Jesus' name.*

The evil spirit in that cure was identified as *hombre tragadero* (swallowing man), and he had a huge hole between his legs. The illness was associated with the evil temptation of unnatural sexual relationships and was banned to the depths of the sea. The baby's mother was held responsible for her role in succumbing to the evil temptation of unnatural sexual relations—relations from the left side of the body.

Flor described another cure that she had performed on a young police corporal who suffered from epileptic seizures. In her description, these juxtapositions of unnatural sex, evil temptation, sickness, and the responsibility of the patient to resist such temptation in order to be cured are clear. Like the cure I witnessed with the baby, Flor cleansed this man in the evening and waited for the evil spirit to reveal itself in a dream. In this case, it was the man's dream that Flor interpreted to discern the cause of the illness and the likelihood of a cure. As Flor recounted his revelatory dream to me:

> [In the dream he was] dancing, dancing, dancing . . . with a young schoolgirl who said to him, "Sleep with me." He said to her, "How can I sleep with you? You are too young for me; you are a schoolgirl. No!" She grabbed him by the waist and [begged him]. "Sleep with me," . . . she insisted stubbornly. Then he said, "You are so stubborn. When the dance finishes, go wait for me outside." She went out. She waited for him outside. The dance finished, and he went out to do it with her. . . . She was dressed in bright red, . . . [but] when he was going to her side, she turned into a black cat. . . . [Then] with all his anger he grabbed [the cat] by the feet and smashed it against the ground. When it was in pieces, . . . he ripped [the head] off. He ripped it into pieces . . . and he took the pieces to a little hole further over . . . and he stuffed the cat, but in pieces, into the hole. He finished burying all the pieces and he covered the hole. . . . He left the cat there then . . . buried. [The cat] was like a bad spirit. Afterward, he told me the dream . . . and I told him that we won [the battle] over evil . . . and the epilepsy left him.

For Yolanda, also, the patient who has become ill is not spiritually close to God but has the sins of many errors and many evils on his or her conscience. On her own path to wellness, Yolanda emphasized, she needed to come closer to God and to separate herself from an unnatural sexual relationship, a relationship into which she had fallen because of love-magic performed against her. What stands out in her explanation is that the victim is not perceived as blameless, but that s/he has a personal responsibility and choice to resist temptation, to become purified, and to come closer to God as a prerequisite for curing. As Yolanda put it, the patients she cures are like "tree[s] grown crooked." They cannot become healed, cannot straighten out or raise themselves up until they undergo the same spiritual rehabilitation which moved Yolanda from illness to health. For both Flor and Yolanda, healing requires purification and depends upon the patient's resolve to overcome temptations that threaten the social and moral fabric of society.

162 These associations, between the social chaos of Shapi's world with its incest, temptation, and evil, and the straightening out of social categories as a prerequisite to healing, also underlay many of Isabel's explanations. According to Isabel, the spiritists and herbalists who are most powerful are those who have pacts with the Devil. Like the famous story of Faust, the exchange is one of power and wealth during a sorcerer's lifetime in return for his/her immortal soul. To seal the bargain and make the pact official, Isabel told me that the spiritist (who takes his/her power from the *ánimas* of the deceased) must have sexual relations with a cadaver. Similarly, the herbalist (who takes his/her power from the below-ground *encantos* that are the Devil's realm) must have sexual relations with the Devil himself. By their actions, these sorcerers pass literally from this world to the other world. They are possessed by evil and effect the *daño* that causes so much pain and suffering because they have lost all sense of moral behavior. Rather, they follow a moral code exactly the reverse of that which regulates life in this world. Not only do they have sexual relations with the Devil, they are also driven to incestuous relations with their closest kin.

Thus, there are differences and similarities between the metaphors and models expressed by the male healers previously described and those utilized by the five women with whom I worked. Both men and women utilize, to a greater or lesser degree, a *mesa,* and both ingest San Pedro to facilitate their healing. Both men and women have incorporated much Catholic symbolism, as well as the absolutist transformations wrought by Catholicism on Andean dualisms, into their healing philosophies. To be more specific, both men and women seem to share a world view in which the fundamental dualisms of down/chthonic/tangled/Demonic and up/celestial/untangled/Godly predominate. But even though these dualisms inform the philosophies of both male and female healers in northern Peru, their approach to these oppositions, both as social fact and as symbolic meaning, are somewhat different. As I will show in chapter 6, these dualisms are utilized differently by Isabel, Yolanda, and Flormira than by either Vicky and Clorinda or the male *curanderos* whose curing has been previously documented. Instead of emphasizing transcendence or domination of opposing categories, these three women use the same dialectic but in a way which emphasizes paradox and synthesis. Like the Catholic reconfiguration of Andean dualisms, this reconfiguration illustrates both the staying power of symbolic categories and their polysemic nature. It also reminds us, as scholars, of something that the users of such symbols have always known, that is, that societies are heterogeneous and cultural forms are emergent. It remains important to remember that symbolic meaning is actively created and negotiated by authors as well as audiences. And, as Bynum recently noted (1986), the time has indeed come to take female symbol-users seriously—both to better understand the social and cultural dynamics involved in the use of symbols, and to evolve our understanding of the symbols themselves.

Sowing Shadows in Sacred Lagoons

*C*hiclayo, July 23, 1989, Journal

Last night, Isabel held a *mesa* for all those who planned to make the pilgrimage to the sacred lagoons to leave their shadows there. There were twenty-two of us at the *mesa*. All were patients who had been to several *mesas* throughout the year and who were, like me, in the final stages of their cures. In her opening invocation, Isabel asked the *mesa* to guide us and watch over us so that no misfortune would befall us on the way.

One by one, we stood at the south end of the corral, looking north towards Huancabamba, invoking God and the saints, the blessed souls of our dead relatives, the four winds, the lagoons, and the mountains. We orally sprayed cane alcohol to clarify the path before us. We sprayed champagne to sweeten and tame the dangerous powers which could over-whelm us. We sprayed *agua florida* and *agua de kananga* to bring good luck along the way. We sprayed our own perfumes, the scents that we had chosen, as our personal offerings to the *encantos*. We also sprayed an offering called "water of the fourteen spirits," which Isabel had specially prepared for the occasion. This mixture included holy water—the flowery essence of the *agua florida* and *agua de kananga*—as well as the fragrant seeds of the plants known as *ishpingo, ashango,* and *amala.* In addition, honey, white flowers, sugar cane and rock-sugar had been added to the mixture.

Isabel then asked me to cleanse each patient with a staff of my choos-ing, to purify and cleanse them for the voyage. I chose the staff Isabel and Olinda call La Marina, which they had found one Good Friday at a nearby port, having followed the directions of the San Pedro from a previous *mesa.* As I cleansed each patient with La Marina, the words came to me   165 like a voice whispered in my ear. I did not feel the need to imitate, to follow Olinda's lead, or to verify my actions with Isabel: I seemed to already know what prayer each patient who stood before me needed.

As soon as all the patients had been cleansed, we were called back to the *mesa* to blow cane alcohol on the *mesa* so that we would be illuminated and guided, and so that our journey would be sure. We were invited to blow champagne on the *mesa* and to repeat Isabel's words so that no waterfall, mountain, or enchanted lagoon would hurt us, and so that there would be no evil rain from here to the Laguna Negra where we would leave our shadows. Then, Isabel asked us to raise *tabaco* through our nostrils. This was another offering to the *encantos*. I knew what I needed to offer:

I go offering my name and shadow, from this sacred mesa *I go raising myself, I go standing myself up, I [I repeated my full name] and Dan [I repeated his full name], so that I won't stumble. I go standing-up my marriage, my future children, my thesis, my work, with this sacrifice, with this penance. That I may be supported by this* mesa.

I was aware of the guidance of San Pedro in every ritual act. When I had drunk my two glassfuls at the beginning of the ceremony, I had prayed, "Come into my heart, San Pedro; open the road before me; open my eyes so that I might see; open my ears so that I might hear." It had felt like a communion, an opening, a surrender and acceptance, and now the words came clearly.

After the raising, we were invited to partake of the *mesa*, drinking or eating whatever "food" we wanted. We all chose from among the champagne, the cane alcohol, the *agua florida,* the *agua kananga,* the holy water, or the *tabaco,* according to our tastes and needs. As we shared in this new communion, Isabel told us to ask the *mesa* for the things that we most wanted. Then she told us to rise from our knees, to cleanse ourselves, and to begin walking around the entire corral as if we were walking through life. We rose and began to walk, each choosing his or her own path, each walking slowly and deliberately. We walked always forward, never turning back to our pasts. We chose each step and felt the footprints that were left beneath us as our feet engaged the dusty earth of the corral.

Isabel looked at the sky and said, "Our road is good; look how the sky is opening." As I looked into the overcast night, a single star broke through the clouds and shone on the *mesa*. The "eye of God," I remembered, and I thought to myself that things would go well. Afterward, Olinda told me that Isabel had conducted this *mesa* as though we were at the lagoon and that all that we had asked for, thanks to her power and to our own offerings, would be granted. The mood had been thoughtful and thankful. We were ready for our trip to the lagoons.

August 3, 1989, Huancabamba

We left for Huancabamba on July 25th, traveling for seventeen hours in the back of a flatbed truck. As we climbed aboard, we each claimed a place on the wooden planks that had been laid over gunny-sacks full of rice and sugar, salted fish, and other coastal products. We bumped along the Pan American highway from Chiclayo to almost Piura, and then at Chulucanas we turned east to follow the tributaries of the Piura River up toward the mountains. At a place called Loma Larga, we left the valley floor and began switchbacking up the face of the mountains into the heart of the mountains. Our ascent was steep—about 3,000 meters in forty kilometers driven—as we crawled at a snail's pace up the narrow ribbon of road, sandwiched between the sheer rock face and the ever-deepening abyss. Having arrived, finally, in Huancabamba the following morning, we rested for most of the day. Thanks to Isabel's ministrations, the trip had been uneventful, if more than a little tiring.

At about three o'clock the following morning, we climbed into the back of a four-wheel-drive pickup for the three-hour ascent to Salalá—the end of the road. There, after a quick breakfast, we rented mules and horses to take us to our final destination, the Laguna Negra. Spirits were high as we began our climb up the muddy trail. We had each brought our supply of offerings, and Isabel could be seen ahead of us on the trail, blowing these as we passed mountains, waterfalls, cave entrances, and swampy marshes—all *encantado*. Isabel had told me that some of these are known places where sorcerers come to make their pacts with the Devil and cohabit with him to seal the bargain. It was a dangerous trip, both physically and spiritually. Isabel made offerings to the mountains as we journeyed, so that they would not take revenge and pull us into their *encantos*. She admonished us to be strong and to have much faith in God. She assured us that her *mesa* would also sustain us on our voyage.

The day was chilly and it threatened to rain, but the offerings seemed to hold the clouds at bay. After about three-and-a-half hours, high above the tree line, we saw Laguna Negra in the distance before us. About a kilometer out we left our mounts and made our final approach to this spring-fed lake on foot. We were almost 4,000 meters above sea level.

Isabel laid a white cloth and began placing the objects from her *mesa* which she had brought on the journey so that when she stood behind the *mesa,* she looked out across the water. She then called us to begin the ceremony. She took the fragrant essences, the grape brandy, the perfumes, sugar, sweet lime, white flowers, white cornmeal, and the *agua florida* and *agua de kananga* which we had all brought for our offerings and began blowing these toward the lagoon, asking that it receive us, that it favor us, that it heal us.

After blowing all these essences, "in the name of all my patients," she threw rock-sugar in the direction of the water so that the spirit of the lagoon would become softer, sweeter, and more amenable. Then, she gave us *artes de levantar,* the seashells from the *mesa,* which she had brought so that we could raise *tabaco.* I was given one of the three first *artes* that Isabel, Olinda, and Miguel had used to make the original *compacto* with the *mesa.* We were told to raise the *tabaco* three times for each nostril. First, we were to raise the left, destroying and constructing new paths for living, strengthening our shadows. She invited us to continue with our own invocations as we raised the liquid, and I prayed:

> *Dear little lagoon, I give you my shadow. Support me and "back" me always, in the name of God and of this sacred* mesa. *Cure me of all illness, all pain, all fatigue. I turn over to you all my confusion and all my indecision. I ask for my future, for my marriage, for my work and health, that all will be successful. Strengthen my own sense of self and my strength of will so that I am sure of myself and so I can live, build, and create from my experiences with joy. I am part of you and you of me; I*

*am connected through you to the forces of creation in the Universe. From
this day forward, I will be joined to you, and because of you I will always
be a part of this sacred* mesa *and it of me. Straighten my entanglements,
so that the path is open and the connections are strong.*

As I raised the *tabaco* through my right nostril I continued praying,
calling on the lagoon to accept the shadows of those I loved who could not
make the trip but whose pictures or clothing I had brought. I named them
all, and said, "I give them to you that you will care for them." I called upon
the lagoon to bless the souls of those who guide Isabel and Olinda in their
work, and I asked blessings to come to them in their work.

As we were raising the third round of *tabaco,* Isabel told us, "The
lagoon wants us naked." The time was coming for our ritual bath to
cleanse and purify body and soul. We undressed quickly and stood shiv-
ering in the wind. It was biting cold, and little whitecaps had formed on
the surface of the lagoon. We raised the last of the *tabaco* "for the bath, so
the lagoon will cure us, washing away all our illness." As we prepared to
walk into the lagoon, Olinda reminded us that we had to have faith in the
cure and faith in the lagoon. If we faltered, it would strike us and make
us sick. We walked two-by-two into the water, and Isabel poured three
conch-shells of water over us. "In the name of the Father and of the Son
and of the Holy Ghost," she intoned. We had been baptized in the living
water. Then she told us to get into the water, to dive beneath the surface,
to drink the water, to take rocks from the bottom and wash ourselves,
throwing the rocks away from our bodies when we were finished.

After a long time, I got out and stood on the shore. The wind stung me
so coldly that the stinging became like an electrical current passing
through me, warming my whole body. I clasped my hands in gratitude and stood thanking the lagoon for having received me, for having
cleansed me, for having heard my prayers. After awhile, Isabel came out
of the water and changed the position of the staffs on her *mesa* so that they
now faced away from the lagoon. After thanking the lagoon and begging
its pardon for turning her back on it, she said, "I want to do my other
ceremony now, so my roads and my future bloom, beginning here, backed
by this lagoon. From here, I go flowering my future." She again took the

fragrant essences that she had used in her offerings, and she blew them toward her house, toward her children, toward her future. Afterward, she invited us to dress and to share a drink of cane alcohol with the *mesa*.

Then, we helped her bathe the *mesa* objects, purifying and cleansing them so that they would be strengthened for another year of work. We had each brought plastic bottles with us to take some water from the lagoon back home with us, and we filled these and busied ourselves with the task of preparing for the return journey. As we climbed onto our mounts and began the descent, Isabel took the lead.

She had ridden cautiously towards the lagoon that morning, admitting that she was afraid of horses and mules. But now, she took off at a trot across the high moors, fearless and energized by the morning's activities. I smiled as I began the ride back and the sun's rays seemed to carry joy to the center of my soul. I intuitively understood Isabel's hurried rush back across the treeless landscape. Like her, I also felt full of energy and anxious to meet the future. Now that I had sown my shadow in the lagoon, I felt the power of creation welling up within me. I remember turning around once to look at the lagoon, which was receding into the distance behind me. As I looked back, the hoofprints of my mount were clearly visible, leading away from the lagoon and down the mountain to my future.

6 ❖ Gender, Healing, and Experience

Just as gender is a constructed category that defines social, economic, and conceptual "realities," gender has also influenced healing philosophies and therapeutic strategies. In this final analytical chapter, I compare and contrast the ritual symbolism used by male and female shamans and suggest that, in the highly patriarchal society that is northern Peru, an emphasis on paradox, synthesis, and the affirmation of life experience provides a better model-of and model-for female shamanism than an emphasis on transcendence. In other words, shamanic symbolism, like religious symbolism, in general, is both polysemic and gendered. But since gender is far from a homogenous construct, in these pages I also explore the regional context of gender for the five women in my sample.

I present the following comparative discussion with a cautionary note. While Vicky's and Clorinda's rituals ostensibly parallel the documented rituals of male *curanderos,* more than either Flor's, Yolanda's, or Isabel's, my brief association with these two women makes any detailed analysis of their rituals difficult. It may very well be that the apparent dualisms of their *mesas* and the patterned sequence of their rituals mean different things to these women than they do for their male counterparts.[1] Only further research among female *curanderas* can corroborate or contest the assertions that follow.

Local Context in the Cultural Construction of Gender and Healing

Local contexts of gender emerge when individuals engage, accommodate, and reshape the constraints of cultural attitudes, social roles, and economic possibilities. These are not, of course, monolithic structures. Urban or rural lifeways, class status, even parenting styles, can and do   171 influence their construction. The five women in my sample, ranging in age from thirty to forty-four years of age in 1989, all grew up in different regions of Peru. While Vicky was raised on the coastal plain of Lambayeque, Yolanda, Flormira, Isabel, and Clorinda spent their early years in rural districts of the northern mountains of Cajamarca and Piura, respectively. At the time of my study, Yolanda and Clorinda still lived in the mountains, but Flormira and Isabel had long since migrated to the coast.

Isabel and Clorinda were born into relatively wealthy farming families. While Isabel's father abandoned his family, leaving her mother as both head of household and manager of the farm, Clorinda grew up with two parents to help spread the load of raising food and family. Flormira also experienced her share of farm living, but as an orphaned child she was shuffled from relative to relative in both town and country. Yolanda's father was a carpenter, and when she was four, he moved the family to the provincial capital so she could attend school. Most of her early years were spent living in town with both her parents and her siblings.

Of the five women, neither Flor nor Isabel had much to report about their fathers. But their fathers were important figures in Yolanda's, Clorinda's, and Vicky's accounts. In fact, Clorinda and Vicky both learned aspects of their profession from their *curandero* fathers. If Yolanda's father had been a *curandero* instead of a carpenter, perhaps he would have had more impact on her own development as a healer. As it was, however, Yolanda, like Flor and Isabel, found her own path to healing.

Educational experiences also varied considerably for these five women. Yolanda, Clorinda, and Vicky lived at home while they attended primary school. Isabel's primary school years were largely spent in residence with her teacher. After primary school, Yolanda stayed in San Miguel until she married. Clorinda stayed on the farm, but couldn't make the daily trek to the secondary school in nearby Huancabamba because of her illness. Vicky's parents sent her to boarding school to learn a trade. Isabel ran away from home and became a domestic servant on the coast, postponing the completion of her formal schooling for many years. Flor, being shuffled between relatives until her marriage at age fourteen, had very little schooling at all.

Among the five women, four had been married and had borne children. Flormira married at age fourteen and had two children before being widowed four years later. Yolanda married when she was sixteen and had four children before separating from her husband. Isabel married in her late twenties after almost fourteen years of service as a chambermaid. She had also separated from her husband, shortly after the birth of her second son. Vicky was married at the time of my study—and was near delivery of their fourth child. Only Clorinda had never married. Rather, she had assumed the role of head-of-household for both her mother and her younger siblings and combined her work as a healer with her obligations to run the farm.

When I knew them, the women's financial situations varied from almost destitute to comfortable. Flormira had been burdened with raising her grandchildren after her daughter's death and often was the sole caregiver for her son's children as well. He contributed to the family income sporadically, but Flormira was the main breadwinner, as well as being mother, father, and grandmother to her grandchildren. At the time of our interaction, she owned neither land nor home, had no garden but raised a few guinea pigs and chickens behind the kitchen, and worked for whatever wages she could manage in both the formal and informal economies.

In some ways, in spite of her economic destitution, Flormira mirrored Clorinda as an "independent" woman. They were both heads of household and neither answered to male authority. But whatever autonomy this social independence afforded Flormira was more than offset by her financial instability. Whereas Clorinda owned her home, had a lovely garden and several pigs and goats, and could rely on the labor of both her mother and younger siblings to help put food on the table, Flormira's grandchildren were too young to contribute much labor or money to the household's meager earnings.

In contrast to Clorinda and Flormira, Isabel, Yolanda, and Vicky all shared expenses, income, and head-of-household responsibilities with their current partners, both domestic and professional. Yolanda lived in a common-law relationship with José, Vicky lived with her husband Emilio, and Isabel lived with her childhood friend Olinda. Yolanda's husband José supplemented her income as a healer with sales of dry goods from the store which they also operated out of their home. Vicky's husband Emilio held a job in Ferreñafe. Isabel and Olinda had previously supplemented their household income with sales from a small store, but they now received enough income from healing to make this less necessary. All three domestic partners also worked as assistants to these *curanderas*. Yolanda, Vicky, and Isabel had all bought or built their homes, which all had, or would soon have, basic amenities like electricity and water (in Isabel's neighborhood, these improvements were anticipated for the near future).

Since the life histories of all five women are quite diverse, it seems fair to ask what, then, are the patterns that reflect or shape how gender has impacted their therapeutic strategies or their ritual cosmology? To find an answer, we must first determine if there are normative structures in northern Peru that define, construct, and constrain gender—and whether these transcend local contexts, that is, do these structures exist beyond, or in spite of, local realities.

The Impact of Patriarchy and Dependence on the Experience of Daño

Most scholars agree that Peru is a highly patriarchal society, as evidenced by the economic, social, and political position of women relative to their male counterparts. This is especially true in the cities. Here, wage labor has replaced subsistence farming; and the lack of available jobs tends to restrict women to informal economic activities (as street-sellers, domestic servants, piece-workers, or prostitutes), all of which are undervalued and undercompensated. Consequently, women in Peru, and especially urban women, are often forced to depend upon men for financial support to feed their families. Moreover, women in Peru are socialized to depend on men. The ideology of *machismo* permeates the legal, social, and emotional landscape. In Peru, a "good woman" is one who does not earn money, but rather stays at home caring for both her children and her husband. A "good woman" also does not give her husband any reason to doubt her emotional, or physical, devotion and fidelity. A "good man" is required to protect the women in his life—his mother, his sisters, and especially his wife—from the advances of other men who would threaten their capacity for goodness. But a complicating paradox in the ideology of *machismo* also requires men to demonstrate their virility by co-opting and possessing for themselves the female devotion which rightly belongs to another. Typical male expressions of intent reflect this: "I'm going to steal you away." "I'm going to conquer you." "I will rob your heart from you."[2] This paradox of chivalry cum conquest can be subtly engaged on many fronts. But in a society in which family honor and female chastity/fidelity are often synonymous, it is conquest, rejection, resistance, and accommodation in the sexual arena that is perhaps the most potent and the most feared manifestation of male *machismo*.

The ideology of *marianismo* as it is applied to Peruvian women also contains paradox and conflict at its core. *Marianismo* requires women to be both virginal and maternal, to be desirable and aloof, to take active responsibility for protecting family and personal honor against would-be invaders, and yet (within her own family) to accept male authority. The reader may recall many examples from chapter 1 that illustrate these ideas. Women in El Bosque, for example, were expected to take care of their families, even though they had little access to traditional female resources like garden plots and domestic animals. Yet they were criticized for working outside the household. Moreover, they were expected to remain loyal to their husbands even while enduring physical and emotional abuse. When Roberta complained about her husband's beatings, her female neighbors supposed that she was to blame. And when Daniela acquiesced to her boyfriend's demands for sex, her loose behavior gave him cause to deny paternity of her unborn child. To explain why the woman is more often blamed than the man when illicit liaisons occur, Isabel once told me, "Man proposes, but it is the woman who decides." In other words, the female ideology of *marianismo* holds women responsible for maintaining chastity, fidelity, purity, and loyalty to family, and this despite the conflicting requisites of *machismo*. The result is a double-bind for women: a woman's claim to be acting in accordance with male demands and to being victimized by male authority does not absolve her of responsibility for her "unwomanly" behavior. Thus, the two ideologies, *machismo* and *marianismo*, both conspire to keep women dependent on men—economically, socially, and emotionally. And in so doing, they define and overdetermine appropriate behavior for women in ways that limit options and often conflict with the imperatives of economic and emotional survival.

The experience of sorcery, as illustrated in the stories told by the women in El Bosque, often reflects these conflicts. Strangers, or members of distinct ethnic or social classes, do not appear as the aggressors in accusations of *daño*. Rather, aggressors are usually those whose actions threaten personal worth, the ability to feed one's family, or the harmony and stability of social relationships. Examples from El Bosque include the "other woman" who charmed Roberta's husband away from her by contracting with a sorcerer to turn Roberta into an alcoholic and a bad mother. Then there was Rigoberta's deadbeat husband, who not only abandoned her but later returned to lay claim, as head of the family, to all the wealth she had accumulated in his absence. And in Violeta's story, presented in chapter 4, it is her husband's "cousin" who is blamed for the stillbirth of her child, the deaths of her farm animals, and the economic, physical, and emotional symptoms that drove a wedge between Violeta and her husband.

Where intimate relationships are combined with overdetermined social roles, conditions of economic uncertainty, structured gender inequalities, and dependence, it can be no surprise that a belief in sorcery "gives voice to the desperation of persons who sense that their trust has been abused, that the face of a friend or lover may disguise betrayal" (Joralemon and Sharon 1993, 256). While women are not the only victims of sorcery in northern Peru, it is also not surprising that women are especially vulnerable in such an environment of suspicion and mistrust.[3]

Life Histories, Love-Magic, and Gender

Love-magic—the artificial manipulation of human sentiment—is a type of sorcery that illustrates the relationship among the etiology of illness, the constraining ideologies of *machismo* and *marianismo,* and the precarious nature of relations of dependence. This is not a new phenomenon. Love-magic has been used as a sorcery technique since at least the early colonial period, when Spanish and Catholic ideologies and institutions, like *machismo* and *marianismo,* first exacerbated the gender asymmetry of the Inca state (Silverblatt 1978, 1980, 1987).[4] Like other forms of *daño,* love-magic is directed toward a specific victim because of envy, jealousy, or revenge. Intended to manipulate or dominate another's will, love-magic is known by many terms, including the *amarrada*, the binding-up, *pisada*, the stepping-upon or mounting, and the *atada*, the tying-up. Like other forms of *daño*, the effects of love-magic occur because the victim's shadow-soul has been called away from the body and commended to another. In this instance, instead of commending the soul to an *encanto* or an *ánima*, the soul is turned over to the perpetrator so the victim will feel irresistibly drawn toward him or her. The final step of this unnatural binding of two souls occurs when the victim absorbs the prepared potion or powder, either directly (by ingestion) or indirectly (through airborne contagion). Drinking menstrual blood that has been surreptitiously mixed in hot chocolate, or donning underpants that have been worked with the hex are two common examples. Alternatively, sympathetic magic may be employed, as when the intended's photograph is placed in the perpetrator's shoe and the *pisada* occurs with every footstep taken.

Neither men nor women are excluded from the negative effects of love-magic. This is particularly true with the manipulation or domination of volition, or will to choose, one's partner, although the results of usurpation do affect male and female victims differently. For male victims, love-magic provides a culturally acceptable explanation for impotence, for an absence of philandering, and for the appearance of subjugation to the will of a dominant female. For the spouses of male victims, love-magic (when perpetrated by the "other woman") gives a culturally acceptable way of justifying a husband's extramarital affairs, as well as his abandonment of the social and financial obligations that come with his role as protector and provider. For female victims, love-magic provides a way to explain infidelity or an unnatural interest in sex, or to justify other "unwomanly" behaviors like inattention to domestic duties, heavy drinking, or lack of caregiving. In short, for male victims, love-magic can justify emasculating, or non-*macho,* behaviors. For female victims, love-magic can justify sexual and other self-serving interests that may be unbecoming to the Marianist image of woman as Virgin and as Mother. For both men and women, love-magic provides a rationale for untoward behavior that does not blame. But in replacing blame and personal accountability by pointing the finger at another, love-magic also creates victims rather than emphasizing agency and the bolstering of self. While love-magic has been used to express resistance to political dominance, social dependence, and over-determined ideologies, because of its victimizing logic, love-magic does 178 not empower. At best, being the victim of love-magic provides a rationale for transition; it then becomes a way station on the path to empowerment, rather than empowerment itself.

To illustrate, recall that both Yolanda and Isabel attributed their mar-riages to love-magic. These women also started on their paths to becom-ing shamans after separating from their husbands. For Yolanda, the perpetrators were her ex-husband's parents. When she expressed no in-terest in the marriage they had arranged for her, they sought out a sorcerer to change her mind. She did, and lived with her husband long enough to have four children, although she didn't love him. Her entry into healing coincided with her awareness that she had been victimized by his actions and by her subsequent decision to leave this man. But her training as a healer was not complete until she renounced her status as a victim and reclaimed responsibility for her actions—until she underwent a spiritual rehabilitation and became morally straight. Although she entered into an-other relationship after she had completed this penance, and after she had begun practicing as a *curandera,* she described her relationship with José as one based on spiritual service to God rather than romance.

For Isabel, the perpetrator of her misfortune was the man who would become her husband rather than his family. Jealous of her long-term ro-mance with a medical student, who not only loved her but whose future profession also assured her of more comforts than any she had previously known, Isabel's perpetrator turned to a sorcerer to charm her into elop-ing with him. Even though he mistreated her emotionally, physically, and financially, she endured her suffering long enough to have two chil-dren. Like Yolanda, Isabel's entry into healing also coincided with her declaration of independence from her husband. Like Yolanda, she found another spiritual partner with whom to share domestic chores and family finances. And like Yolanda, she often insisted that healing could not occur until one accepted personal responsibility for one's actions. As Isabel lec-tured one patient, "No one is the victim of anyone else."

Flormira also reported having suffered the effects of love-magic. In her case, the perpetrator was not her husband, whom she loved very much and who lived up to his responsibilities to both provide for and protect her. In this case, the perpetrator was the "other woman," whose favors Flormira's husband had rejected. Because of her jealousy of Flor's good fortune, this woman had contracted a sorcerer to have Flor's husband killed. It was only after his death that Flormira's suffering began. But it wasn't until her daughter had also been "robbed" from her, persuaded to elope at the young age of thirteen, that Flor began to practice the vocation God had given to her as a young child.

In contrast to Yolanda, Isabel, and Flor, neither Clorinda nor Vicky reported having suffered the effects of love-magic. Could the first three women's shared experience serve as a kind of pointer to gender stresses that neither Clorinda nor Vicky faced? Clorinda's position as an accomplished, unmarried, *curandera* holding both property and a position of authority in her natal family had allowed her to acquire economic and social power that transcended the constraints of gender. Vicky's position as a *curandera* whose husband revered her power and accepted her financial contributions to the family gave her a certain economic autonomy and social power despite her married status. By contrast, the experiences of Yolanda, Isabel, and Flormira had all diverged from the normative structure of male/female relationships. They had been economically and emotionally dependent on their husbands, as "good women" should be. But their husbands had not provided the financial and/or emotional support expected of them. In addition, for whatever reasons, these women had felt the stresses of their dependence (and the constraints of a patriarchal system which overdetermines women's roles) more acutely than had Vicky or Clorinda.

By comparing the experiences of Yolanda, Isabel, and Flor with those of Clorinda and Vicky, we see that gender is a constructed category that both defines and reflects social, economic, and conceptual realities. Therefore, it is not unreasonable to posit that engendered realities also influence constructions of illness and models for healing. In the case of these five women, there are striking similarities and differences in healing philosophies between the three who suffered from love-magic and the two who did not. I believe this shared experience of love-magic can be interpreted as an expression of frustration in the face of heteronomous and overdetermined social roles. For Isabel, Yolanda, and Flor—who felt this

frustration most acutely—the healing philosophies and therapeutic strategies they advocate share an important feature. They all associate spiritual
power with accepting and revaluing life in this world, or as one feminist
scholar recently put it, with "coming into [a] relationship with reality"
(Ochs 1983, 10).

Perhaps another case history of *daño* can best illustrate these ideas. José
and his wife Rosa had come to see Isabel in early May 1989 because of
José's headaches. He had suffered on-and-off for years, had been to various
doctors (without relief), and at thirty had given up hope of a cure. Now,
he had come to Isabel for a diagnosis, and she saw in the tarot cards that
sorcery was to blame: he needed a *mesa*. Isabel advised me that she told
José that he should bring a woolen hat to the *mesa*. She also explained that
although it was not apparent until the night of the *mesa*, the sorcery had
precipitated economic and emotional problems for José, in addition to the
headaches. A bright child, his family had envisioned that he would attend
college and study a profession. But something had happened when he
entered adolescence. During the next several years, he had shown little
interest in study and had dropped out of high school to work in a sugar
mill. He had met and married Rosa, and they had had a couple of children.
But now there were tensions in the marriage. She suspected he was having
an affair. He was tired of her complaints about his mother and sisters.

During the ritual, Isabel saw the cause of his affliction. When he was
seven years old, she said, he had lost a woolen hat. "Where did it happen,"
she asked? He replied that he remembered losing a hat one day when he
carried lunch to his father in the field. Someone—Isabel didn't say who—
had a grievance against his father and had seized upon the hat as an
opportunity to make the family suffer. Taking the hat to a sorcerer, his soul
had been called, manipulated, and commended to an *encanto*. The hat had
been stuck through with two hundred pins to cause the headaches. José
had been rendered indecisive by this act. In addition to the headaches,
José found it difficult to concentrate, to think, and to remember. Because
his spirit had been commended to the *encanto* of a *sitán,* an intermittent
waterfall, the headaches and the other symptoms were intermittent. At
times, José would be motivated, assertive, and anxious to succeed. But
then, when things got tough, he would become depressed and lose interest. He could never seem to get ahead. Instead of pursuing a profession,

and despite his intelligence and the aspirations of his parents, José still worked as a common laborer. His family was disappointed in him. He was disappointed in himself.

José asserted that Isabel's diagnosis was correct. Then, Isabel asked that he be cleansed by four volunteers. I stepped forward, along with his wife Rosa and two others. As we began rubbing him with the staff, Isabel said,

> *"They are cleansing you . . . so you will repent of all that was . . . and so destroy all that you were, the victim of a daño. . . . [They are cleansing you] so that your spirit is purified, so that you are closer to God, and so that the will of God goes within you, and within your thoughts . . . and you will thus be made so strong that when they try to harm you they cannot. Your spirit will not be called away, because the spirit of God will fill you."*

After this, Isabel instructed José to stamp on the hat he had brought with him and to say:

> *For more than thirty years [sic] I have been suffering these pains. Now, in this moment, all is destroyed. They barred my path, my future, in this hat. But now I destroy all those thoughts, all those bad ideas. . . . All my life I have lived in anger because of all the things I never did. But now I will triumph. Thanks be to God, all my problems are in the past. Now I am being cured.*

Now Isabel told everyone at the *mesa* to run and stamp on the hat and to say:

> *That which was, was. It is in the past. Now I will make something of my life. . . . I go constructing my future. . . . Out, out, all evil, all pins. . . . They did not want me to triumph, to have my own thoughts. . . . But they will not win.*[5]

Then Isabel turned to José and said: "Now go and make something of your life. You're still young; study for a career."

Later in the same *mesa*, Isabel had directed her attention toward José's wife Rosa: "There's something else here. . . . Who can change it, the wife, the sons, or who? Is your mother-in-law a bitch? Don't lie." At first, Rosa had denied the tension in her relationship with José's mother, but Isabel pressed and Rosa recanted. With José's encouragement, Rosa admitted that there had been problems getting along with José's mother and his sisters. She and José had often fought about where his allegiance lay. Then Isabel said,

182

> *Here, let's be clear; nobody is the victim of anybody else. . . . She brought him up to be served, and you, as his wife, can't change that. Do you understand? He may be your husband, but he's his mother's son. She may be a bitch; she may be the worst person in the world, but she is still a mother. The same with your sisters-in-law. They are as they are, but they are still the children of a home. And that is to be respected. . . . You were born to be his wife. Love him, respect him, because you won't find another like him. . . . Do you understand what I'm telling you? . . . You are mistress of the household, you are mistress of your husband, but don't abuse [that role.] Never abuse it. He put on the shirt, but not the ankle-length overcoat.[6] He does as he wishes. As a son. As a brother. And that is as it should be. Whatever was doesn't matter. It is what will be that matters, . . . and the two of you must tighten your belts [and accept your roles.] All right? Okay, you're both cured.*

In this lecture to her patients, Isabel had placed the responsibility for their misfortune squarely on their shoulders. José could choose to overcome the obstacles in his life by relinquishing the position of the victim. Rosa needed to come to terms with her role as good wife and mother, even though this meant resigning herself to a double-standard that gives her husband privileges and freedoms she doesn't have.

Women and Daño in Northern Peru

Isabel's acknowledgment of the double-standard for men's and women's roles in Peruvian society is shared by the male healers of Joralemon and Sharon's sample. But her suggestion that women should accept and resign

themselves to the structural inequalities of an inherently *machista* society
is problematic. It can be argued that this attitude masquerades accommodation as pragmatic action, mystifying rather than clarifying relations of
oppression. Indeed, Joralemon and Sharon argue that it is this ideology of
machismo and of oppression that puts women "in harm's way," and that
the healing rituals of *curanderos* empower women by *challenging* that ideology. They do this by "providing a hidden transcript of resistance," in
which patriarchy is critiqued. For, although the healer may tacitly rein-
force oppressive stereotypes and double-standards, Jorelemon and Sharon
argue that "repeated instances were found in which the *curandero* critiqued, sometimes with severe language, the behavior of men that caused
their spouses/mates to suffer" (1993, 265). But Joralemon and Sharon
also caution,

> In the Peruvian case, it is important not to overstate the redressive power
> gained by women through the agency of curanderos. Many of the cases
> we documented were inconclusive; the ongoing suffering they indicate is
> evidence that women gain moral leverage, not control, by the intervention
> of a curandero. Still, in a social system that only minimally constrains the
> actions of men in regard to women, anything that provides pressure for
> moral accountability is a strategic resource. (1993, 268)

In José's case there is no challenge to male patriarchy. Neither is there
an inversion or transcendence of prescribed social roles. Rather, there is
an admonishment to Rosa to be a good wife and a good daughter-in-law.
Isabel counsels her to live within the parameters of her expected social
role. This strategy does not negate patriarchal authority. But it does insist
that this authority is conditional. If Rosa fulfills the social mandates required of her, the implication is that neither her husband nor her mother-
in-law will have reason to abuse their power (nor will their abuse be
tolerated by others). This approach provides for resistance, not to the first
principles of patriarchy, but to the manner in which authority is applied.[7]
It also replaces futility and victimhood with a sense of agency.

In societies like Peru's, where gender inequality is structured and sys-
temic, the awakening of agency requires a prior recognition and accep-

tance of "what is" (Cooey 1990, 11; Wendell, 1990, 15; Ulanov 1981, 151–73). This is not the same as justifying or condoning the circumstances of oppression. Rather, it is a way for women to reclaim identity, rather than to be defined by external forces (Wendell 1990, 15; Ulanov 1981, 165).

184

This paradox of agency/submission is expressed in spiritual terms by Isabel, Yolanda and Flor. For these three *curanderas,* the assertion of agency and control over life circumstances requires submission to "God's will" and a letting go of control. For all three women, the process of coming closer to God is synonymous with the decision to live within the parameters of socially defined behavior that promotes both family and community survival. It is this letting go that awakens and harnesses power. As Isabel explained it, sorcery—the ability to call, capture, and imprison one's soul—can only occur if one is empty of the spirit of God. It is then that one's spirit can be called away from the body and captured by an *encanto.* It is also then, when one is "empty," that one is a victim. But "when one accepts God's will, the will of God will inhabit your empty soul and you will be so strong that no harm can touch you."

Isabel calls this paradox of acceptance and agency, "living in the Grace of God rather than in *desgracia.*" According to Isabel, *desgracia* is a rejection of life, of being, and of the experience of living (which includes suffering as well as joy). Not only is *desgracia* misery and disdain, it also describes a life outside God's Grace, a life "apart."

Shamanic Symbols, Religious Experience, and Gender

In a recent article summarizing the impact of gender on the experience and representation of religious symbols, Carolyn Bynum concludes:

Men and women of a single tradition—when working with the same symbols and myths, writing in the same genre, and living in the same religious or professional circumstances—display certain consistent male/female differences in using symbols. Women's symbols and myths tend to build from social and biological experiences; men's symbols and myths tend to invert them. Women's mode of using symbols seems given

*to the muting of opposition, whether through paradox or through
synthesis; men's mode seems characterized by emphasis on opposition,
contradiction, inversion, and conversion. Women's myths and rituals tend
to explore a state of being; men's tend to build elaborate and discrete
stages between self and other. (1986, 13)*

It has long been argued that shamanism and organized religion are
closely related phenomena. Both are belief systems that mediate with
unseen worlds on behalf of human communities. Both fill psychological
needs for their practitioners and the communities they serve by giving
form and explanation to the inchoate: "Why has misfortune befallen me/
us? What must I/we do to allay misfortune and restore harmony? What
wonders/terrors lie beyond the edge of my/our experience, and how can
I/we be prepared for the unknown?" These are the questions for which
both the priest and the shaman must provide answers. Additionally, both
organized religion and shamanism provide guidelines for correct behavior as well as negotiating the gulf between individual desires and social
needs. These similarities suggest a question: might there be a correlation
between gender difference in the use of religious symbols and gender differences in shamanic philosophy and therapeutic strategy? Indeed, this
would seem to be the case with Yolanda, Isabel, and Flormira. All three
women emphasized the paradox of agency and submission rather than
transcendence of oppositions. It is true that all three also shared a dichotomous understanding of "this" world and the "other" world—of human
and spirit domains, and of the juxtapositions of Godly/moral/up/fragrant
qualities versus Demonic/amoral/down/putrid qualities (and in Yolanda's
case, the additional qualities of right versus left). Still, the emphasis was
not on mastery or transcendence of these categories. Rather, for these
three *curanderas* at least, these oppositional dualisms were juxtaposed to
illustrate their differences and to persuade patients to make a choice.

In other words, these women did not heal "on behalf of their patients,"
but insisted that patients actively participate in their own cures and take
responsibility for the causes of their suffering. Instead of treating their
clients as passive victims, dependent upon the shaman's power to transform their suffering, these women emphasized the agency of the sufferer,

both in facilitating and overcoming their own illnesses. They emphasized that healing does not come through the vanquishing by the healer of an unseen enemy, but rather that healing is only achieved through acceptance of life circumstances and through a kind of "getting right" with the forces of the universe. The healer's role is only to guide the patient to a conscious understanding of this task. For Isabel, particularly, "experience" plays a key role in this awakening.

During my first *mesa* with Isabel, she told me that I was empty inside, that I had spent too many years trying to "find myself" by looking outward for direction and validation. Because of my outward-looking orientation, I had "experienced" very little. Since I had allowed my life to be defined by others rather than choosing my own path, I had neither self— *yo personal*—nor volition or intent—*decisión propia*. Like so many of the Peruvians she had cured through the years, I too had allowed my sense of purpose and my worth to be defined by my fears about what others would think or say, rather than what I knew to be important.[8] I had, to use one of her favorite analogies, been "walking through life without leaving any footprints." Unless I began to live by a different set of rules—rules in which I became an active participant in the construction of who I was, rather than a victim of someone else's expectations and definitions—at the end of my life I would look back and see that I had never "made a difference." In looking back, I would find that I had neither been transformed by my life experiences, nor would I have had any impact on those around me. By relinquishing agency, in letting my worth be defined by what others had thought of my actions, I would find my life had not "been worth the effort," to use another of Isabel's favorite phrases.

A Feminine Approach to the Divine

These ideas find resonance in twentieth-century feminist theology and feminist spirituality.[9] Whatever the origins or manifestations of gender difference,[10] feminist scholars suggest that women are unlikely to find themselves or their life experiences reflected in traditional Judeo-Christian definitions of the divine. Rather, in Judeo-Christian philosophies seekers of the divine will find an emphasis on nonphysicality, transcendence of the natural or physical world, even a renunciation of the physical world. As Ochs summarizes it,

> *God's own non-physicality makes the physical suspect, if not absolutely*
> *evil. . . . The world itself, so material, so physical, and so sexual, is*
> *viewed as unreal and as a potential trap for the would-be seeker of God.*
> *To achieve enlightenment . . . one must be otherworldly [and] life ceases to*
> *be intrinsically valuable (1983, 21).*

As a kind of rejection of "what is," this approach to spirituality renounces and turns away from the realities of this world. This is quite the opposite of what Isabel, Yolanda, and Flor advocate, for it proposes escape rather than acceptance. In Isabel's words, this is the path of *desgracia*.

Furthermore, for women living under patriarchy where their economic possibilities, social roles, and even self-definitions are constructed and limited by men, transcendence is simply not an option. As Alcoff puts it,

> *Woman's nature has overdetermined her behavior, the limits of her*
> *intellectual endeavors, and the inevitabilities of her emotional journey*
> *through life. . . . [Thus] the place of the free-willed subject who can*
> *transcend nature's mandates [and approach the divine] is reserved*
> *exclusively for men. (1994, 96–97)*

The response of feminist scholars to this dilemma has been varied. On the one hand, cultural feminists (represented by writers such as Mary Daly and Adrienne Rich) have reappropriated (and revalued) the denigrated side of these structural dualisms (e.g., nature/culture, physical/spiritual, object/subject, irrational/rational) in order to illuminate the "miracle and paradox of the female body" (Alcoff 1994, 99). On the other hand, poststructural feminists have attempted to problematize both the category and the concept of woman.

Scholars of feminist spirituality have taken similarly divergent paths (Davaney 1987). Ironically, whether reinvigorating the feminine side of theological dualisms, or deconstructing and contextualizing feminist spirituality, both camps have emphasized the embodied (rather than the nonphysical), lived (rather than otherworldly), relational (rather than solitary, competitive, or adversarial), processual (rather than goal-oriented), and immanent (rather than transcendent) aspects of divinity, albeit for

188   different reasons. A hallmark of both approaches has been an insistence that feminist spirituality is the process of coming into a relationship with lived reality and embracing, rather than defying, the actual experience of living in this world.

As a result of this relational emphasis, dialectical oppositions are commonly challenged by feminist scholars. Not surprisingly, such scholars warn against interpreting feminist spirituality as the flip-side of male spirituality (which simply inverts existing categories rather than claiming the power to construct something new). Thus, traditional theological dualisms like transcendence and immanence come under close scrutiny. As Ruether insists,

> *We [feminist theologians] reject both the image of nature or matter as*
> *static immanence and the concept of spirit as rootless or anti-natural,*
> *originating in another world beyond the cosmos. . . . We also reject the*
> *false conflation of nature or created being with the ontological foundations*
> *of the existing oppressive social order. Feminist theology affirms a vision*
> *of exodus, of liberation and new being, but emphasizes that these must be*
> *rooted in the foundations of being and body, rather than as an antithesis*
> *of nature and spirit. (1987, 67)*

When applied to a discussion of gender difference in shamanism, instead of focusing attention upon transcendence as the key legitimizing feature of the journey, or on shamanic power as the ability to go "beyond the boundaries of himself" (Sharon 1978, 49) this vision emphasizes something that Houston and Stuart call coessence (1989). Coessence, in contrast to both transcendence and immanence, locates shamanic power and the spiritual energy upon which shamans draw neither within nor without the boundaries of this world. Instead, coessence implies that this power is shared. In other words, the life essence which animates all living things flows between worlds. When the shaman taps into this source of power, she is not transcending dichotomies and she is not healing "on behalf of" her patients. Instead, she is facilitating a reestablishment of the energy flow between spirit and matter, between individual and group, and between shaman and patient. Shamanic power and the shamanic voyage is, thus, inherently relational.

Immanence, Coessence, and Umbilical Cords: The Flow of Life

One metaphor (although certainly not the only one) for understanding the difference between coessence and either immanence or transcendence as these relate to spiritual journeys can be found in an analysis of motherhood. As one scholar of feminist theology summarizes it,

> *The [spiritual] insights that occur naturally in the course of mothering [include], the need to give oneself over completely, for a time, to the physical and spiritual care of the infant; the need to know by empathetic understanding; the need to endure some discipline; the easy acceptance of the natural development through error to correctness; the necessity to love the child not as a possession but as belonging to itself; and, perhaps the most difficult insight of all, the necessity of letting go. (Ochs 1983, 32)*

According to Ochs's reinterpretation of Evelyn Underhill's classic discussion of mysticism and the spiritual journey toward enlightenment (1961), the journey, which also draws on the analogy of motherhood, is a five-step process that requires and instills (1) self-abnegation, (2) development of empathy for another, (3) discipline, (4) forgiveness and the acceptance of imperfection and limitations, both externally and internally imposed, and (5) the ability to let go. Instead of the classical shamanic journey that transcends the mundane, masters the challenges of a supernatural world, and then returns to impart this wisdom, the coessent model of shamanic power/spiritual empowerment requires the shaman to undergo the following steps: (1) awakening/acceptance; (2) purgation/ penance; (3) illumination/awakening; (4) extended commitment and endurance of the trials of life, and (5) the formation of a new self that is defined by relationship.

The personal journeys of Yolanda, Flor, and Isabel have all been informed by these five steps. As we shall see, these steps are also at the core of the healing philosophies the five women share with their patients. Perhaps their own experiences as mothers have informed their philoso-

phies. Certainly, the emphasis on experience, agency, and the validation of women's roles that this model encourages has positive implications for feminine spirituality and empowerment.

For Isabel, the relational emphasis on spirituality, the shared life force, and the metaphor of mothering are made explicit. She used the analogy of an umbilical cord to describe both her shamanic journey and the process of healing her patients go through. Intensely physical and embodied, this relationship is of this world. It is a nexus of "being." Perhaps the purest metaphor of coessence, the umbilical cord allows for a transfer of energy, blood, and life between two beings which are connected yet separate, and with two different pasts, futures, and life trajectories.

Each of Isabel's *mesa* objects contains spirit power, which is derived from their connection to the charmed or enchanted places of their origin. At the end of each *mesa* ceremony, this energy leaves the *mesa* objects and returns to rest in what Isabel refers to as the *mama,* or womb, of the mountain, spring, or other *encanto* where they originated. When reactivated, this power surges back into the *mesa* objects along an umbilical cord-like conduit that exists between worlds. Similarly, when a victim's spirit is captured and bound to an *encanto,* it too travels along this conduit. Because one end of the conduit is tied to the *encanto* while the other end remains connected to the victim's body, the victim's soul can be called away from his/her body at will by the *encanto,* and the natural flow of the life force between the two worlds is interrupted. In her cures, Isabel calls the victim's soul back into his body along this conduit. But the cure is not complete until she is able to sever the cord from the interfering *encanto* and reattach it to an *encanto* that has not been manipulated by a sorcerer so as to interrupt the flow of energy between worlds.

The reader will recall that as Violeta stood before Isabel at the *mesa,* Isabel chided her for being weak, saying that she needed Violeta's force of will so that she could see her shadow and see the way the *daño* had been effected. As long as Violeta's shadow was not in her body, but at the other end of the umbilical cord-like conduit, Isabel could not ascertain the things she needed to know in order to help Violeta. Isabel called upon Violeta to be strong, to have the strength to will her shadow to come back along this conduit.

As Isabel later explained, she needed Violeta's spirit in her body so she could send it back in time and space to the *mesa* of the sorcerer who had called, captured, commended, and tied it to the *encanto*. As Violeta's spirit traveled back along the conduit, Isabel could follow it to discover the agent(s), instruments, and mechanisms by which the *daño* had been effected. To protect Violeta while she sent her spirit back along this conduit through time and space, Isabel utilized the power contained within her *mesa* artifacts. Thus, when Violeta's spirit traveled back in time and place to the *mesa* of the sorcerer who had effected the harm, her spirit was accompanied by the power of the staff from Isabel's *mesa*, which Isabel had given to her.

Once she had discovered the sorcerer who had captured Violeta's spirit, and once she had discovered the specific *encanto* or *ánima* to which it had been bound, Isabel called upon the power of her *encantos*—the spirit-essences from the places where her own spirit has been "tied"—as well as the power of her *mesa* objects to cut the ties that afflicted Violeta. When these had been severed, Violeta's spirit could no longer be called away at will. Her energy, volition, and the vital essence which animates her being were returned to her own control. Even so, she remained in a weakened state because of the forced and intermittent separation of body and spirit, so Isabel had provided her with "secrets," which would fortify and protect her against future harm. By so doing, Isabel forged new ties between Violeta and the spirit-powers of nature, ties which would protect Violeta should an offending sorcerer try to call her spirit away at some time in the future.

This focus on coessence presupposes an intimate, symbiotic relationship between the parallel human and spirit worlds. To Isabel's way of thinking, the umbilical-like connection between individuals and the spirit world are never completely severed; neither are they available only to the shaman. Rather, these pathways are conduits which nourish and sustain all living things, whether that thing is an object on Isabel's *mesa,* an *encanto* with whom one has a special pact, or any person during sleep.[11] The conduits are the paths the spirits take to return to the source

192   of life, to rest and regenerate so that they (and we) may be animated and refreshed with each new day.

While Isabel is the only healer I met who uses an umbilical-cord model to express the coessent relationships, both Yolanda and Flor also emphasize the shared vitality that exists between healer and patient, healer and spirit-force, patient and spirit-force, and healer and *mesa,* all of which are certainly implied by the concept of coessence. One reason Rolando's symptoms intensified on Tuesday and Friday nights, according to Yolanda, was because these were the very nights that the sorcerer responsible for Rolando's *daño* laid his *mesa* and renewed his evil work. During these twice-weekly sessions, the sorcerer was calling upon the *encanto* to draw Rolando's spirit away from his body again and again. Similarly, an emphasis on untying, unraveling, and unwinding to straighten and reopen the coessent conduits between worlds is an especially prominent feature of Yolanda's ceremonies.

This idea of embodied physicality and coessent energy underlies much of Andean cosmology, social and political organization, and ideology as well. As Allen describes it, it is this exchange of *sami*—the animating essence of life—between distinguishable but complementary categories that keeps the world alive. The *reciprocal* exchange of *sami,* between individuals, couples, communities, and the "enlivened" natural world is described as the "pumping mechanism at the heart of the Andeans' circulatory cosmos" (1988, 208; see also Bastien 1985). Whether the exchange is hostile or friendly, *sami* provides the mechanism for moving the flow of life. The circulation of *sami* underlies all cultural activities, from religious ritual, to economics, to politics. In this world view, all existing things—people, llamas, mountains, potato fields, houses, whatever—are imbued with life. *Sami* can be transmitted from one living thing to another. The flow of *sami* is dependent upon some material medium, which might include coca leaves, corn beer, or cane alcohol, all of which are ritually exchanged and offered in sacrifice. There are no disembodied essences in the Andean universe (1988, 207).

One advantage in this reconfiguration of the shamanic voyage as coessent rather than transcendent is that it revalidates the overdetermined nature of women's social roles, as these have been constructed in Peruvian society. Instead of removing the shaman's power from the present world, it locates it somewhere between worlds, between healer and patient, between patient and community. Like Ruether's discussion of the feminist reinterpretation of the Catholic sacrament of communion, the power to heal comes, not through transcendence, but "by celebrating our ordinary life." (1993, 202).

Transforming the Victim: Healing and Agency in Shamanic Ritual

In the preceding pages, I have suggested that, just as gender is a constructed category that defines social, economic, and conceptual realities, gender also influences constructions of illness and models for healing. The classical shamanic journey—and the spiritual journey of the initiate that it reflects—is one example of such a model which is neither gender-neutral nor value free. Specifically, in classic shamanism the emphasis on transcendence and mastery—on the limitations of natural or physical existence as well as the ascription of active/passive roles to healer and patient, respectively—reveals a distinctly male bias.

In northern Peru, as in many patriarchal societies where women's identities and social roles are overdetermined and heteronomous,[12] transcendence, resolution or dominance of theological dualisms, and the pitting of "self" against "other" may be a path to empowerment and spiritual mastery for male shamans, but this path does not lead to the same ends for women. Thus, female shamans—and especially those who most acutely feel the constraints of overdetermined gender roles—will adopt a different approach to healing. For Yolanda, Isabel, and Flormira, this alternative approach emphasizes coessence rather than transcendence, and grounds spiritual power in the realities of this world. It utilizes metaphors that reflect and revalue their roles as mothers, wives, sisters, and daughters—metaphors that emphasize lived experience, the participation and the building of community, and the successful integration of individual desires with the needs of children, husbands, and brothers. It associates spiritual power with accepting and revaluing life in this world, even while accepting the constraints of overdetermined gender roles and structured social inequality.

Ochs's Five-Part "Mothering" Model and Female Healing

The messages of acceptance, penance, illumination, determination and coessent union imparted by Isabel, Yolanda, and Flormira empower their patients by awakening both the awareness and possibility of agency. In this regard, Och's five-part relational model of "mothering" illustrates that an analysis of gender differences in healing can provide a useful window for examining local contexts of gender and illness. But more importantly, it can provide insight into how patterns of resistance and accommodation are used to creatively engage the structured inequalities of patriarchal societies. Finally, it can suggest how taking experience seriously, through an emphasis on engaged participation, personal responsibility, and agency rather than victimhood, can positively impact relations with the social and the natural world.

Acceptance and Awareness

In Ochs's[13] reconfiguration of the shamanic or mystic journey to fit the metaphor of mothering, she uses the term "awakening" to define the first of five stages. For the mother, this awakening comes with the birth of a child and the realization that one must now redefine oneself in terms of another life rather than stubbornly refusing to accommodate such a momentous change in identity. As she put it, the first imperative in awakening a feminine spirituality is that one must "come into a relationship with reality" (1983, 10). Similarly, Yolanda, Flormira, and Isabel all emphasize the need for "acceptance" as a first step to empowerment and healing. Flormira described this acceptance in terms of her willingness to accept God's will for her life. As she told me, God tests this acceptance and this faith every day by bringing her poverty instead of riches: "When I have wanted to change things [He] says no. Be happy with what I give you. Don't want what others have. Be happy with what I give you. I am God." Flor sees the precarious condition of her poverty as evidence of her faith and her acceptance. She relies on God to feed her family. "I ask God and He helps me. I don't have anything and I say, 'God, God, what will I do? With what will I feed these innocent children? And then their bread appears." Similarly, every patient who approaches her must write a letter like the one I wrote, beseeching God to give permission for the cure. And the letters always end with the phrase, "I give you thanks and I will accept the decision that you give your servant, doña Flor."

Likewise, during my first *mesa* experience with Isabel, and on repeated occasions after that, she told me that I had to learn "that what is red is red and what is green is green" instead of trying to force my own vision on the world around me. This acceptance was a necessary prerequisite for more than being happy; it was necessary for "being" itself. In the oppositional metaphors of good/evil, lifegiving/lifetaking, God/Devil, or "this world" and "the other world," Isabel equates the former with "reality" and the latter with "fantasy." In her description of "this world" and the "other world," God is not only aligned with what is "good" and the Devil with what is "evil," God is also aligned with what is "real." As Isabel told one patient, "Your moodiness is worth nothing. . . . You are gruff and scornful [like an old lady]. Nobody will love you like that! [Rather,] accept life, live contentedly . . . do your part. Don't scorn anymore and don't curse life. Be happy. . . . Where can evil enter in a household that is thus? . . . Those who live in God's grace recognize the beauty of life and know how to live it in harmony with the Divine, while those who don't, *manan kanchu*." (Translated, this phrase means "they are not.") As long as you are rebelling against God, you are rebelling against life itself, according to Isabel. Literally, you don't exist.

Purification and Penance

According to Ochs, "When we think of the word 'purgation,' images of fasting, ascetic practices, and long vigils come to mind, . . . yet what is essential to purgation is not some extreme practice, but character formation. The self that has been awakened must now be strengthened" (1983, 127). In terms of the motherhood analogy, this can best be found in the daily acts of childcare—in the feeding, diapering, and bathing that create an environment where love can be nurtured. For Yolanda, Isabel, and

Flormira, the purgation that follows acceptance is symbolized by action rather than resignation. Acceptance leads to acts of penance and purification because it requires one to take responsibility for one's behavior. Perhaps Yolanda described it best when she said that one could not become healed without undergoing a spiritual rehabilitation. Only by becoming morally straight, and by becoming conscious of God's will, can one begin to be healed. For Flormira also, illness often accompanies the inability to resist evil thoughts or evil temptations. In her cure of the baby, Flormira blamed the arrival of the swallowing man who had come to claim the baby's soul on the mother's participation in some (unidentified) immorality. And as Isabel told one patient, "They are cleansing you with San Cipriano [one of her *mesa* staffs] so you will repent of all that was . . . ; and so you destroy all that you were—victim of an evil; so that you [will] become other; so that your spirit is purified; so that you are closer to God; and so that the will of God goes within you."

By way of analogy, Isabel once compared humankind to the Cross. "Every earthly being is like a Cross," she said. "We have our arms and our legs, just as animals have theirs. Every being is a Cross." As she said this, she stood erect and held her arms straight out from her body, drawing our attention to the vertical and horizontal axes. She reminded us that health, right thinking, morality, and life are described in terms that connote the straight lines of these two axes, whereas illness is characterized by the nonlinear, the crooked. "But what is the Cross?" she continued. "The Cross is grace and the Cross is dis-grace. But the thing is, how should one carry the Cross?" She explained that the commitment to live according to God's will, or what she called the right path, is represented by the straight lines of the Cross. The Cross can also symbolize living outside of God's grace. If one insists on rejecting reality, one comes face-to-face over and over again with doors that are "closed" or "barred," with paths that are "locked"—in short, with obstacles that keep one apart from "reality." But, if one accepts God's will, as Christ did, if one is willing to carry the burden of the Cross in penance and in sacrifice, then one becomes "filled" with the spirit of God. One is no longer empty and can no longer be compared to a lifeless rag doll. Instead, one is filled with the essence that is spiritual vitality. In accepting God's will, one becomes filled with *yo personal,* or "self."

The symbolism of the Cross proliferates in Isabel's curing geography. In the corral behind her house where she conducts her rituals, she lays her Mesa Novata in a vertical line from north to south. Her Mesa San Cipriano is laid at the east end of the corral, and a *mesa* which she calls Espiritu Santo, but all of whose objects she has not yet obtained, will one day sit at the west end of the corral. In describing the source and extent of her power, Isabel invokes the four winds and the four roads. This is common in Peruvian curing. But, in addition to cardinal reference points, she labels these four directions as *costa, sierra, selva,* and *donde vaya.* In other words, her powers come from the coast (to the west), the mountains (to the north), the jungle (to the east) and the path to one's future, which is situated to the south. Isabel sits with the mountains at her back and faces her future. While the focus of her ritual in the northern, eastern, and western quadrants of the corral is on the ground objects of her *mesas* or on the sea (to the west), the focus at the south end of the corral is on the stars, through which the Eye of God looks down on the participants, and from which rivers and roads stretch from the corral into the future. Isabel's patients stand in the center of the corral to receive her ministrations. On the path from past to future, this spot represents the present moment, where choice exists and where, at the structural center of limbs and trunk, the human heart throbs.

Isabel uses the cross to describe human form as well as the process by which to live. By standing at the center, her patients receive and participate in a flow of spirit power between worlds as well as between yesterday and tomorrow. At the nexus of these four roads lies the one quality which Isabel cannot give to her patients, although she expends a good deal of energy during every curing session counseling them to seek it for themselves. Ultimately, Isabel knows, the bridge from the past to the future can only be crossed by the patient him or herself. Isabel calls that bridge "experience."

Awakening and Illumination

For Isabel "experience" is the most important factor underlying every part of her healing philosophy. Epistemologically, "experience" stands somewhere between an external reality (whatever we take that to be) and its representation through expression. It is, in this sense, an essential component of human consciousness. But for Isabel, experience is not something that happens to all of us in equal measure. It is something we must actively choose, in order to "leave footprints" as we walk through life. To illustrate, when Isabel directs her patients to walk or run around the corral where her *mesas* have been set up, she is asking them to begin following what she sometimes calls the "path to healing." When they (we) would sometimes ask her for directions—should we run toward the left or towards the right?—she would chidingly answer, "It's up to you which way to go. It's your life, your own decision!" Like the male healers discussed above, Isabel's exhortations are symbolically charged. When she admonishes the yawning patient for being "tired of life," or warns him away from retracing his footsteps because "that was yesterday and yesterday is past," she is clearly communicating the correspondences between the ritual performance of the *mesa* and the social and physical worlds represented there. But, for Isabel, healing also requires the patient's active engagement: the journey is one's own to make.

Yolanda expressed similar views when she insisted that she and I collaborate actively and *participate* in Rolando's cure. She knew that the harder we stamped out the images of evil that kept appearing in the swirls of dust beneath our feet, the more effective the cure would be. Yolanda views her role as one of helping her patients choose the "living road," although she counsels and advises her patients to repair their relationship with God, she cannot undergo the spiritual rehabilitation for them. This is the patient's responsibility alone. And it is only when one has developed a spiritual state borne of consistency and commitment that one can really see the reality of how things are. As she told me,

> It makes me very happy when a patient does what I tell him to, what I counsel him to do, because what I want to do is to give him the hand that takes him out of the abyss. . . . But when he sees himself as living in a paradise, all of a sudden he can forget and eat of the forbidden apple that is sin.

For Isabel and Yolanda—and for Flormira as well—their own calling also followed this path. The power to see and travel into the spirit world required an active and ongoing decision to "follow God's living road" (Isabel, Yolanda) and to "renounce" temptation (Flormira). Only then would the spirit of God fill them; only then would the power to see become incarnate. For all three women, it is this God within, which emerges when agency replaces victimhood and penance makes one worthy, that transforms, fills, and empowers. Such a definition of experience transforms and changes. It is life-affirming rather than victimizing. It is a natural outgrowth of accepting reality and of taking responsibility for our actions. When we engage it, we awaken the "self," and something else, which Isabel calls *decisión propia*. But for this awakening to have transformative power in our lives, as Isabel admonished me so many times, we need to continually work at staying "on the right path."

The Dark Night of the Soul

From early October of 1988 to late June of 1989, Isabel admonished me, prodded me, chided me, advised me, and, through it all, forgave me. The task she had laid out for me was a seemingly simple one. I had only to let go of my stubborn insistence on living in a fantasy world where Carlos and I would somehow be reunited and live happily ever after. I had only to accept the reality that I was a married woman and accept responsibility for my future actions. And yet, time and again, I demonstrated— despite my insistence that I had and would take her advice—that I refused to choose and commit to following "the right path"—"the path of no more suffering," as she called it. I was stubborn and unwilling—perhaps fearful is a better word—to let go of an illusion of control. I was immensely attached to the role of the victim and completely unprepared for the commitment of taking responsibility for my actions. It was so much easier to blame my misfortunes on upbringing, family loyalties, even love-magic (all of which I had claimed as explanations for letting my relationship with Carlos die in the first place) rather than on my own actions. I had been too concerned with external validation and with what others (my family, his family, Carlos himself) would think. I had thus been unable to assert myself and advance my own interests at a time when it might still have been possible to change the future. Once I had married another, there was no going back, as far as both Carlos and Isabel were concerned. Now, the most important concern, from both their perspectives, was the future of my own family. If I did leave Dan, Isabel assured me, Carlos would treat me with all the disdain of one who has been deeply hurt by a woman's rejection, and all the scorn reserved for the woman who would defile her husband's honor (what would keep me from thus betraying him at some future time?). Carlos himself lamented to one of my friends that forging a future relationship from past attachments was completely impossible because I had chosen my life's path and that path had not included him.

Certainly, this perception of a married woman's choice, or lack of choice, is culture-bound. The importance of "family" to economic and emotional well-being was emphasized throughout my research by all five *curanderas*, as well as many of the women I interviewed in El Bosque. They also emphasized the importance of resisting any behavior that would weaken the family.[14] Illicit sexual liaisons, argumentative dispositions, and even overdependence on the productive capacity of a single individual are all included in this category of dangerous behavior. Women, as I was often reminded, are responsible for keeping their families together. Not surprisingly, it was this emphasis on the synthesis of male/female, rather than on transcendence of dualistic oppositions, that stood out when I began to analyze each of the women's cures.

At the first ceremony I attended with Isabel, there were thirteen people present, including herself. She sat in the center of the group, at the head of the Mesa Novata, and spent some time rearranging those who were seated on either side of her so that an equal number of men and women, two and four, respectively, were seated to her left and to her right. Additionally, whenever a patient was to be cleansed in front of the *mesa*, Isabel often asked for four *mesa* participants—two men and two women—to perform the cleansing. When there was not an equal number of men and women who could participate, she would often ask one of those assisting to symbolically change genders while performing the cleansing. Similarly, if the patient required a raising of *tabaco,* Isabel gave the men and the women different shells from her *mesa* with which to perform the raising. Women would raise the *tabaco* in bivalve shells (which are "female"), and men would raise the *tabaco* in spiral "snail" shells (which are "male"). Any person who had been instructed to change genders to ensure equal pairings of male and female was asked to raise the patient with the shell-type appropriate to the gender they were enacting. Isabel also insisted that the *mesa* objects should all be paired. When I asked her why, she said that in order to live well, male and female are both necessary.

Given the same triangle between Dan, Carlos, and me but in a different cultural context, I might have divorced Dan and married Carlos. But, regardless of the cultural context, my actions still would not have erased the consequences of past choices. In any context, I would still have needed to face that reality and let go of the fantasy.

Coming to terms with this need to let go, and suffering the despair, fatigue, doubt, and internal battles that result in what Ochs calls "the dark night of the soul." It is the fourth stage of Ochs's metaphor of motherhood. Children grow up and leave home. They may come to despise their mother as they lose their illusions about her power and perfection, and come to see her as a fallible being like themselves. Learning to divorce one's own sense of worth from such affronts (especially when your very identity has been defined by this mother/child relationship) while also still loving those who despise you is the true work of motherhood—and of healing. But, forgiving, accepting fallibility, in both oneself and in others, and even embracing this fallibility as a part of life is an important part of spiritual development in another sense as well. This acceptance of imperfection and of the backsliding that makes us human is a necessary part of empowerment. It is an especially important component of feminist spirituality because it allows us to accept ourselves, even when we fall from those pedestals of chastity, honor, virtue, and the like that have been built by others to showcase and celebrate the feminine.[15] As Ochs describes it, "We do not travel on a straightforward, linear path. The insight we gained yesterday may not be with us today. . . . [Rather than refusing to distort experience to make it conform to the model] we must be similarly open to our own experiences" (1983, 123).

Empowerment, Embodiment, and Union with the Divine

Isabel, Flormira, and Yolanda, like Vicky and Clorinda as well as most of the male healers documented, are devout Catholics. In their devotion, and in their application of Catholic concepts to pre-Columbian traditions of healing, they are not unusual. But all three women embody and are filled with the Godhead, claiming that their ability to heal, as well as their patients' own empowerment, is a direct result of this union with the Divine. The coessent model of spiritual empowerment previously discussed seems also to find expression in this concept of divine union. Isabel distinguishes between two kinds of healers: those who don't really see the causes of illness but rather heal by simply becoming proficient in the technique of manipulating *mesa* objects, and those who are truly filled with the spirit of God. She puts herself in the latter category, and she illustrates the source of her power by recounting stories about revelations she has received, both at her *mesa* and in dreams, directly from San Pedro himself, who *is* the Holy Spirit. Flormira also emphasizes that her ability to cure comes directly from God—from revelations she receives when his spirit fills her in both dreams and waking-visions. Yolanda and Isabel both express the degree to which they also embody the patient's pain by drawing a parallel between their own suffering and that of Christ for humankind. As Yolanda described it, she feels the pain of each patient like a *cruz cargada* (a cross which she bears). "How I have suffered!" she told me. "Just like Christ on the Cross. One time in a session a *compadre* told me, 'Comadre, I see blood streaming from your hands, as though you were nailed.' Like that he told me. But I realized why he said it, because my suffering is like being nailed [to the Cross]." For these women, the sharing and empathy that ties them to their patients, to the communities in which they live, and to spirit-power of the *encantos,* the *ánimas,* and of the Catholic Godhead itself, is expressed relationally. They explain their relations in coessent terms. Instead of evoking the infallibility of the Godhead—or of Mary, for that matter—they draw on the Catholic doctrine of Christ as God and man. It is a paradox that synthesizes and embodies spirit and matter, the divine and the human, individual suffering and communal pardon. This emphasis on embodiment and relation—as shared experience, shared pain, and shared love—is also found in the analogy of motherhood. As Ochs concludes:

> *Traditional spirituality offers us a model of the individual self in a*
> *solitary struggle for salvation. . . . Inherent in [this] . . . is the notion of*
> *a goal. [But] women's experience of mothering places value in the*

process, . . . *in knowing through being.* . . . *The image of the mother suggests that true worship is not to give thanks but to do thanks—to pass on the gift."* (1983, 138–43).

For Yolanda, Flor, and especially for Isabel this "passing-on" of the gift is at the core of "experience." It is what makes the difference between "just passing through" life and transforming it. It is the key to finding—and claiming—the volition, will, and sense of self that makes life worth living. In a world where gender inequality is structure and women's power to define themselves is muted, it is through accepting this responsibility to "pass-on" the gift rather than resigning oneself to the status of "victim" that agency is reclaimed. And on a more personal note, this exhortation to "step firmly" through life so that—upon reflection—I might see how living had been "worth the effort" was Isabel's most liberating and most precious gift to me.

vi *The* Seguro *as Embodied Self*

$\mathcal{A}$ugust 7, 1989, Chiclayo

At last night's *mesa,* as a final stage in the healing process, those of us who had entered into pacts with the lagoon last week were told it was time to "activate" our *seguros.* These bottles of herbs, which we had purchased from an herbalist in Salalá, are full of "living plants," according to Isabel. Every plant contained in the *seguro* has a spirit, and by activating these we will have a permanent connection, both to Isabel's *mesa* and to the enchanted lagoons from which these plants have been taken. As I stood at the *mesa,* blowing offerings of champagne to the *mesa* and to the bottle of herbs before me, I suddenly felt very cold and realized that this was the frigid water of the lagoons in which I had recently bathed. At that moment, a woman standing next to me complained of the cold and Isabel remanded her sharply, "Of course you are cold; you have recently bathed in the lagoon!" Then Isabel passed around some holy water and told us to "refresh the herbs at their source in the lagoons, in the name of your *seguros.*"

We knelt before the *mesa,* as before, blowing our offerings to the lagoons, to the herbs, and to the *mesa.* As one of the patients performed the offerings, she became nauseated, and then the smell of toothpaste permeated the air. "No," Isabel told her, "you are not ready for your *seguro* yet. I can't give it to you because you are still sick." To the rest of us, she told us to blow some of the liquid from our *seguros* onto the *mesa* as we held the bottles in the path of the spray. I brought the bottle close to my lips; it smelled not of perfumes but of rich, black soil. I drew in the liquid and held the *seguro* before me as Isabel said, "The mother always goes before us." I thought of how the "connective" pathways that we had opened with

205

our pacts were generative, like the power of maternity. Finally, it was time to raise our *seguros.* Like the plants which sprout from seeds within the fertile ground, we would raise the power of our souls which we had planted in the lagoon. As we absorbed the liquid through our nostrils, I thought of the *pacha mama,* the earth mother, who is revered throughout the Andes as the feminine, the fecund, the generative power of earth and water. I felt a strength, a peace, and a satisfaction that reminded me of the feeling I had had while standing naked in front of the lagoon, aware of the paths which had been opened between my body and the spirit essences of these places. Isabel told us:

> *Speak to the* seguro *as though you are speaking with yourselves. It is a friend, a lover; it is your own being well, backed by the lagoons, by its herbs which have been placed by God and which must be respected as you respect yourselves. . . . Never forget God; pray for the Evil to be destroyed and the Good constructed.*

Then she gave the breath of life to each of our *seguros.* She told us to cleanse ourselves, from feet to head, talking to the *seguros* and telling them our life stories. When we were finished, she told those of us whose cures had involved "freeing ourselves from two loves" to stand up and move to the south side of the corral and to continue "cleansing" ourselves, rubbing the *seguros* over our bodies. A few of the patients, including myself, immediately stood and left the *mesa,* but some remained behind, unsure of her instructions. She chided them, saying that perhaps they didn't want to be free of their second loves. Still they remained kneeling at the *mesa* and she exploded, "Make up your minds about your lives! You must have *decisión propia,* it is now or never!"

After awhile, she called us before the *mesa* again and told us:

> *Now you have your* seguros, *but you must make them live, make them work. You must work together with them and not wait for the world to come to you with a full cup. It makes me so mad when people think that now that they have a* seguro *it will put the food on their table. You are not lame, or blind, or deaf. You can't just wait to be given your due like*

fools. Stand up, move around. . . . You are the ones who have to make life happen!

Isabel told me that she was glad to see me go, for I had graduated. From now on, she said, I would be more sure of myself. She told me, "You will have much success in your life because you have your life's purpose planted firmly within you. You have the internal spirit of your *yo personal,* and when you say 'yes' or 'no,' you will say it with the conviction of your *decisión propia.* I am happy to bless you. Wherever you go, you will be backed always by my *mesa.*" With her benediction, I felt light-hearted and content. She told me that as long as I remained motivated by this limited pride, which is God's gift to me, I will own myself.

Isabel had imparted this gift of self-worth, self-knowledge, and self-love to me and our engagement with one another had also made her stronger. "I am proud that you are going," she told me. She had become stronger, wiser, and more content through the part that she had played in awakening me to myself. By her action, she had extended the path of creation, and her own soul had been nourished by the experience as well.

She turned to me and told me to come to her side of the *mesa* and to kneel. As I recalled in my fieldnotes, she told me:

Have you really changed? If you have, I give you my mesa. *Ask it anything you wish, but think well on it. Take it as a mother before whom you ask forgiveness, one who will listen and will counsel you. I give you my* mesa. *The* artes *are all alive. Ask for whatever you will.*

As I knelt before the mesa I realized that the cure that I had embarked upon had no end; it would never be complete. Acceptance, surrender, self-assessment, penance, self-knowledge, was an ongoing process like the flow of power and energy along the pathways between ourselves and others, between this world and the next. My prayer was simple: "Accompany me always. Give me discipline and memory; never let me lose my awareness of what I have been given or awareness of what I have to give."

⁞ Epilogue

Seven years have passed since that "final" prayer at Isabel's *mesa*. In the interim, as Isabel would put it, I have stepped firmly. I have changed and been changed by the experience of that stepping. The completed degree, the job in academe, the renewed ties of blood and marriage, the experience of becoming a mother have left deep impressions along the path of these past seven years. Yet, if I have learned anything in the interim, it is that the process of healing, like the flow of life itself, is full of fits and starts, disappointments and setbacks. It took three full years to complete the dissertation and receive my degree; motherhood came only after four more miscarriages. It took almost seven years to forge a new, more appropriate place, in Carlos's family. But, setbacks notwithstanding, I have moved on. And so has he.

In the summer of 1996 I returned to Peru to celebrate Isabel's forty-eighth birthday. Much had changed about the details of her curing ceremony—a product of her own stepping along life's path. But, as Olinda reminded me, Isabel's emphasis on "reforming lives" and on renewing family bonds of commitment—the bonds of women to their husbands, the bonds of men to their families, and the bonds of children to their parents—still forms the basis of her healing philosophy. She was pleased when I told her of my plans to become a godmother to Carlos's daughter. My relationship to Carlos, tied as it once was to the remorse of "what could have been," had once threatened to destroy both our futures. Now, rooted in the separateness of our married lives, my decision to become a god-mother to his child would solidify the socially appropriate ties between our two families.

"You need to know, regardless of the way we've fought, or of the things that have happened over the years, that you will always be a member of

209

our family." The voice on the other end of the telephone line belonged to Carlos's sister Rosa. Earlier, these same words would have had a different impact, would have been filtered through an entirely different emotional lens. But now, I am ready to hear them and to accept their intent as well as their impossibility. Isabel showed me that healing requires the acceptance of this kind of paradox—of being dependent and independent; of letting go and of being sustained; of being a part of, and of accepting myself as a Being apart. But the work of acceptance has come mostly through the daily grind of compromise, of "choosing the path of no-more-suffering," of taking responsibility for my choices, and of learning to be content with the process rather than the product of living. I have begun to accept the gift—the *don*—of living, and of experience. Having said that, I can only add that I still have a long way to go . . .

Notes

1. See Desjarlais (1994), Turner (1985, 226), and Steedly (1993, 26) for recent discussion of etymological origins and common-sense meanings of the term.
2. See Desjarlais (1994) for a good discussion of ontological/epistemological approaches to "experience."
3. See Pratt (1986) and Glass-Coffin (1993) for further discussion.
4. See Marcus and Fischer (1986, 68), Geertz (1988, 129–49), and Picci (1983) as quoted in Pratt (1986, 30) for further discussion. See also Haraway (1991, 109–24), Mascia-Lees (1989), and Steedly (1993, 25, 242–43) for discussions about why a focus on "experience" is particularly problematic for feminist scholars.

Chapter 1

1. See Bankes (1977); Lumbreras (1974, 99–111; and Moseley (1978, 53–59).
2. A shaman (from the Tungusic word *saman*) is a magical-religious specialist who intercedes with the spirit world on behalf of the human community. Eliade defines shamanism as a technique of ecstasy in which the shaman's soul, or spirit, leaves his body during the trance-state to undertake a mystical journey into the spirit realm (1964). Broader definitions, as discussed below, do not limit the shaman to this element of a mystical "journey" or magical "flight" into the spirit realm. According to the broader definition, ecstatic trance may also be experienced as a "possession" by spirits. Unless

211

otherwise noted, I will be using Eliade's definition because "soul flight" rather than "possession" characterizes the form of shamanism practiced by those contemporary Peruvian shamans whose work has been documented. See Peters and Price-Williams (1980) for a good review of the various schools of thought pertaining to these broad and narrow views of shamanism.

3. See Chiappe (1970) for a discussion of the urban/rural and coastal/highland dynamics of sorcery.

4. See Taussig (1980, 1982), Glass-Coffin (1992b), and Joralemon and Sharon (1993, 246–56) for more detailed discussion of this paradox.

5. Unless otherwise noted, all translations of Spanish-language publications are my own.

6. See Harris (1978), Isbell (1978), Bourque and Warren (1981), and Allen (1988) for further discussion.

7. All of the names of the women whom I interviewed are pseudonyms.

8. "Black, half-breed foodseller," a derogatory term.

9. See Del Valle (1985), Barrig (1988b), and Bunster and Chaney (1989) for a general discussion of these issues.

10. See Boddy (1989) for a discussion of how similarly "overdetermined" social roles affect women's perspectives on healing in a very different part of the world.

11. See Sharon (1978, 23–29), Chiappe, Lemlíj and Millones (1985), Glass-Coffin (1992b), and Joralemon and Sharon (1993, 196–98, 246–69) for discussions of this "psycho-functionalist" interpretation of the sorcery syndrome and for criticisms of this approach.

12. See Sharon (1978), Sharon and Donnan (1977), and Polía (1988a) for discussion of the iconographic representations of the San Pedro cactus in pre-Colombian pottery.

13. Throughout Latin America, foods are classified according to their "hot" or "cold" nature—which has nothing to do with temperature. In Peru, foods may be "hot," "cold," "heavy," or "fresh."

14. Much of the discussion that follows is based on understandings gained from conversations and recorded interviews with the five

female healers who formed the basis of my investigation. However, as the above-mentioned quote by one of Polía's male informants makes clear, the perceived separability of body and soul is not a gender-specific concept.

15. More correctly, the first is called by the term *encanto* and the second by the term *calicanto*. See León Barandiarán (1938, 26), Skillman (1990), Polía (1988a, 67–83; 1994, 313–20), and Joralemon and Sharon (1993, 150–51) for definitions and further discussion.

16. See Bastien (1985) and Allen (1988) for a discussion of similar human/spirit relations in the southern and central Andes, respectively.

17. Today, the *encanto* of Chicuate is said to attack humans who venture too near. See Polía (1990), Ramírez (1969), and León Barandarián (1938) for examples and more details regarding the parallel, subterranean worlds of *encantos*.

18. The term "shadow" is often used interchangeably with "spirit" to refer to the victim's vital essence because, like the appurtenance used to summon it, it is also a kind of image or reflection of the victim.

19. See Glass-Coffin (1992a, 19–23) and Polía (1994, 317–20) for discussion about these two types of *daño*.

Chapter 2

1. Archivos Arzobispales del Diocese de Trujillo, 1786 [hereafter cited as AAT]. Full text appears in Glass-Coffin and Vásquez Guerrero (1991).

2. Exceptions to this generalization include Varvara Ferber, who apprenticed herself to a female herbalist (who specializes in guinea pig cleansings and the ritual care of ancestors but who uses neither a *mesa* nor San Pedro in her work) in Trujillo (see Ferber 1993), and Laura Larco, who is in the process of completing a dissertation, at the University of Maryland, on the *mesa* tradition.

3. This contrasts with the earliest and most detailed records describing rituals of the Central Andes, where, in any case, religious traditions had not been fragmented by recent and recurrent conquest

(Millones 1982). Examples of northern Peruvian chronicles include Calancha (1639), Carrera (1644), and Medina (1650).

4. Exceptions include Hocquenghem (1977, 1987), Hocquenghem and Lyon (1980), Rostworowski de Diez Canseco (1983, 1988), Gareis (1994), and Glass-Coffin and Vásquez Guerrero (1991).

5. Duviols (1986, lvi–lxvi), Silverblatt (1980, 157; 1987, 67–80), Huertas Vallejos (1981, 73), and Rostworowski de Diez Canseco (1983, 72–73; 1988, 10). For contemporary references to these dualisms see Allen (1988), Earls and Silverblatt (1978), and Bastien (1985).

6. A good summary of the other deities in the pantheon and the ways in which they were worshipped can be found in Duviols (1986, 268).

7. For a summary of alternate versions of the origin myth of Paucaritambo, see the introduction to Betanzos (1987, lxxviii–lxxix).

8. See Mills (1997: 127–28) for discussion of the persecution of sorcerers by the Inka state. It should also be noted that soul-calling as a preamble to doing sorcery is discussed in colonial accounts as early as 1547 (AGI).

9. I do not mean to imply that this conquest was absolute or that women did not actively engage this process in creative and dynamic ways. In fact, as shown by authors like Griffiths (1996) and Mills (1997), quite the opposite is true.

10. In 1493 Pope Alexander VI mandated the conversion and Missionization of the Indians in his Bull entitled "InterCoetera." In the Concilio Limense of 1551–52, Peruvian priests received their first orders to rigorously punish *"umos o hechiceros, a los adivinos, y demás magos"* (Valcarcel n.d., 97). The Holy Office of the Inquisition was instituted in Peru in 1570 to prosecute Spanish, *mestizo,* and black idolaters and heretics (Medina 1887; Lea 1922), but it also brought cases against Indians living in urban centers (Millones 1982, 232). Archbishop Lobo Guerrero refined doctrines pertaining to heretics and idolaters in 1609 and ordered the first visits to rural *doctrinas* (Tauro 1966), ushering in the era of the "campaigns to extirpate

idolatries" which lasted through the first half of the seventeenth century (Duviols 1977, 1986).

Chapter 3   215

1. All names in this chapter, except those of the healers and their partners who asked me to use their first names, are pseudonyms.

2. This is the tropical forest region of northern Peru and southern Ecuador, where the Aguaruna and other "Jivaro" (Shuar) tribes live. They are known for their very famous and powerful *brujos,* and many healers try to obtain *artes* from this region in order to tap into this power.

3. Isabel told me that one is only in danger of being attacked by evil spirits or by the *sombras* (shadows) of opposing *brujos* when one is under the influence of the *hierba.* Thus, by conducting *mesas,* she and Olinda were opening themselves up to attacks to which they were immune in a normal waking state.

4. In the highlands, *huaca* has retained more of its pre-Columbian meaning as a "manifestation of the sacred." On the coast, *huaca* refers to man-made structures, to the adobe temples and tombs which pre-Columbian civilizations left as evidence of their occupation.

5. Clorinda told me that some people believe that if a person takes San Pedro while he is in mourning, the dead person will "step on" him, or *pisarlo.*

6. The Huancabamba region is also a very popular destination for European and North American visitors interested in traditional forms of healing. The region is quite remote: the ride from Chiclayo to the town of Huancabamba takes seventeen hours in the back of an open, flatbed truck since these are the only "buses" from Chiclayo. From Huancabamba to the "jumping-off" point for the lagoons is another four-hour ride standing in the back of an open pickup. From there, pack animals can be "rented" for the journey up to the lagoons (three or more hours, depending on the lagoon that one visits). In spite of this, the region has become the destina-

tion of so many Europeans and North Americans that it is not uncommon for prices to be quoted in dollars.

216   *Chapter 4*

1. All of the patient names in this chapter, except my own, are pseudonyms.

2. Isabel actually had two *mesas*. She called her original *mesa* the Mesa Novata and used the *artes* and staffs from this *mesa* to cleanse her patients. Her second *mesa* was called San Cipriano, and it stood on the east side of the corral. Each of the objects on this *mesa* served a purpose similar to those on the Mesa Novata, but they were used *only* to cleanse Isabel, Olinda, and a few other select assistants. The symbolism of these two *mesas* will be discussed in detail in chapters 5 and 6.

3. An "account" is the history of a healer's relationship with spirit-entities. When this history is sung or chanted at the mesa ceremony, this narrative act both brings that spirit-power into the *mesa* objects and allows the healer to dominate that power. To send the power back out of the *mesa* objects and close the ceremony, the healer "unaccounts" (again through chanting or singing) that power by verbalizing the action of its return from the *mesa* to the enchanted "place of origin" (place in nature) where that power resides. See Glass-Coffin (1992b) for further discussion.

4. Vicky referred to the fragrances that she used for raising patients and for making offerings to the *artes* of her *mesa* as "spirits."

5. "*Shucar*" and "*jacar*" are verbs which refer to magically produced harm effected by places that are "charmed" [the noun form may either be *shuco(a)* or *jaco(a)* depending on the dialect of the speaker]. See Polia (1988b) for a detailed description.

Chapter 5

1. Exceptions include Holmberg (1983), Atkinson (1989), Oosten (1986), and Tsing (1993).

2. This emphasis on "soul-travel" is found throughout much of western South America (see Seaman and Day [1994], and Langdon and Baer [1992] for summaries).

3. The use of Joralemon and Sharon (1993) to cite Myerhoff (1976) is   217
   not accidental. In their book, Joralemon and Sharon use a somewhat shortened version of Myerhoff's account of the shamanic journey to compare and contrast their own findings concerning the stages of the *mesa* ceremony to those of Myerhoff. Since my own data on female shamans in Peru will be compared with Joralemon and Sharon's data for male healers, and since they emphasize these particular elements of Myerhoff's descriptions, it is more appropriate to cite their summary of her account.

4. See also Joralemon (1983, 1984, 1985), Joralemon and Sharon (1993), and Polía (1988b).

Chapter 6

1. In other words, although gender-specific patterns may account for differences between male and female healers, they should not be interpreted as inflexible or all-encompassing. Just as Clorinda and Vicky emphasize healing philosophies that are more in keeping with the male patterns described by Joralemon and Sharon, so also some male healers emphasize healing philosophies that fit more closely with the patterns I describe for female healers (Sharon, personal communication, 1996).

2. In Spanish: *Te voy a raptar, te voy a conquistar, tu corazón te lo voy a robar.* My familiarity with these phrases comes not so much from informant accounts, but from the personal experience of hearing them directed toward female friends as well as toward me.

3. In Joralemon and Sharon's recent study of the patients of four male healers in northern Peru, 62 percent of those patients seeking the services of a *curandero* were women, whereas 38 percent were men (1993, 199).

4. For colonial examples of love-magic in the central and southern regions of Peru, see Millones (1982, 254–56), Huamán Poma de

Ayala (1978, 73), Polo de Ondegardo (1922, 224–27), and Montesinos (in Valcarcel n.d., 87). In northern Peru, a peasant woman called María Francisca was tried in an Ecclesiastic Court in 1771 for effecting love-magic against her husband so that he would "treat her with kindness" (AAT 1771c).

5. See Glass-Coffin (1992a, 255–56, 273–74) for more detail.

6. *"El se viste—a su camisa pero no el saco hasta los talones."* This is a veiled reference to the epithet *saco largo,* which translates loosely as "henpecked," or more literally as "long scrotum." *Saco* translates as both overcoat and scrotum in the colloquial Spanish of this region.

7. See Stern (1995) for a discussion of this strategy for resisting and accommodating patriarchy in colonial and contemporary Latin America.

8. During one *mesa* Isabel made this point graphically when she asked me, "You are Bonnie *y qué* ["and what else"]? I thought she was asking me my middle name, so I responded, "My middle name is Kay." "That's fine," she told me. "You are Bonnie Kay, but from now on you will be Bonnie '*y qué.*'" I didn't understand the reference, so I asked what she meant by "*y qué.*" Olinda replied, "*Y qué* is like saying, '*Y qué mierda te importa*' [what the hell should it matter to you]." The implication was that I should not be concerned with what other people might think: what should it matter what others might think [*qué dirán*] . . . ; the important thing is to find validation and worth within.

9. Although these are related disciplines, they are not philosophically conflatable. Feminist theologians challenge "traditional" theological theory and practice while working from within the framework of "great" religious traditions. Examples include work by Elisabeth Schüssler Fiorenza and Rosemary Ruether (on Catholicism); Carol Ochs and Judith Plaskow (on Judaism); Rita Gross (on Buddhism); Ada María Isasi-Díaz and Yolanda Tarango (on *mujerista* and Latin American liberation theology); Toinette Eugene (on African American womanist theology); and Riffat Hasan (on Islam), among others. Breaking from these traditions to assert their allegiance to "thealogy" (*Thea* = Goddess) rather than "theology" are femi-

218

nist writers and scholars of the "feminist spiritualism" vein like Mary Daly, Carol Christ, Margot Adler, Charlene Spretnak, Naomi Goldenberg, and Starhawk. Other scholars of feminist spirituality include those who seek "spiritual" models in Native American religions (see, for example, Paula Gunn Allen, Marla Powers and Dhyani Ywahoo), the human/nature relationship (Carolyn Merchant comes to mind), literature (Adrienne Rich, Annie Dillard, Audre Lorde, Tillie Olsen, Maya Angelou, and Alice Walker, among others), and other genres of worship outside "great" religious traditions. For good bibliographies and summaries, see Carson (1986), Spretnak (1982), Keller and Ruether (1995), and Yates (1983).

10. There exists a vast literature on this topic. For an introduction to the biological, socioeconomic, structural, and symbolic arguments about gender differences, see Fausto-Sterling (1986), Ortner and Whitehead (1981), and Sanday (1981). For an excellent review of recent debates in feminist theory as it relates to feminist spirituality and theology, see Alcoff (1994).

11. Recall from the discussion in chapter 1 that a person's "vital essence" is believed to leave the body during sleep to travel in this parallel world of spirit entities and *encantos*. These spirit-voyages refresh/re-energize the body because of the spirit's nightly return to the power-sources that animate all life. They also provide the substance of dreams.

12. Cooey (1990, 11) defines heteronomy as "the role played by Otherness in the formation of the concept 'woman'. . . . Women who for whatever reasons, whether of necessity or choice, reject the role of other-directedness challenge the patriarchal framework established to control them."

13. The following discussion of Ochs's five-part model and its analogies with motherhood is taken from her book (1983, 123–33).

14. See also Allen (1988), Isbell (1976), Giese (1989), and De la Torre (1986) for a discussion of how gender-pairing is an integral part of economic and social dialectics in Peru.

15. On this point many scholars of feminist spirituality agree with Ochs. The same Catholic doctrine that sanctifies the Virgin and

removes Mary from human fallibility has provided an unfortunate model, especially visible in the as yet predominately Catholic countries of Latin America, for women's spirituality. As long as women are imagined and idealized as infallible and "Mary-like," forgiveness for the accidents of living will not be forthcoming. Of paramount importance to scholars of feminist spirituality is the reworking of feminine identity in a way that restores the sanctity of ambiguity and that does not tie inherent worth to perfection. See Saiving (1960), Plaskow (1980), Christ (1980, 1989), Sanford and Donovan (1984, 160–76), Wendell (1990), Belenky et al. (1986), Cooey (1990), and Pheterson (1986) for further discussion.

Glossary of Spanish Terms and Place Names

agua—Water.

agua de kananga—A type of perfumed water, red in color.

agua florida—A type of perfumed water; Florida water.

amarrar—To tie up.

ánima(s)—Spirit, soul. Refers to Christian ancestors in contrast to "pagan," or pre-Hispanic, ancestors.

arranque—A potion given at the end of a *mesa* to "cut" the influence of the San Pedro (from *arrancar*: to pull out by the roots).

arte—Art; a *mesa* object, power object.

atada—A type of sorcery (from *atar*: to bind, fasten).

ayllu—A kinship-based and residence/territory-based social community.

banco—Bank, bench, area, field of the *mesa*.

banco de gloria—Right-hand field of the *mesa*; *gloria* = heaven.

bastón—Walking stick.

brujería—Sorcery.

brujo(a)—Sorcerer (male or female).

cacique/cacica—Indigenous leader (male or female).

campesino(a)—Peasant, one who works the land for a living.

capullana—A pre-Hispanic female leader, so called because of her hood or veil.

carretilla—A three-wheeled cycle with a large wooden box in front of the handlebars, commonly used as a type of transport among the small-scale vendors in and around Chiclayo.

ceviche—A pickled fish delicacy common to coastal Peru.

chicha—Fermented corn beverage indigenous to Peru.

Chimu—Generic term for the coastal empire, centered in Trujillo, which fell to the Inca in the mid-fifteenth century.

221

china—Common nickname for women of mixed ancestry. Its use can be derogatory or affectionate, depending upon the context.

chupa—Sucking out.

comerciante—Merchant, trader.

compacto/pacto—Pact, deal, contract.

compadre/comadre—Co-father/co-mother; one who has a godfather/ godmother relationship to a close relative of the speaker.

compañero(a)—Companion.

compromiso—Engagement, social engagement.

conopa—Pre-Hispanic house god.

contra—Counter; something which stands in a relation of opposition.

curandero(a)—Curer, shaman (shamaness), healer.

daño—Intended harm, sorcery.

daño por aire—Sorcery by means of the air.

daño por boca—Sorcery by means of the mouth.

decisión propia—Personal decision, will, volition.

despachar—To "dispatch." Refers to the act of orally spraying mesa objects with alcohol or Holy Water to cleanse and to "send" noxious substances on their way that have been extracted from patients during *limpias*.

doméstica—Domestic servant.

don—Gift, talent.

El Bosque—Literally, "the Forest." Name for a neighborhood of Chiclayo.

El Niño—Literally, the [Christ] child. The geophysical reversal in the Humboldt current that reverses weather patterns along the normally dry coast of Peru; it is so named because of its December or January appearance.

encanto—Charm; enchantment; the spirit-essence and power of objects/places.

entrega—A surrender; a giving over; to relinquish control.

espiritisto(a)—Spiritist (male or female).

florecer/floreciendo/florecimiento—Literally, to flower/flowering/to be "flowered". To magically cultivate luck and good fortune by offering sweet-smelling substances to *encantos*.

forastero—An outsider.

ganadero—A herdsman (*ganado* = livestock); one who "wins souls" for
the Devil (*ganar* = to win); one name for the left side of a *mesa*.

gigante(ón)—Giant.

gringo(a)—North American man or woman.

Grupo de Mujeres, Fanny Abanto Calle—Women's group in El Bosque.

hacienda—Agricultural estate.

hierbatero(a)—Herbalist (male or female); a shaman(ess) who works
with spirit forces of the natural world.

hombre tragadero—Swallowing man.

huaca—Shrine; power or force of the deity associated with a shrine;
archaeological ruin or temple mound.

huachuma/achuma—Other names for the San Pedro cactus.

Huancabamba—Mountain town in northern Peru.

Huari—Autocthonous deity associated with the underworld, with caves
and darkness, with water, and with fecundity.

Huaringas—(Or Las Huaringas) Series of lagoons sacred to Peruvian
shamans.

interesada—Self-serving.

jacar (see *shucar*)

jugada—Played, manipulated; an act of sorcery.

La Victoria—Neighborhood of Chiclayo.

Laguna del Rey Inga—Lagoon of the Inca king.

Laguna Negra—Black Lagoon.

levantada—A raising; a ritual act performed by nasally imbibing
tobacco that has been macerated in cane alcohol to strengthen the
object or person being "raised."

limpia—A cleansing; a ritual act to "pull out" and purify, performed by
rubbing the person to be "cleansed" in an up-to-down motion with a
mesa object or staff.

llacuaz—Outsider; invader; class of deities associated with upper world.

loca—Crazy; amoral.

machismo—Ideology that stresses male supremacy, virility, and power. It
requires men to be providers, protectors, and patrons.

machista—Full of machismo; a male chauvinist.

maestro(a)—Teacher or master (male or female); shaman.

mal aire—Evil air.

mal daño—Evil harm; sorcery.

mal ojo—Evil eye.

maleficio—Evil act; sorcery.

malero(a)—Evildoer; sorcerer (male or female).

mallqui—Mummy-bundle; ancestral spirit.

marianismo—Marianism; an ideology that stresses female purity, chastity, sacrifice, and identification with the Virgin Mary.

Mercado Moshoqueque—Chiclayo market.

mesa—Table; the curing altar of Peruvian shamans.

Mesa Negra—Black *mesa;* the name for the "defending" side of Clorinda's *mesa.*

Mesa Novata—Literally, "rookie." Isabel's name for her main mesa.

misha—Multicolored; generic term for Datura (sp.) and Brugmansia (sp.) hallucinogens.

Moche—*An ancient coastal civilization in Peru (ca. 100 B.C. to A.D. 700).*

muñeco/muñequeando—"As lifeless as a rag doll."

novena—Literally, "a nine-day period." Ecclesiastic term for an annual celebration to honor specific representations of the Virgin.

Perú Mujer—A development organization.

pisada—The stepping-on; sexual possession or mounting; a maleficent act, carried out against a victim by a *huaca* or by the *encanto* of a power place.

pago—Payment; ritual offering.

rastreo—Divination.

Reina del Páramo Blanco—Queen of the White Mountain Moor.

remolino—Whirlwind or whirlpool.

Ricardo Palma—Famous Peruvian folklorist who published widely during his lifetime (1833–1919).

salud—"To your health."

sami—Animating essence.

San Antonio—Saint Anthony.

San Cipriano—Saint Ciprian; the patron saint of Peruvian shamans.

San Martín—Saint Martin of Porres (1579–1639). Born in Lima to a Spanish nobleman and a freed daughter of Panamanian slaves, this

patron saint of Peru is revered throughout the Americas for his
commitment to racial and social justice during his lifetime.

San Pedro—Saint Peter; also the mescalin-bearing San Pedro cactus.

seguro—Security; talisman; a jar of herbs and other "charmed" objects   225
that secures a person's spirit to the power of certain *encantos.*

Sendero Luminoso—The Shining Path, a guerilla group based in Peru.

Señor de los Milagros—Lord of Miracles; an image of the crucified
Christ.

shuca(o)/jaca(o)—The word form varies according to the dialect of the
speaker. A magical attack directed against those who neglect to give
offerings to the spirit entities (*encantos*) of plants and/or *huacas.*

susto—Magical fright that results in soul-loss; perpetrated by spirit
entites, not sorcerers.

tabaco—Tobacco leaves macerated in cane alcohol and used in
levantadas.

tarea—An assignment.

tarjo—A power-song.

tinku—Encounter; confluence; ritual battle.

trabajo—Job, work; an act of sorcery.

vinagre bully—A type of vinegar which, like rubbing alcohol, is used to
"*despachar*" after a ritual cleansing.

virtud—Virtue; spirit-power.

vista—Sight; vision; ability to see into the spirit-world and to perceive
objects and events that exist beyond sensory reality.

vista en virtud—The visual manifestation of an *encanto.*

yo personal—Personal-I; the self.

yonque—Cane alcohol.

References

Manuscripts

AAT: Archivos Arzobispales de la Diocese de Trujillo, Trujillo, Peru.
AGI: Archivo General de Indias, Seville, Spain.
AHN: Archivo Histórico Nacional, Madrid, Spain.

La querella de don Francisco Sánchez Curuzano ante el Licenciado Cepeda sobre que dice que un negro suy le quiso matar con hechizo con induzimiento de unas indias. AGI Justicia 451, folios 877v–889 (1547).

Relacíon que hizo Felipe de Medina de las idolatrías descubiertos en Huacho. AGI Audiencia de Lima #303 (March 25, 1650).

Transcription of *cargos* and *capítulos* in the case brought against Juan Santos Reyes by Lima Tribunal of the Holy Inquisition. AHN Sección de Inquisicion, no. 1647, Doc. 44 (1738).

Autos seguidos contra un indio nombrado Marcos Marcelo por el delito de su escandaloso ejercicio de supersticiones y hechicerías (Pueblo Nuevo). AAT Legajo DD, Extirpación de Idolatrías (1768).

Autos criminales seguidos contra Domingo Atuncar, indio del pueblo de Moche; don Miguel de Cruz Chumbe Guamán, oriundo del pueblo de este nombre y contra Juan Catacaos, por el delito de practicar la hechicería (Moche). AAT Legajo DD, Extirpación de Idolatrías (1771a).

Autos criminales seguidos contra María Isidora Asnarán, india del pueblo de Santiago de Cao, por el delito de hechicería. AAT Legajo DD, Extirpación de Idolatrías (1771b).

Autos seguidos contra María Francisca, india de Calipuy, acusada de hechicería. AAT Legajo DD, Extirpación de Idolatrías (1771c).

References

Doña María Antonia de Azabache, india principal de el Puerto de Huanchaco, en los autos criminales que sigo contra María Asunción Coronel, india mitaya de dicho pueblo, por las calumnias injuriosas de superticiones que le ha inferido. AAT Legajo DD, Extirpación de Idolatrías (1778).

Expediente seguido contra María de la "O" Perfecta, del pueblo de San Pedro, sobre superticiones é irreligión. AAT Legajo DD, Extirpación de Idolatrías (1786).

Autos seguidos contra Juan Pablo Arispe, operario de la Hacienda "Colpa", comprensión de Lucma por prácticas de hechicería. AAT Legajo DD, Extirpación de Idolatrías (1804).

Sobre la acusación formulada contra Faustina Gavino, vecina de la Hacienda de Nepén, por hechicerías. AAT Legajo DD, Extirpación de Idolatrías (1825).

Printed Sources

Abu-Lughod, Lila. 1991. Writing against culture. In *Recapturing anthropology: Working in the present,* edited by R. Fox. Santa Fe: School of American Research.

Alcalde Lucero, Nélida. 1988. *Mujer y economía familiar: La mujer y el hilado en la economía familiar del pueblo joven: "El Bosque" de Chiclayo.* Lima: Ediciones Video Impres, S.A.

Alcántara Salazar, Gerardo. 1977. *El extraño mundo de la brujería: Estudio sociológico de casos verídicos registrados en la zona campesina de Cajamarca.* Lima.

Alcoff, Linda. 1994. Cultural feminism versus post-structuralism: The identity crisis in feminist theory. In *Culture/Power/History: A reader in contemporary social theory,* edited by Nicholas B. Dirks, Geoff Eley, and Sherry B. Ortner. Princeton: Princeton University Press.

Allen, Catherine J. 1988. *The hold life has: Coca and cultural identity in an Andean community.* Washington D.C.: Smithsonian Institution Press.

Andreas, Carol. 1985. *When women rebel: The rise of popular feminism in Peru.* Westport, CT: Lawrence Hill and Company.

228

Arriaga, Pablo Joseph de. 1968. *The extirpation of idolatry in Peru*. Lexington: University of Kentucky Press.

Atkinson, Jane Monnig. 1989. *The art and politics of Wana shamanship*. Berkeley: University of California Press.

———. 1992. Shamanisms today. *Annual Review of Anthropology* 21:307–30.

Ayto, John 1990. *Bloomsbury dictionary of word origins*. London: Bloomsbury.

Bankes, George. 1977. *Peru before Pizarro*. Oxford: Phaidon Press.

Barrig, Maruja. 1988b. *Investigación sobre empleo y trabajo femenino*. Lima: ADEC-ATC (Asociación Laboral Para el Desarrollo).

Bastien, Joseph W. 1978. *Mountain of the condor: Metaphor and ritual in an Andean ayllu*. Prospect Heights, IL: Waveland Press.

Belenky, Mary F., et al. 1986. *Women's ways of knowing: The development of self, voice, and mind*. New York: Basic Books.

Betanzos, Juan de. [1551] 1987. *Suma y narración de los Incas: Con transcripción notas y prólogo por María del Carmen Martín Rubio*. Madrid: Atlas.

Boddy, Janice. 1989. *Wombs and alien spirits: Women, men, and the Zar cult in northern Sudan*. Madison: University of Wisconsin Press.

———. 1994. Spirit Possession Revisited: Beyond Instrumentality. *Annual Review of Anthropology* 23:407–34.

Bourque, Susan C., and Kay B. Warren. 1981. *Women of the Andes: Patriarchy and social change in two Peruvian towns*. Ann Arbor: University of Michigan Press.

Briggs, Sheila. 1987. Women and Religion. In *Analyzing gender: A handbook of social science research*, edited by Beth B. Hess and Myra Marx Ferree. Newbury Park, IL: Sage.

Browner, Carole, and Ellen Lewin 1982. Female Altruism Reconsidered: The Virgin Mary as Economic Woman. *American Ethnologist* 9 (1):61–75.

Browner, Carole H. 1983. Male Pregnancy Symptoms in Urban Colombia. *American Ethnologist* 10 (3):494–510.

———. 1989. Women, Household and Health in Latin America. *Social Science and Medicine*. 28 (5):461–73.

229

References

Bruner, Edward. 1986 Introduction to *The anthropology of experience,* edited by Victor Turner and Edward Bruner. Urbana: University of Illinois Press.

Bunster, Ximena, and Elsa M. Chaney. 1989. *Sellers and servants: Working women in Lima, Peru.* Granby, MA: Bergin and Garvey.

Bynum, Caroline W. 1986. "The Complexity of Religious Symbols," Introduction to *Gender and religion: On the complexity of symbols,* edited by Carol W. Bynum, Steven Harrell, and Paula Richman. Boston: Beacon Press.

Calancha, Antonio de la. 1639. *Crónica moralizada del orden de San Agustín en el Perú . . . Barcelona.* Pedro Lacavalleria, 1639–53, 2 vol.

Camino Calderón, Carlos. 1942. *El daño: Novela de la costa Peruana.* Lima: Gil S.A.

Carrera, Fernando de la. [1644] 1939. *Arte de la lengua Yunga.* Tucumán: Instituto de Antropología, Universidad Nacional de Tucumán.

Carson, Anne. 1986. *Feminist spirituality and the feminine divine: An annotated bibliography.* Trumansburg, NY: The Crossing Press.

Chiappe, Mario. 1979. Nosografía Curanderil. In *Psiquiatría folklórica,* edited by Carlos Seguín. Lima: Proyección Cristiana.

———. 1969. Psiquiatría folklórica Peruana: El curanderismo en la costa norte del Perú. *Anales del Servicio de Psiquiatría* 11 (1–2).

———. 1970. El síndrome cultural de daño y su tratamiento curanderil. In *Psiquiatría Peruana,* edited by Carlos Seguín. Lima: Amauta.

Chiappe, Mario, Moises Lemlij, and Luis Millones. 1985. *Alucinógenos y shamanismo en el Perú contemporaneo.* Lima: Editorial El Virrey.

Christ, Carol. 1980. *Diving deep and surfacing: Women writers on spiritual quest.* Boston: Beacon Press.

———. 1989. Embodied thinking: Reflections on feminist theological method. *Journal of Feminist Studies in Religion* 5 (1):7–16.

Cieza de León, Pedro de. 1959. La crónica del Perú. In *The Incas,* edited by Victor W. von Hagen. Norman: University of Oklahoma Press.

Clifford, James. 1988. On Ethnographic Allegory. In *The predicament of culture: Twentieth century ethnography, literature and art,* edited by James Clifford. Cambridge: Harvard University Press.

Cooey, Paula M. 1990. Emptiness, otherness, and identity: A feminist perspective. *Journal of Feminist Studies in Religion* 6 (2):7–24.

Davaney, Sheila Greeve. 1987. Problems with feminist theory: Historicity and the search for foundations. In *Embodied love: Sensuality and relationship as feminist values,* edited by Paula M. Cooey, Sharon A. Farmer, and Mary Ellen Ross. San Francisco: Harper and Row.

De la Torre, Ana. 1986. *Los dos lados del mundo y del tiempo: Representaciones de la naturaleza en Cajamarca indígena.* Lima: Centro de Investigación, Educación y Desarrollo (CIED).

Del Valle, Delma. 1985. El empleo en el Perú y la mujer. In *Mujer, trabajo y empleo,* edited by Maruja Barrig. Lima: ADEC.

Desjarlais, Robert. 1994. Struggling along: The possibilities for experience among Boston's homeless mentally ill. *American Anthropologist* 96 (4):886–901.

De Soto, Hernando. 1987. *El otro sendero: la revolución informal.* Lima: Instituto Libertad y Democracia.

Dobkin de Rios, Marlene. 1976. The Relationship Between Witchcraft Beliefs and Psychosomatic Illness. In *Anthropology and mental health: Setting a new course,* edited by Joseph Westermeyer. The Hague: Mouton.

———. 1979. Curanderismo psicodélico en el Peru: Continuidad y cambio. In *Psiquiatría folklórica,* edited by Carlos Seguín. Lima: Proyección Cristiana.

Donnan, Christopher. 1976. *Moche art and iconography.* Los Angeles: UCLA Latin American Center.

Dow, James. 1986. Universal aspects of symbolic healing: A theoretical synthesis. *American Anthropologist* 88 (1):56–69.

Duviols, Pierre. 1977. *La destrucción de las religiones Andinas (durante la conquista y la colonia).* Mexico: Universidad Nacional Autónoma de Mexico.

———. 1986. *Cultura Andina y represión: Procesos y visitas de idolatrías y hechicerías, Cajatambo, siglo XVII.* Cusco: Centro de Estudios Rurales Andinos "Bartolomé de las Casas."

Earls, John, and Irene Silverblatt. 1978. La realidad física y social en la cosmología Andina. *International Congress of Americanists* 4:299–325.

231

References

Ehrenreich, Barbara, and Deirdre English. 1973. *Witches, midwives, and nurses: A history of women healers.* Old Westbury, NY: The Feminist Press.

Eliade, Mircea. 1964. *Shamanism: Archaic techniques of ecstasy.* Princeton: Princeton University Press, Bollingen Series 76.

Fausto-Sterling, Anne. 1986. *Myths of gender: Biological theories about women and men.* New York: Basic Books.

Ferber, Varvara. 1993. The magical and medicinal lore of herbal healing in Peru: metaphors of highland folklore—flowers from Maria. Ph.D. diss., University of California, Los Angeles.

Fernández Villegas, Oswaldo. 1989. Las capullanas: Mujeres curacas de Piura siglos XVI–XVIII. *Boletín de Lima* 11 (66):43–50.

Figueroa, Blanca, and Jeanine Anderson. 1981. *Women in Peru.* London: International Reports.

Finerman, Ruthbeth D. 1985. Health care in an Andean community: Getting the best of both worlds. Ph.D. diss., University of California, Los Angeles.

Forsberg, Margarita, and Marfil Francke. 1987. Situación socio-económica de la mujer costeña. In *La costa Peruana: Realidad poblacional,* edited by Roger Guerra García. Lima: AMIDEP.

Frisancho Pineda, David. 1986. *Curanderismo y brujería en la costa Peruana.* Lima: Lytograf.

Gareis, Iris. 1994. Una bucólica andina: Curanderos y brujos en la costa norte del Peru (siglo XVIII). In *En el nombre del señor,* edited by Luis Millones and Moises Lemlij. Lima: SIDEA.

———. 1995. Como el diablo llegó a los Andes. Paper presented at the 17th International Congress of the History of Religions, Mexico City, Mexico.

Geertz, Clifford. 1986 Making Experience, Authoring Selves. In *The anthropology of experience,* edited by Victor Turner and Edward Bruner. Urbana: University of Illinois Press.

———. 1988. *Works and lives: The anthropologist as author.* Stanford: Stanford University Press.

Giese, Claudius. 1989. *"Curanderos," Traditionelle Heiler in Nord-Peru*

(Kuste und Hochland). Müncher Beiträge zur Amerikanistik, Band 20. Hohenschaftlarn: Klaus Renner Verlag.

Gillin, John. 1947. *Moche: A Peruvian coastal community.* Washington, D.C.: Smithsonian Institution.

Glass-Coffin, Bonnie. 1992a. The gift of life: Female healing and experience in northern Peru. Ph.D. diss., University of California, Los Angeles.

———. 1992b. Discourse, *daño,* and healing in north coastal Peru. In *Anthropological Approaches to the Study of Ethnomedicine,* edited by Mark Nichter. Philadelphia: Gordon and Breach Science Publishers.

———. 1993. Portrayals of experience in ethnography: Situated knowledge or Castaneda's revenge? *Anthropology UCLA* 20 (spring):105–25.

———. 1995 The meaning of experience: Theoretical dilemmas in depicting a Peruvian *curandera's* philosophy of healing. Paper presented at the 17th International Congress of the History of Religions, Mexico City, Mexico.

Glass-Coffin, Bonnie, and Rafael Vásquez. 1991. La brujería en la costa norte del Peru del xiglo XVIII—El caso de María de la O. *Journal of Latin American Lore* 17:103–30.

Grandón, Alicia. 1987. Organizaciones populares de mujeres: Movilización y prácticas. In *Crisis y Organizaciones Populares de Mujeres,* edited by Alicia Grandón et al. Lima: Pontificia Universidad Católica del Perú.

Griffiths, Nicholas. 1996. The cross and the serpent: religious repression and resurgence in colonial Peru. Norman: University of Oklahoma Press.

Guerrero Torres, Nexar D. 1969. Supersticiones y medicína empírica. Unpublished manuscript, Escuela Normal, Jaén, Peru.

Gushiken, José. 1977. *Tuno: El curandero.* Lima: Universidad Nacional Mayor de San Marcos.

Haraway, Donna. 1991. Reading Buchi Emecheta: Contests for 'women's experience' in women's studies. In *Simians, cyborgs, and women.* New York: Routledge.

Harris, Olivia. 1978. Complementarity and conflict: An Andean view of women and men. In *Sex and Age as Principles of Social Differentiation,* edited by J. S. LaFontaine. New York: Academic Press.

233

Hocquenghem, Anne Marie. 1977. Les Representations de chamans dans l'iconographie Mochica. *Nawpa Pacha* 15:123–30.

———. 1987. *Iconografía Mochica*. Lima: Pontificia Universidad Católica del Perú.

Hocquenghem, Anne Marie, and Patricia J. Lyon. 1980. A class of anthropomorphic supernatural females in Moche iconography. *Nawpa Pacha* 18:27–47.

Holmberg, David. 1983. Shamanic soundings: Femaleness in the tamang ritual structure. *Signs: Journal of Women in Culture and Society* 9 (1):40–58.

Houston, Stephen, and David Stuart. 1989. *The Way Glyph: Evidence for "co-essences" among the Classic Maya*. Washington D.C.: Center for Maya Research.

Huamán Poma de Ayala, Felipe. 1978. *Letter to a king: A Peruvian chief's account of life under the Incas and under Spanish rule*. New York: E. P. Dutton.

Huertas Vallejos, Lorenzo. 1981. *La religion en una sociedad rural Andina, siglo XVII*. Ayacucho: Universidad Nacional de San Cristóbal de Huamanga.

Iberico Mas, Luis. 1971. *El folklore mágico de Cajamarca*. Cajamarca: Universidad Nacional de Cajamarca.

Instituto Nacional de Estadística. 1989. Peru: Compendio Estadístico 1988. Lima, Instituto Nacional de Estadística.

Isbell, Billie Jean. 1976. La otra mitad esencial: Un estudio de complementariedad sexual Andina. *Estudios Andinos* 12:37–56.

———. 1978. *To defend Ourselves*. Austin: University of Texas Press.

Jackson, Michael. 1989. *Paths toward a clearing: Radical empiricism and ethnographic inquiry*. Bloomington: Indiana University Press.

Joralemon, Donald. 1983. The symbolism and physiology of ritual healing in a Peruvian coastal community. Ph.D. diss., University of California, Los Angeles.

———. 1984. Symbolic space and ritual time in a Peruvian healing ceremony. *San Diego Museum of Man Ethnic Technology Notes* 19:1–20.

———. 1985. Altar symbolism in Peruvian ritual healing. *Journal of Latin American Lore* 11:3–29.

Joralemon, Donald, and Douglas Sharon. 1993. *Sorcery and shamanism:*

234

Curanderos and clients in northern Peru. Salt Lake City: Utah University Press.

Karlsen, Carol F. 1987. *The devil in the shape of a woman: Witchcraft in colonial New England.* New York: W. W. Norton and Company.

Keller, Rosemary Skinner, and Rosemary Radford Ruether. 1995. *In our own voices: Four centuries of American women's religious writing.* San Francisco: Harper.

Klaits, Joseph. 1985. *Servants of satan: The age of the witch hunts.* Bloomington: Indiana University Press.

Kosok, Paul. 1965. *Life, land, and water in ancient Peru.* New York: Long Island University Press.

Kramer, Heinrich, and James Sprenger [1486] 1970. *Malleus maleficarum.* New York: Benjamin Blom, Inc.

Langdon, E. Jean Matteson, and Gerhard Baer. 1992. *Portals of power: Shamanism in South America.* Albuquerque: University of New Mexico Press.

Lea, Henry Charles. 1922. *The Inquisition in the Spanish dependencies.* New York: The Macmillan Company.

León Barandiarán, Augusto. 1938. *Mitos, leyendas y tradiciones lambayecanas.* Lima: np.

Lewis, Ioan M. 1971. *Ecstatic religion: An anthropological study of spirit possession.* Harmondsworth, U.K.: Penguin.

———. 1986. *Religion in context: Cults and charisma.* Cambridge: Cambridge University Press.

———. 1989. *Ecstatic religion: A study of spirit possession and shamanism.* 2nd edition. London: Routledge.

Levi-Strauss, Claude. 1963. *Structural Anthropology.* New York: Basic Books.

Lumbreras, Luis. 1974. *The peoples and cultures of ancient Peru.* Washington, D.C.: Smithsonian Institution Press.

Macera, Javier. 1989. Medicina tradicional y curanderismo en las comunidades campesinas de Mórrope y Salas. *Alternativa* 11:117–35.

Marcus, George, and Michael M. J. Fischer. 1986. *Anthropology as cultural critique: An experimental moment in the human sciences.* Chicago: University of Chicago Press.

References

Mascia-Lees, Francis E., Patricia Sharpe, and Colleen Ballerino Cohen. 1989. The postmodernist turn in anthropology: Cautions from a feminist perspective. *Signs: Journal of Women in Culture and Society* 15 (1):7–33.

McClain, Carol Shepherd, ed. 1989. *Women as healers: Cross-cultural perspectives*. New Brunswick, NJ: Rutgers University Press.

Medina, José Toribio. 1887. *Historia del tribunal del santo oficio de la Inquisición de Lima (1569–1820)*. Santiago: Imprenta Gutenberg.

Mills, Kenneth. 1997. Idolatry and its enemies: colonial Andean religion and extirpation, 1640–1750. Princeton: Princeton University Press.

Millones, Luis. 1982. Brujerías de la costa/brujerías de la sierra: Estudio comparativo de dos complejos religiosos en el area Andina. *Senri Ethnological Studies* 10:229–74.

Millones, Luis, and Moises Lemlij. 1994. *En el nombre del señor.* Lima: SIDEA.

Molina, Carlos. 1986. Don Hermógenes Miranda: Un curandero llamado "Pato Pinto." *Revista Antropológica* 2:344–86.

Montoya Peralta, Eddy. 1988. *Lambayeque.* Chiclayo: Editorial Kemoy.

Moseley, Michael. 1978. *Peru's golden treasures.* Chicago: Field Museum of Natural History.

Myerhoff, Barbara. 1976. Shamanic equilibrium: Balance and mediation in known and unknown worlds. In *American Folk Medicine,* edited by Wayland D. Hand. New York: Harry N. Abrams, Inc.

Ochs, Carol. 1983. *Women and spirituality.* Totowa, N.J.: Rowman and Allanheld.

Polo de Ondegardo, Juan. 1922. Instrucción contra las ceremonias y ritos que usan los indias, in *La Medicina Popular Peruana: Contribución al Folklore Médico del Perú,* edited by H. Valdizán and A. Maldonado. Lima: Torres Aguirre.

Oosten, Jaarich. 1986. Male and Female in Inuit Shamanism. *Etudes/ Inuit/Studies* 10 (1–2):115–31.

Ortner, Sherry, and Harriet Whitehead. 1981. *Sexual meanings: The cultural constructions of gender and sexuality.* New York: Cambridge University Press.

Pagels, Elaine. 1988. *Adam, Eve, and the serpent.* New York: Vintage Books.

Peters, Larry, and Douglass Price-Williams. 1980. Towards an experiential analysis of shamanism. *American Ethnologist* 7:397–448.

Pheterson, Gail. 1986. Alliances between women: Overcoming internalized oppression and internalized domination. *Signs: Journal of Women in Culture and Society* 12 (1):146–60.

Pimentel Sevilla, Carmen. 1988. *Familia y violencia en la barriada.* Lima: TIPACOM.

Plaskow, Judith. 1980. *Sex, sin and grace: Women's experience and the theologies of Reinhold Niebuhr and Paul Tillich.* Washington, D.C.: University Press of America.

Polía, Mario. 1988a. *Las lagunas de los encantos: Medicina tradicional Andina del Perú septentrional.* Lima: Gráfica Bellida.

———. 1988b. Glosario del curanderismo Andino en el departamento de Piura, Perú. *Anthropológica* 6 (6):177–238.

———. 1990. Apuntes de campo: Cinco mitos huancabambinos. *Perú Indígena* 28: 12 (28):95–109.

———. 1994. El curandero, sacerdote tradicional de los encantos. In *En el Nombre del Señor,* edited by Luis Millones and Moises Lemlij. Lima: SIDEA.

Pratt, Mary Louise. 1986. Fieldwork in common places. In *Writing culture: The poetics and politics of ethnography,* edited by James Clifford and George E. Marcus. Berkeley: University of California Press.

Quezada, Félix 1976. *Diccionario Quechua: Cajamarca—Cañaris.* Lima: Ministerio de Educación.

Ramirez, Miguel Justino A. 1969. *Acuarelas huancabambinas: Fiestas, danzas, brujería.* Piura: np.

Rodríguez Suy Suy, Victor Antonio. 1973. La medicina tradicional en la costa norte del Perú actual. *Boletín Chiquitayap* 1 (1).

Rostworowski de Diez Canseco, María. 1983. *Estructuras Andinas del poder: Ideología religiosa y política.* Lima: Instituto de Estudios Peruanos.

———. 1988. *La mujer en la época prehispánica.* Lima: Instituto de Estudios Peruanos.

Ruether, Rosemary Radford. 1987. Spirit and matter, public and private: the challenge of feminism to traditional dualisms. In *Embodied love:*

sensuality and relationship as feminist values, edited by Paula M. Cooey, Sharon A. Farmer, and Mary Ellen Ross. San Francisco: Harper and Row.

Saiving Goldstein, Valerie. 1960. The human situation: A feminine view. *Journal of Religion* 40:100–12.

Sanday, Peggy Reeves. 1981. *Female power and male dominance: On the origins of sexual inequality.* Cambridge: Cambridge University Press.

Sanford, Linda Tschirhart, and Mary Ellen Donovan. 1984. *Women and self-esteem: Understanding and improving the way we think and feel about ourselves.* Garden City, N.J.: Anchor Press.

Seaman, Gary, and Jane S. Day. 1994. *Ancient traditions: Shamanism in central Asia and the Americas.* Denver: University Press of Colorado and Denver Museum of Natural History.

Seguín, Carlos Alberto. 1979. Introducción a la psiquiatría folklórica. In *Psiquiatría folklórica,* edited by Carlos Seguín. Lima: Centro de Proyección Cristiana.

Sharon, Douglas. 1972. The San Pedro cactus in Peruvian folk healing. In *Flesh of the Gods: the Ritual Use of Hallucinogens,* edited by Peter Furst. New York: Praeger.

———. 1976. Distribution of the *Mesa* in Latin America. *Journal of Latin American Lore* 2:71–95.

———. 1978. *Wizard of the Four Winds: A Shaman's Story.* New York: Free Press.

———. 1979. A Peruvian *curandero's* seance: Power and balance. In *Spirits, Shamans and Stars: Perspectives from South America,* edited by David L. Browman and Ronald A. Schwarz. The Hague: Mouton.

Sharon, Douglas G., and Christopher B. Donnan. 1977. The magic cactus: Ethnoarchaeological continuity in Peru. *Archaeology* 30 (6):374–81.

Shirokogoroff, Sargiei. 1935. *Psychomental complex of the Tungus.* London: Routledge and Kegan Paul.

Silverblatt, Irene. 1978. Andean women in the Inca empire. *Feminist Studies* 4 (3):37–61.

———. 1980. The universe has turned inside out. . . . There is no justice for us here: Andean women under Spanish rule. In *Women and colonization: Anthropological perspectives,* edited by Mona Etienne and Eleanor Leacock New York: Praeger.

——. 1983. The evolution of witchcraft and the meaning of healing in colonial Andean society. *Culture, Medicine, and Psychiatry* 7 (4):413–27.

——. 1987. *Moon, sun, and witches: Gender ideologies and class in Inca and colonial Peru.* Princeton: Princeton University Press.

——. 1991. Interpreting Women in States: new feminist ethnohistories. In *Gender at the Crossroads of Knowledge: Feminist Anthropology in a Postmodern Era,* edited by Micaela di Leonardo. Berkeley: University of California Press.

Skillman, R. Donald. 1990. Huachumero. *San Diego Museum of Man Ethnic Technology Notes* 22:1–31.

Spretnak, Charlene. 1982. *The politics of women's spirituality: Essays on the rise of spiritual power within the feminist movement.* Garden City, N.J.: Anchor Books.

Steedly, Mary Margaret. 1993. *Hanging without a rope: Narrative experience in colonial and postcolonial Karoland.* Princeton: Princeton University Press.

Stern, Steve. 1995. *The secret history of gender: Women, men, and power in late colonial Mexico.* Chapel Hill: University of North Carolina Press.

Tauro, Alberto. 1966–67. *Diccionario enciclopédico del Peru.* Lima: Editorial Mejía Baca.

Taussig, Michael. 1980. *The devil and commodity fetishism in South America.* Chapel Hill: University of North Carolina Press.

——. 1982. El curanderismo popular y la estructura de la conquista en el suroeste de Colombia. *América Indígena* 42 (4):559–614.

Tsing, Anna Lowenhaupt. 1992. *In the realm of the diamond queen: Gender, marginality, and state rule in an out-of-the-way place in Indonesia.* Princeton: Princeton University Press.

Turner, Victor. 1985. *On the edge of the bush: Anthropology as experience.* Tucson: University of Arizona Press.

Tyler, Stephen. 1986. Post-modern ethnography: From document of the occult to occult document. In *Writing Culture: The Politics and Poetics of Ethnography,* edited by James Clifford. Berkeley: University of California Press.

Ulanov, Ann Belford. 1981. *Receiving woman: Studies in the psychology and theology of the feminine.* Philadelphia: The Westminster Press.

References

Underhill, Evelyn. 1961. *Mysticism.* 12th edition. New York: Viking Press.

Valcarcel, Luis E. nd. *Historia del Perú Antiguo.* Lima, Editorial Juan Mejía Baca.

Van Maanem, John. 1988. *Tales of the field: On writing ethnography.* Chicago: University of Chicago Press.

Vásquez, Rafael. 1988a. Las causes sociales en el curanderismo y causas que motivan su asistencia. Segundo Congreso Internacional de Medicinas Tradicionales, Lima, Peru.

———. 1988b. El curanderismo: Terapia y participación de clases sociales en la costa norte del Perú—Trujillo. Thesis, Universidad Nacional de La Libertad, Trujillo.

Yates, Gayle Graham. 1983. Spirituality and the American feminist experience. *Signs: Journal of Women in Culture and Society* 9 (1):59–72.

Wendell, Susan. 1990. Oppression and victimization: Choice and responsibility. *Hypatia* 5 (3):15–46.

Index

241